Performing an Operational and Strategic Assessment for a Medical Practice

Performing an Operational and Strategic Assessment for a Medical Practice

Reed Tinsley, CPA
Joe D. Havens, CPA

John Wiley & Sons

New York • Chichester • Weinheim • Brisbane • Singapore • Toronto

Library of Congress Cataloging-in-Publication Data:
Tinsley, Reed.
    Performing an operational and strategic assessment for a medical
practice/by Reed Tinsley and Joey Havens.
        p. cm.
    Includes index.
    ISBN 0-471-29964-2 (cloth : alk. paper). — ISBN 0-471-29964-2 (cloth :
alk. paper)
    1. Medicine—Practice—Management. 2. Medical offices—Management.
3. Physicians—Finance, Personal. I. Havens, Joey. II. Title.
    [DNLM: 1. Practice Management, Medical. 2. Financial Management—
methods. 3. Management Audit—methods. 4. Efficiency, Organizational.
W 80 T592p 1999]
R728.T55 1999
610'.68—dc21
DNLM/DLC
for Library of Congress   98-42396
                                                                    CIP
Printed in the United States of America.

10 9 8 7 6 5 4 3 2 1

Reed Tinsley, CPA

Reed Tinsley, CPA serves as shareholder in charge of Horne CPA Group's Houston, Texas office and is instrumental in the firm's Physician Services Division. He works closely with physicians, medical groups, and other delivery systems with managed care contracting issues, operational matters, strategic planning, and growth strategies. His entire practice is concentrated in the healthcare industry.

Reed has published numerous articles in national and regional publications and is frequently asked to speak on a variety of healthcare topics, including managed care contracting, risk accounting, and related topics. He is a member of the Editorial Advisory Board for *Physician's Marketing and Management* and editor of the *CPA Health Niche Advisor*. He is also co-chair of the CPA Section of the IPA Association of America. His articles have been published in the *Journal of Medical Practice Management, MGMA Journal, Hospital Physician, Texas Medicine Family Practice Journal*, and *Group Practice Journal*.

Both the American Medical Association and the Southern Medical Association have sponsored Reed's risk sharing seminars. In addition to his consulting and speaking projects, Reed has also written two books, *Medical Practice Management Handbook for CPAs* and *Medical Practice Management: A Strategic Operations and Contracting Guide for Physicians and Managers*, both published by Harcourt Brace.

Joe D. Havens, Jr., CPA

Joe D. Havens, Jr., CPA is a shareholder in charge of Horne CPA Group's Hattiesburg office and a member of the board of directors. He also serves as the firm's Director of Physician Services.

Joe leads a team of healthcare consultants providing services to physicians, medical groups, IPAs, hospitals, and other managed care organizations as they develop strategies for healthcare reform. His experience includes managed care strategy, mergers, practice efficiencies, and integration issues.

Joe has recently completed a five-part video series on healthcare issues sponsored by Westcott Communications. This series is being promoted nationally to CPAs, consultants, and healthcare professionals. He serves on the National CPA Committee for TIPAAA (The IPA Association of America) and co-authored TIPAAA's *Financial Accounting Manual for IPAs*. Joe coauthors *HealthBeat*, a quarterly physician's newsletter and has published numerous articles in national publications. He gives frequent presentations on healthcare reform, managed care, strategic planning, and integration to both regional and national associations.

Joe recently served on the Advisory Committee of the Center for Research in Ambulatory Health Care Administration) to publish *Medical Group Practice Chart of Accounts*, first edition, 1996. He was a panelist on the Accounting Television Satellite Network, sponsored by the American Institute of Certified Public Accountants on a program titled "The Changing World of Health Care." Joe was a recipient of the Mississippi Business Journal's 1996 "Top 40 Under 40" Leadership Award.

Introduction

Medical practice operations are being reviewed, analyzed, and re-designed like never before. As the healthcare industry matures, revenues stagnate and overhead continues to rise. This loss of profitability has definitely turned up the spotlight on medical practice operations. Every practice must strive for maximum efficiency. In addition to efficiency pressures, government and third-party issues have brought coding and billing compliance pressures to bear. With substantial civil fines and criminal penalties risk, medical practice billing operations are under the microscope for compliance issues.

These pressures, as well as good management principles, dictate a closer look at medical practice operations. This usually leads to the need for an objective third-party review of operations. This is commonly referred to in the industry as a medical practice assessment and evaluation.

Oftentimes a practice administrator, physician manager, a healthcare consultant, or a certified public accountant is called on to perform an assessment or review of a medical practice. This often happens for many reasons: (1) an operational problem; (2) acquisition; (3) merger; (4) creditor review; (5) efficiency concerns; (6) compliance issues; (7) good business sense; (8) embezzlement; and (9) change in management. In some situations, the manager or the practice owners might want an independent verification of how well the practice is really doing and what, if anything, can be done to improve it.

There is usually a call for an assessment and evaluation when a problem is suspected. Simple causes include when receivables begin to grow unexpectedly, cash flow slows down or decreases, there are concerns about practice production and growth, or when some operation issue is brought before practice management. For example, problems at the front desk could result in an assessment and evaluation of not only this particular area of the office, but its entire operations as well.

So what is a *medical practice assessment and evaluation?* Think of it again as when a person goes to his or her family doctor for a complete physical checkup. Think of it as the owner taking his car to the dealership for its annual tune-up. Think of it like getting your car tuned up each year and whatever problems there are, they get fixed. A medical practice evaluation is a comprehensive diagnostic review of all aspects of a medical practice, or as you will see throughout this book, any specific aspect of office operations. This review can cover just a few of the following areas:

1. Current Practice Finances and Benchmark Comparison

2. Billing and Collection Process

3. Practice Referral Patterns, if applicable

4. Physician Production Patterns

5. Practice Collections

6. Practice Fee Schedule

7. Evaluation and Management Coding

8. CPT Coding

9. Chart Documentation

10. Front Desk Collections

11. Payer Reimbursement

12. Timing of Insurance Payments

13. Accounts Receivable Management

14. Personnel/Staffing

15. Physician Compensation

16. Insurance Claims Filing

17. Internal Controls

18. Compliance Plan Readiness

19. Organizational Structure

The chapters that follow are intended to show you how to assess and evaluate these practice areas. The ultimate objective of a medical practice assessment and evaluation is to diagnose problems and provide an action plan to correct them. An assessment can take place at any time, but generally such a project is undertaken annually or for some, even quarterly. The concepts, actions, and recommendations of medical practice assessment and evaluation apply to any size of practice, big or small. While many feel the engagement is suited for, and mainly needed by, smaller medical practices (i.e., those that are less than ten physicians), it is quite helpful for the larger practices as well. This is because as practices grow, they sometimes tend to breed inefficiencies and in addition, specific problems are not detected as fast as they are in smaller offices. In fact, many existing problems are often overlooked in larger practices. A medical practice assessment and evaluation is one definitive way to detect and solve problems in any medical office or operation.

The healthcare industry is rapidly changing. In addition to impacting the daily operations of medical practices, these changes have resulted in heightened competition for patients, in continuous attacks on physician reimbursement, and in increased government regulation and intervention. The result is that practice profits and physician incomes are being squeezed; practice revenues are stagnating or declining while overhead continues to rise. All of this has caused practice owners and their managers to take a closer look at their medical practices. This is a main reason why a medical practice assessment and evaluation is so important in today's ever changing practice climate.

ENGAGING AN INDEPENDENT THIRD PARTY TO CONDUCT THE ASSESSMENT

The owner or owners of a medical practice may want an independent third party to conduct an assessment and evaluation of their entity. This could be a qualified certified public accountant or a qualified healthcare consultant. If so, it is important to spell out the terms of the project in what is typically called an "engagement letter." The engagement letter addresses what the scope of the engagement will be, as well as the fee structure. The following is a sample letter for a practice assessment and evaluation:

Date

PERSONAL AND CONFIDENTIAL

Name
Practice Name
Address
City, State, Zip

Dear _____:

Our Firm would like to propose our medical review engagement for your medical practice. The objective of any practice management review is to diagnose and assess the financial "health" of a medical practice. Our review of the practice's performance, personnel, practices, policies, and efficiency will allow you and the other practice owners, along with our assistance, to develop a program of action items in priority sequence requiring implementation. The practice review is presently expected to address at a minimum the following areas and issues:

[INSERT HERE AREAS TO BE COVERED BY THE ENGAGEMENT; THE FOLLOWING ARE SAMPLES]

- Current Practice Finances and Benchmark Comparison
- Billing and Collection Process
- Practice Referral Patterns
- Practice Collections
- Practice Fee Schedule
- Visit Coding
- Other Coding Patterns
- Front Desk Collections
- Payer Reimbursement
- Timing of Insurance Payments
- Accounts Receivable Management
- Personnel
- Insurance Claim Filing
- Closing Books/Records and Related Reconciliation
- Other Issues Identified By You

QUALIFICATIONS OF THE FIRM AND ENGAGEMENT PARTNER

[Insert information about the firm or company proposing on the engagement]

PROPOSED FEE STRUCTURE

[Insert proposed fees. This could be hourly billing or a fixed project rate]

SCOPE LIMITATIONS

[Insert here any limitations on the scope of the project. The following is sample language pertaining to fraud detection]

Our engagement cannot be relied upon to detect and disclose any errors, irregularities, or illegal acts, including but not limited to, fraud, embezzlement, or defalcations. Therefore, we cannot be held liable for any direct, indirect, or consequential damages, losses, or penalties arising from the discovery or lack of discovery of any errors, irregularities, or illegal acts. It is your responsibility to appropriately apply and implement any recommendations we may give you concerning this area of practice management if such recommendations become part of our engagement.

TERMINATION OF THIS AGREEMENT

[Insert how agreement may be terminated by either party]

This agreement can be terminated immediately at any time by either you or us, without reason or cause, and without advance notice. Notice can be given either orally or in writing. Once the agreement is terminated, our obligations to you cease and any unpaid, and accrued but unbilled, charges become immediately payable.

APPROVAL OF SERVICE AGREEMENT

If this service agreement agrees with your understanding of the terms, nature, scope, and limitations of our services we intend to provide to your medical practice, then your signature and date on this agreement will indicate your approval for us to begin your work. A copy of this agreement is enclosed for your retention.

Once I receive your executed copy, I will call your office to schedule our on-site visit.

I have also enclosed a copy of our standard Data Request Form. You will need to gather this information for us since the information is needed for our engagement. You can either mail this information to me before we begin the engagement or have it ready for us when we arrive at your office. [Generally a data request list will be presented by the firm or company. This information is to be gathered by practice personnel and will be used to complete the assessment project]

Thank you for the opportunity to propose our services. I look forward to receiving this executed agreement in the very near future.

_____

Signature

CLIENT APPROVAL:

_____   _____

Signature   *Date*

DATA NEEDED TO PERFORM THE ASSESSMENT

The following is the basic information you will need, or have access to, in order to perform your evaluation and assessment engagement. This information is usually gathered and assembled before the assessment begins.

1. Financial statements and tax returns for the last five years

2. If a group practice, copies of physician compensation worksheets for the last three months if practice pays its doctors on a productivity basis

3. If the practice receives capitation and the practice is a group practice, a description of how the doctors distribute the capitated dollars in its compensation formula

4. If applicable, physician compensation worksheets showing how Stark-related ancillary services are distributed to the doctors

5. Copies of physician employment agreement and physician buyout agreement

6. Charges, collections, and adjustments for the past five years and current year-to-date (by doctor)

7. Current detail aged accounts receivable listing

8. Current aged accounts payable listing

9. Copy of practice fee schedule

10. Copy of insurance follow-up documentation form

11. Year-to-date and prior year CPT Frequency Report for practice and by individual doctor

12. Listing of current managed care contracts

13. If applicable, the referring doctor report for most recent year-end and current year-to-date

14. Copy of any prior assessment reports

15. Copy of office charge ticket

16. Copy of inpatient/surgical charge ticket(s)

17. Copy of new patient registration form

18. Breakdown of current payer mix as follows:

a. ____% Medicare
b. ____% Medicaid
c. ____% Commercial
d. ____% PPO fee for service
e. ____% HMO fee for service
f. ____% Self pay
g. ____% Capitated plans
h. ____% Other

<u>100%</u>

1. List of current employees, including job description, pay rate, and last year's W-2 compensation.

2. Explanation of Benefits (EOBs).

3. Copy of any payer audit reports.

The following chapters outline and discuss the step-by-step process to conducting a medical practice assessment and evaluation. As previously stated, the assessment can be conducted by internal practice personnel or by an independent third party. Not only do these chapters discuss how to perform the engagement, but they provide solutions to detected or possible problems as well.

Contents

The Financial Analysis

This first step in the assessment and evaluation process is to perform a financial analysis of the practice. There is an old saying in the CPA and consultant community that for medical practices, "NUMBERS DON'T LIE." What we mean by this is that many practice problems can be detected simply by a thorough analysis of its financial performance. This includes both past and present performance. There are many financial benchmarks within the healthcare industry for medical practices, most of which will be discussed in this book. If a medical practice is attaining these benchmarks, then most likely there will not be too many problems related to these particular issues. However, if they are not, the financial analysis will allow you to not only spot potential problems, but lead you to those areas where additional investigation is needed.

The following is how to perform a financial analysis and what to look for when doing so. This analysis applies to all sizes of practices. While it may seem to be tailored to smaller types of practices, these analysis tools can easily be applied to larger practices as well. For multi-specialty groups, this analysis should be performed on a department-by-department basis. For large single-specialty practices, these tools are equally applicable as you will soon see. This analysis will provide you with valuable clues for the rest of the assessment and evaluation.

DEFINING THE PAYER MIX

The first step in performing a financial analysis is to define a breakdown of the practice's current payer mix. This is important because where a practice

1

receives its revenues often defines its financial performance. For example, suppose a practice treats only Medicare patients. Since it is known what Medicare pays for the practice's services, the evaluator for example can easily define what would be a reasonable gross collection percentage and contractual percentage for the practice. In other words, the practice's payer mix will have a direct impact on the practice's ability to attain certain specific financial benchmarks.

The following is a sample breakdown of a practice's payer mix (⌘ TAB01.DOC). The total should equal 100 percent. The figures should be based on production generated, not production collected.

Payor mix % of patients in each insurance class:

Medicare	_____	%
Medicaid:	_____	%
Champus	_____	%
Workmens Comp:	_____	%
HMO FFS	_____	%
PPO FFS	_____	%
Capitation	_____	%
Blue Cross	_____	%
Commercial	_____	%
Self Pay	_____	%
	100 %	

Most practices' computer or information systems can provide you with this breakdown, but believe it or not, many cannot. Many systems can print a report showing production generated by specific payer class. This is important because you will want to see percentages based on production generated and not on collections. This is because many of the benchmarks based on payer mix breakdown are production based. What if the practice's computer system cannot produce this information? The next best step is to estimate the payer mix breakdown. Some information is better than no information at all. The administrator, billing personnel, or even possibly a doctor can provide a "best guess estimate" from where the practice generates its production. Sometimes a sample of medical claims can aid in evaluating or determining the practice's payer mix.

One objective of the payer mix breakdown is to assess how much of the revenues are generated by "fixed-fee production." If portions of the revenues are fixed fee in nature, like from Medicare and managed care services, the evaluator knows he or she should see a certain level of contractual adjustments and also be able to predict a target gross collection percentage as a benchmark. On the other hand, if the practice treats numerous indemnity type of patients, the evaluator would expect lower contractual allowances and a higher gross collection percentage than those practices operating in a fixed-fee patient environment.

The payer mix information is also critical if you are going to benchmark the practice's financial results with some of the published benchmark data that we will discuss later in the book. Obviously, a practice which is 80 percent Medicare cannot be benchmarked with data based upon 60 percent indemnity business. The evaluator must be careful in their analysis of the financial data.

In today's environment, where thousands of patients can actually change providers overnight with the stroke of a pen, it is vital that a practice monitor its payer mix constantly. You cannot afford to wait a year before reacting to significant fluctuations in a practice's payer mix. Most administrators and consultants also find this information extremely valuable in strategic planning and especially with marketing analysis.

If the evaluator is a independent third party, such as a certified public accountant, he or she can take this payer mix information and compare it with other clients of the same medical specialty. If a similar client can be found, the financial performance of one practice can be compared to the one being assessed. This allows the evaluator the ability to see how other practices have performed financially with the same or nearly the same payer mix. If the practice being assessed is performing below these other practices, the evaluator is obviously going to ask why and hopefully find out the reasons.

SUMMARIZING PRACTICE FINANCIAL PERFORMANCE

The easiest way to assess financial performance, and as such to detect potential issues that may need further investigation, is to summarize specific financial statistics in a month-to-month comparative worksheet. The worksheet shown in Exhibit 1.1 (📄 CH0101.DOC) is a suggested method for summarizing the practice's recent and past financial performance. You should summarize data for the immediate twelve-month period. You can and should also summarize annual data if available. This allows the evaluator to review periods together, therefore assessing if production is increasing, stagnating, or declining, and whether collections are performing in the same manner.

As previously mentioned, this worksheet can and should be completed for each department in a multi-specialty group practice. Since indi-

Exhibit 1.1
Financial Analysis and Comparative Worksheets

FINANCIAL ANALYSIS WORKSHEET

Practice Name: _____

Worksheet Preparation Date: _____

For the month beginning _____ and ending the month of _____ , 19 _____

Month	Production	Collections	Gross Coll %	Contractual Adjustments	Adjustments %	Net Coll %
Month 1						
Month 2						
Month 3						
Month 4						
Month 5						
Month 6						
Month 7						
Month 8						
Month 9						
Month 10						
Month 11						
Month 12						
Total						
Monthly Avg						

Accounts Receivable Balance: $ _____ (As of _____)

Accounts Receivable Ratio: _____ (see section below on A/R analysis)

COMPARATIVE WORKSHEET

Practice Name: _____

Worksheet Preparation Date: _____

Month	Production-Current Year	Production-Prior Year	Variance	Collections-Current Year	Collections-Prior Year	Variance
Month 1						
Month 2						
Month 3						
Month 4						
Month 5						
Month 6						
Month 7						
Month 8						
Month 9						
Month 10						
Month 11						
Month 12						

vidual departments often perform differently financially, or have their own specific issues, and as such, could have an adverse impact on the group practice as a whole. It allows the evaluator to see if one department is underperforming, especially when compared to other departments. It also can indicate and isolate potential problems with one or more specific departments.

By evaluating individual department performance, the evaluator has more insight into the basic fairness of the compensation system, as well as more information for the need of having consistent policies and procedures throughout the clinic.

Since physicians are very autonomous by nature, you will often find in larger practices where departments have deviated from the standard policies adopted by the clinic as a whole. This also can help isolate specific specialty reimbursement issues or even coding and compliance problems within one department of the clinic. This first rule and last rule in evaluating a medical practice is: Make No Assumptions!

In addition, this worksheet can be completed on a doctor-by-doctor basis. This information can show you if certain doctors are performing at a substandard level when compared to the other physicians, or if the financial performance of one or more doctors is below an acceptable standard. These are common issues that can affect the overall financial performance of the practice.

The following is a brief description of each column of the Financial Analysis Worksheet; as you will see, it is very difficult to obtain this information if the practice is not using a computerized information system.

Production

This is the practice's actual gross charges, no matter how the charges are posted to the computer or other patient records. For example, some practices will record Medicare charges at the Medicare allowable charge while some other practices will record the contract reimbursement allowables for managed care plans when these patients are treated. Gross production should also include charges related to capitated patients.

Collections

This column records actual collections posted to the practice's computer system for each month, including capitation revenues received. This should be collections related to billed production only. It should not include miscellaneous income such as honorariums, income from medical directorships, and so on. However, if possible, collections should be reduced by patient refunds. Some medical billing software systems will net patient refunds against gross production figures if these refunds are posted to patient accounts in the system.

Gross Collection Percentage

This statistic is calculated by dividing total collections by total production as both were defined above.

Adjustments

Record the practice's "contractual adjustments" in this column. A contractual adjustment is defined as the difference between what a practice bills a third-party payer and what it is legally entitled to receive. In other words, it is the difference between what the practice bills and what the payer contractually pays for the particular service.

> *Example:* Practice bills a managed care plan $500 for a procedure performed on a patient. The plan's allowable for the same procedure is $300. In this instance, the plan would reimburse the practice $300 (assuming no copayments or deductibles) and the practice would record $200 as a contractual adjustment.

When calculating contractual adjustments for a medical practice, it is important to remember two categories should not be included: Bad debts and professional courtesy. Bad debts occur when a practice decides to write off a patient's account as uncollectible. It is not a contractual adjustment because nobody legally makes the practice write them off; it has chosen to do so on its own.

In other words, these amounts are in fact collectible, but the practice has chosen for some reason not to continue its collection efforts. As you will see later, this could have a direct impact on the net collection percentage.

Professional courtesy occurs when a doctor performs a service for free (i.e., no charge), usually for a colleague's relative, an employee, or his or her own relative. For example, when a doctor treats the wife of another physician, he or she usually doesn't bill for the service. It is usually written off as a professional courtesy adjustment.

A question often arises in those practices that see an inordinate amount of charity-type patients. In effect, these patients are self pay but in reality because of their financial situation, they cannot pay for medical care. In this situation, offices generally write off these charges immediately as a credit adjustment called "charity care"; there is almost always no attempt at collection. This is a common practice by medical offices owned by nonprofit hospitals or by offices located in very rural areas. Should these adjustments be considered a "contractual-type" adjustment or should they be considered a bad debt–type of adjustment? The answer depends on each practice's own facts and circumstances. If the office treats numerous charity patients, these write-offs should be considered contractual in nature simply because the office will never attempt to collect them. However, if an office treats charity patients on a sporadic or "hit-and-miss" basis (e.g., Poor patients treated in the emergency room), the office should treat these write-offs as bad debts. In other words, the practice has made the decision not to collect the patient's receivable, even though it could have.

Before calculating the contractual adjustment amount that goes onto the worksheet, be sure you review carefully each credit, and even debit, adjustment amounts. A mistake that is often made is when debit and credit adjustments are included in the worksheet when, in fact, they should not have been, or when a debit or credit adjustment is incorrectly categorized on the worksheet. One good example is debit/credit adjustments related to obstetrical services.

In many ob/gyn offices, the full charge for a child's delivery is posted to the parent's account at the time of the first appointment. This is so that the practice can track payment of what the parent or parents owe as a co-payment. In most ob offices, they want the copayment paid in full by the seventh month of pregnancy. When the mother finally delivers, her account shows the normal ob charge less the copayments that were made. In this situation, the practice needs to back out the balance so it can bill the mother's insurance for the full ob delivery fee. Keep in mind most computer billing software systems will show only the net amount. Getting to the correct amount to bill the insurance company is done through a series of debit and credit adjustments. The following is an example.

$2,000 delivery fee: Posted as debit adjustment at the time of the mother's first prenatal visit.

$400 copayment: Paid to the practice by the mother since this is her copay amount.

$1,600 credit adjustment at time of delivery: To back out net amount so that delivery fee can be billed to the mother's insurance company.

$2,000 delivery fee: Billed at time of delivery using appropriate CPT code.

In this situation, you have a $2,000 debit adjustment, and a $1,600 credit adjustment. For purposes of the worksheet, these should be ignored. Why? Because the $2,000 billing after the delivery will show up as gross production on the computer printouts and the $400 copayments as cash received. Inclusion of the related credit and debit adjustments inflate the figures.

The point again to be made is that you need to carefully review all debit and credit adjustment accounts to assess whether or not they should be included on the worksheet. The most common posting error by employees is posting adjustments as contractual when they are not. For example, a practice gets behind on billing some of its services and does not file the claim within the established deadline. It is inevitable due to the practice's oversight. Often the errors will erroneously be posted as contractual adjustments. Even more common, are the simple write-offs of uncollectible accounts as contractuals. Incorrect inclusions or exclusions could result in an incorrect analysis of the financial performance of the practice, as will be shown later on in this chapter.

Adjustment Percentage

This statistic is calculated by dividing total contractual adjustments by total production as both were previously defined above.

Net Collection Percentage

This statistic is calculated by dividing total collections by the net amount of production (Gross production less contractual adjustments). This is considered one of the most important practice management statistics for a medical practice. It indicates how much of the practice's "collectible" dollar is actually getting collected. As you will see, a substandard percentage is often an indicator of problems in the practice's billing and collection processes.

Accounts Receivable Ratio

Practices, and their accountants and their consultants, often need to know what is a reasonable accounts receivable balance for the medical practice. In particular, they want to make sure the current accounts receivables balance is not too high and is manageable. This statistic is calculated by dividing the current accounts receivable balance by the *average* of the prior twelve months of practice gross production.

You will also want to complete the comparative worksheet also shown in Exhibit 1.1. The financial analysis worksheet is basically a one-year snapshot of the financial activity of the practice. To improve and assist in your ability to analyze the practice, you will want to create and complete a similar comparative report. This report uses the same columns but adds prior year information next to it, along with related variances. This is an excellent way to monitor financial trends and increase your ability to detect problem areas.

After completing the worksheets, the next step is to analyze each column and their financial performance. *This analysis allows you to detect problem areas that need your immediate investigation and attention.* Again, remember one key concept: NUMBERS DON'T LIE. Medical practice achievement and financial success can usually be tied directly to the numbers it produces. Poor statistics usually indicate poor performance somewhere in the practice. Good numbers indicate good performance; it is that simple.

ANALYZING PRACTICE FINANCIAL PERFORMANCE

Once the financial analysis worksheet is completed, it is now time to analyze it (the comparative worksheet will be discussed later on). For larger practices, the worksheet should be completed for the practice as a whole and by each individual physician and/or department. It's important to understand each column of the worksheet, shown in Exhibit 1.2, and how to use this analysis to detect problem areas that might need further investigation.

Exhibit 1.2
Financial Analysis Worksheet

PRODUCTION COLUMN

Month	Production	Collections	Gross Coll %	Adjustments	Adjustment %	Net Coll %
Month 1						
Month 2						
Month 3						
Month 4						
Month 5						
Month 6						
Month 7						
Month 8						
Month 9						
Month 10						
Month 11						
Month 12						
Total						
Monthly Avg						

This column includes all gross production, including production related to capitated arrangements. When taking a look at a practice's gross production, the main objective is to look for overall consistency. For almost any established medical practice, production should be consistent from month to month and even year to year for that matter. Gross production should not fluctuate materially each month, especially for those practices that have a consistent volume of clinical services from month to month and from year to year. Exhibit 1.3 is an example of inconsistent production.

Inconsistent production often results in "sister" problem with practice collections. This is because if production fluctuates, corresponding collections generally have a tendency to fluctuate as well. In other words, if production gets billed on a timely basis, collections, assuming a good collection system within the practice, will be received on a timely basis.

A medical practice can ill afford a situation where it does not know whether or not a certain level of collections will be received in a particular month. This often has a direct impact on the practice's ability to pay vendors (i.e., overhead) and physician compensation.

Therefore, your objective in this part of the financial analysis is to make sure production is consistent so that practice collections will be consistent. If production appears not to be consistent from month to month, the following are some possible reasons (most will be discussed also in chapter 4 on billing and collection processes):

Exhibit 1.3
Inconsistent Production

Month	Production
Month 1	89,121
Month 2	120,100
Month 3	91,667
Month 4	73,917
Month 5	98,333
Month 6	85,867
Month 7	100,981
Month 8	88,222
Month 9	99,005
Month 10	79,111
Month 11	111,321
Month 12	103,667

The Practice Fails to Bill Its Services on a Timely Basis

Work performed in one month should be posted and billed as soon as possible. This in particular applies to insurance billing. The following are the most common billing benchmarks for medical practices:

Office visits: These should be billed on average within two to three days from the date of service. Of course it would be nice to get them billed the next day but this is often impractical for many offices, especially smaller ones.

All other visits: These should be billed on average within five to seven days. This is particularly true for any hospital service, including hospital visits and surgical procedures.

There is absolutely no reason why any medical service cannot be billed within seven days from the original date of service.

EXPLANATIONS FOR CLAIM FILING PROBLEMS

So why can't an office prepare and file a claim form and transmit such claim form to the patient's insurance company? The following are common reasons:

There is an Inadequate Number of Billing Personnel

This is a common problem in small offices. In many instances, there just isn't the number of personnel needed to efficiently bill for the practice's services. Many doctors want to keep overhead low, so they attempt to minimize the number of people employed by the practice. Unfortunately, the practice's owners, and even its management, often do not realize the negative impact this has on the financial performance of the practice.

The Medical Group Management Association produces an annual survey of practice statistical information. In this survey is the number of business office personnel utilized per full-time physician equivalent. A basic rule of thumb in the marketplace is that you need at least one billing/collection person per two full-time physicians. However, keep in mind employee surveys are only a starting point in your analysis. Most physician practices are different in their operation and needs, and as such, you should strive to have the right number of billing personnel to get the job done correctly, efficiently, and on a timely basis.

Simply said, the practice should have the exact number of billing (and office personnel for that matter) necessary to get the job done right! It will be different numbers for different medical offices.

The Practice's Billing Personnel Lacks Billing Expertise

It is very difficult today to find and hire good, qualified billing personnel for a medical practice. This is particularly true in rural communities and small urban communities where the qualified labor pool is not that large. As a result of their individual experience and abilities, some employees can prepare insurance claim forms more quickly than others can. For example, why is it that one billing employee can prepare twenty claims for a day while a similar person in the same office can only prepare eight claim forms a day?

Other Job Duties Get in the Way

In smaller offices, there will be times when billing personnel have to perform other job duties: Answering the telephone, performing secretarial work, filling in for another employee, or performing other administrative duties. Make sure this isn't a consistent problem occurring from week to week. Oftentimes it is the result of not having enough personnel in the office to make it operate efficiently.

Turnover in Staff/Management

Medical practices are notorious for frequent turnover for a variety of reasons. This turnover leads to billing backlogs and inconsistent production. This may indicate an employee turnover problem.

Train, train, and train. Most insurance and billing clerks have not received adequate training to carry out their responsibilities. Most of what they learn about the process is based on trial and error. In addition, the staff is not cross-trained. So when an employee is out, that specific pile of charges goes unprocessed. Insignificant production can be a clear sign of frequent absenteeism with inadequate cross training or the general lack of training for the billing staff.

The Physician is Hindering the Claim Filing Process

Be alert to situations in which the volume of claims prepared is being impaired by something the physician is doing to hinder the billing process. For example, the physician may not be communicating to the staff exactly which procedures he or she is performing at the hospital. The physician may not be dictating notes on a timely basis, like an operative report. We have even seen situations where the physician does not fully complete the office charge ticket at the time of a patient's visit, so therefore the staff must go back and complete it.

A Decline in Service Volume

Managed care encourages the "management" of clinical care. When managed care begins to penetrate a particular service market, many physicians see their volumes decrease. This is because either the managed care plan can and often does decline a service when it must be "precertified" or the primary care "gatekeeper" physician does a more effective job of "managing" the condition of the patient before such patient is referred to a specialist. Also competition can reduce production, especially in those situations where a particular group obtained an exclusive managed care contracting relationship and the related patients of the practice were transferred to this group. There could be "personal" reasons why a doctor's production has dropped off, like taking too much time off for continuing medical education and vacations. Referrals from other doctors could have declined, which in turn has caused a decline in production.

One simple reason for a decline in service volume is because a doctor has not signed up with managed care plans. If managed care begins to penetrate a service area and the area's employers begin to contract with these plans for their health insurance needs, doctors will begin to lose patients if they are not a credentialed provider on the plans.

To analyze service volume, reformat the Service Analysis Worksheet shown in Exhibit 1.4 (🖥 CH0104.DOC). Pay particular attention to new patient office visits and procedures that were performed. This worksheet should be prepared for the practice as a whole and for each individual physician.

A Word About Production for New Medical Practices

For new medical practices, production should increase every month. This indicates that the practice is growing. Production should definitely increase for a new medical practice that is receiving a financial subsidy from a hospital as part of a new physician recruitment agreement. Many new doctors do not feel the need to produce immediately because their income, at least in the first year, is subsidized in some way by the hospital. This often lulls the doctors into a false sense of security. Many fail to realize they are going to be on their own within a relatively short period of time. If the

Exhibit 1.4
Service Analysis Worksheet

For the month beginning _____ and ending the month of _____, 19__

Physician Name _____

Month	NP Visits	EP Visits	Hosp Admits	Hosp Visits	Procedures	X-Rays	Lab Tests
Month 1							
Month 2							
Month 3							
Month 4							
Month 5							
Month 6							
Month 7							
Month 8							
Month 9							
Month 10							
Month 11							
Month 12							
Total							
Monthly Avg							

doctor's production isn't increasing during the first year, his or her compensation will decrease. The practice's production can be monitored using the practice Financial Analysis Worksheet as well as the Service Analysis Worksheet.

If a new practice's production is stagnating or not increasing at the desired level, make sure this is investigated for the reasons why. This is why a budget should be prepared and actual results in the first year compared to these figures. This will be another indicator that the practice is not growing. If revenue is lagging, the practice may need to develop a strategic marketing plan to increase its revenue.

The column in Exhibit 1.5 lists the collections each month (and by doctor on a separate worksheet) or collections for a specific time period (e.g., quarterly). This includes both collections from fee-for-service production as well as capitated payments.

The gross collection percentage is one of the most important statistics to the practice because it indicates how much of the office's production is actually going into its bank account. Keep in mind that if the practice can increase its gross collection percentage in any way, its cash flow will increase accordingly. Thus, the first step is to assess whether or not the per-

Exhibit 1.5
Gross Collections

COLLECTIONS COLUMN

GROSS COLLECTION PERCENTAGE COLUMN

Month	Production	Collections	Gross Coll %	Adjustments	Adjustment %	Net Coll %
Month 1						
Month 2						
Month 3						
Month 4						
Month 5						
Month 6						
Month 7						
Month 8						
Month 9						
Month 10						
Month 11						
Month 12						
Total						
Monthly Avg						

centage is reasonable, after taking into account the special characteristics of the practice.

The following are sample gross collection percentage benchmarks we have seen around the country:

	Primary Care	*Specialty*
Concentrated fixed-fee environment	60–80%	45–60%
Moderate fixed-fee environment	65–80%	55–70%
Indemnity insurance dominates	75–90%	70–85%

The gross collection percentage will be unique for each medical practice since each will have its own special characteristics that affect the gross collection percentage. Some characteristics have a direct impact on the practice's ability to meet the benchmark ranges, such as whether or not the practice is operating in a concentrated fixed-fee environment. For example, this characteristic relates to the practice's actual payer mix. Where the practice will fall within these categories will depend on its own unique payer mix (i.e., the breakdown of revenues between such payers as Medicare, Medicaid, commercial insurance, workers' compensation, and managed care):

Payer mix percent of patients in each insurance class:

Medicare:	_____%
Medicaid:	_____%
Champus	_____%
Workmen's Comp:	_____%
HMO FFS	_____%
PPO FFS	_____%
Capitation	_____%
Blue Cross	_____%
Commercial	_____%
Self Pay	_____%

The more weighted production is toward fixed-fee payers, the more likely the gross collection percentage will be smaller than expected.

Also, the practice's fee schedule has a direct impact on the gross collection percentage. This percentage assumes a fee schedule that is at or near what is usual, customary, and reasonable for a particular service area. If the fee schedule is significantly below these reimbursement amounts, the practice's actual collection percentage may be artificially high when compared to the benchmarks. For example, if a practice has a high gross collection percentage and the practice's revenues mainly come from managed-care patients, the practice fee schedule probably is too low. The same is true for practices that have very high fees. In this case, the practice's gross collection percentage may appear too low, when in fact it would score within an acceptable range if the practice would just adjust its fee schedule downward to the usual, customary, and reasonable amounts.

How a practice bills its services to Medicare patients and other fixed-fee payers could also impact the gross collection percentage. Most practices bill all services at their regular standard fee and adjust off the difference between this amount and the amount actually allowed for payment by the payer. For example, some practices bill Medicare at their standard fee while others bill Medicare at the amount Medicare will pay for the service. Some practices even set up in their computer and bill the contracted reimbursement rates for each of its managed care plans. In these instances, the gross collection percentage will seem to be higher than what it really is because the production column on the worksheet has been collapsed by the way the practice posts its charges. We recommend billing and posting all charges at the practice's standard fee because it removes the possibility of error when trying to set up and maintain multiple fee schedules. More important, however, is the fact that you want to assess how much revenue is actually getting into the bank account based on the practice's own payer mix. The objective is to increase this percentage and thus increase the practice's cash flow.

There are two other disadvantages of booking production on the expected payment amount. If you are going to benchmark the physician's production with other same specialty physicians, you need production calculated at usual and customary fees. By booking production at the reduced levels, the physician's production could appear to be less than comparable benchmarks or the physician compensation/production ratio would be artificially high. Secondly, it is imperative the medical practices measure one managed care plan to the next. If you book production at the contractually collectible amounts, you cannot compare the actual discounts you are taking with each managed care plan. The biggest benefit to booking this production at the collectible amount is that accounts receivable is not overstated as much with the usual contractual adjustments. Overall, we feel it is more appropriate to bill usual and customary to everyone. The exception to this is oncology, where various billing rules apply on drugs, as well as the numerous individual cancer policies held by patients. This specialty does warrant consideration of using basically three or four fee schedules, depending upon the payer.

Another important characteristic is the practice's medical specialty. For example, a cardiology or neurology practice in which most of their revenue comes from treating Medicare patients cannot be expected to have a gross collection percentage greater than 80 percent in most circumstances because the practice's Medicare payment profile prohibits it. A practice that has a large number of patients with indemnity coverage, however, could and should expect to have a higher gross collection rate. Practices operating in a managed care environment often have higher gross collection percentages than similar practices operating in rural areas where there are primarily Medicare, Medicaid, and self-pay patients. Primary care practices, such as pediatrics, often have higher gross collection percentages than do specialty type practices, such as pulmonology, because of better reimbursement structures. The type of medical specialty will give you insight on the practice's payer mix, which in turn will allow you to assess the reasonableness of the financial statistics on the financial analysis worksheet.

If the practice's collections and related gross collection percentages do not meet expectations or expected benchmarks, the following are possible reasons you should look for.

A Detected or Undetected Shift in the Practice's Payer Mix

In some service areas, the penetration of health plans can suddenly switch from commercial insurance to managed care. Some service areas for example have been known to go from 20 percent managed care penetration to 70 percent within a 12-month period. If managed care begins to penetrate a service area, and because managed care plans pay less (the contracted fee is less than the office's normal indemnity fee schedule), the practice's gross collection percentage should decline accordingly. Many offices fail to identify when their payer mix is shifting until it is too late to do anything about it. Keep in mind employees and other people do move in and out of health plans throughout the year and this could have a direct short- and long-term financial impact on the practice.

The following is an actual example of a shift in payer mix (▣ TAB02.DOC); this occurred in the southeast part of the United States:

	Payer Last Yr.	This Yr.
Medicare	11%	13%
Medicaid	5%	6%
Commercial Plans	68%	50%
PPO Plans	10%	22%
HMO Plans	1%	5%
Workers' Compensation	0%	0%
Self Pay	5%	4%
Other	0%	0%
Total	100%	100%

In the above example, a shift in the payer mix resulted in the practice having more insurance payers that reimburse less than what the practice was getting paid in the prior year. This will result in both declining revenues for the medical practice and a declining gross collection percentage.

If a shift in payer mix has occurred, you should first get a detailed breakdown of the current payer mix, as shown in the example above. In other words, determine what percentage of the revenue is now being derived from managed care, commercial insurance, self-paying patients, Medicare, Medicaid, and other insurance programs. Once this information is obtained, you will need to determine how the practice can shift its mix of patients to the type of patients for whom reimbursement is the highest. One way to do this is by designing marketing strategies that target a specific payer class. The success of this project will depend largely on the demographics of the practice's area and the willingness of the physician to participate in marketing activities. For example, if the practice is in an area that has moved toward managed care, there may not be much of an opportunity to change the practice's payer mix. The physician is stuck with managed care reimbursement simply because no other alternatives are available.

Decline in Reimbursement Rates

This is an alarming trend in our industry since many insurance companies are changing the way they pay physicians. As a result, doctors are receiving less for their services than they were before. For example, many commercial insurance carriers and managed-care plans are adopting Medicare's resource-based relative value scale (RBRVS) system as a way to pay their physician providers. They then select conversion factors that will place the new reimbursement rate structure as a percentage of the current Medicare fee schedule. The following is an example of a recent change to RBRVS by a major health plan and the resulting new rate structure:

Evaluation/management services	125% of current Medicare rates
Surgical services	105% of current Medicare rates
All other services	125% of current Medicare rates

This switch caused a 40 percent decline in surgical reimbursement rates in this service area! Some payers in some areas of the country are even paying contracted rates less than Medicare's rates. It is important to keep in mind that as Congress keeps changing Medicare rates each year, this will have a direct impact on all other payer rates that are based on the RBRVS payment system. This is because the practice's managed care rates will change as Medicare RBRVS changes each year. Government programs, such as Medicare, Medicaid, and state workers' compensation have seen their rates lowered almost annually in some cases.

As payers reduce what they pay physicians, you can expect a decline in both the practice's overall collections and related gross collection percentages over time.

Poor Follow-up on Unpaid Insurance Receivables

Practices that file a large amount of their charges to insurance companies often incur some type of problems from time to time. Oftentimes payers attempt to delay payment or an error by the office results in delayed payment. Failing to timely follow up on these unpaid charges is a common systems breakdown in many medical offices and it affects cash flow. Practices should be receiving payment on an average of 45 days from the date of service (See chapter 4 on billing and collection processes for further discussion). The longer it takes to get paid by insurance companies, the more you will have a fluctuation in monthly collections and a resulting fluctuation in related gross collection percentages. Keep in mind one major overall objective is to have consistent cash flow from month to month. If this is not occurring, the inability to collect timely insurance receivables could be the problem.

Poor Front Desk Collections

For certain medical practices, such as primary care practices (family practice and pediatrics for example), a "payment at the time of service" policy should be in place. If patients do not make payments at the time of their office visit, insurance has to be filed for these services and, consequently, the office must wait for its payment. As a result, collections will fluctuate and the related gross collection percentages will not be as good as they could have been if these payments were secured at the time of the visit. (See chapter 4 on billing and collection processes). That is why the explanation of benefits (EOB) review discussed in chapter 3 is so important. Low collection percentages can be a direct result of not filing clean claims.

Poor Claims Filings

Significantly lower collection problems can be the result of the practice not filing clean claims initially. We recently reviewed a practice where the rules had changed to meet medical necessity guidelines. The medical practice did not make this adjustment to comply with the change, and consequently received numerous claim rejections. These rejections were either not followed up on, written off as contractual, or hidden.

Failure to Send Out Patients' Statements

This could be either failing to send them out on a timely basis or even sending them out at all. Patients who do not receive statements every month cannot pay on their accounts. If the statements are not mailed at the same time each month, cash flow could become erratic (See chapter 4 on billing and collection processes).

Poor Patient Receivables Management

Poor patient receivables management situations include those in which patients are not called about their overdue accounts, collection letters are not used, or a collection agency is not used properly. Patients may arrive at the physician's office with an unpaid balance on their account. Many offices fail to collect this overdue amount when the patient is in the office. All of these factors could contribute to poor collections and poor gross collection percentages (See chapter 4 on billing and collection processes).

New Physician or Provider Added to Practice

If the practice has added a provider or several providers, you should expect a dip in the collection ratio. Whenever a new physician starts the practice, there will be a delay in collections that will adversely affect the production's gross collection percentage.

Possible Embezzlement

If the practice has a good payer mix, same or increasing production from that of the prior year, and all the right business systems are in place, a declining rate could be the result of possible employee embezzlement. Instead of collected revenue ending up in the practice's bank account, it is being diverted to an employee's own personal account.

One example was a general surgery practice where production increased $300,000 over that of the previous year but collections were the same in both years. After a change in reimbursement structure was analyzed in detail, the next step was to look for embezzlement, which was found.

The columns in Exhibit 1.6 list the amount of contractual adjustments posted for the period and the related contractual percentage for the same period. The purpose of these two columns is twofold:

1. To compare the amounts written off as contractuals against the practice's current payer mix. Does this appear reasonable?

Exhibit 1.6
Contractual Adjustments Worksheet

CONTRACTUAL ADJUSTMENTS COLUMN

CONTRACTUAL PERCENTAGE COLUMN

Month	Production	Collections	Gross Coll %	Adjustments	Adjustments %	Net Coll %
Month 1						
Month 2						
Month 3						
Month 4						
Month 5						
Month 6						
Month 7						
Month 8						
Month 9						
Month 10						
Month 11						
Month 12						
Total						
Monthly Avg						

When looking at and knowing what the practice's payer mix is (as we have defined in our discussions above), does the amount of contractual adjustments appear reasonable? Practices with a majority of their revenues coming from fixed-fee payers should have a larger amount of contractual adjustments than those that do not. If the practice's contractual adjustments appear larger than what they should be, it could be because an employee is embezzling. Embezzlement through contractual adjustments is arguably the number one way money is stolen from a medical office.

Want to know how? Here is an example:

Erin Granberry has surgery for a neurological problem; the surgery costs $5,000 and Erin has an 80/20 indemnity policy. The neurosurgeon mails the insurance claim form to her insurance company and the practice posts an accounts receivable due from Ms. Granberry of $5,000. Three weeks later the office receives a check from the insurance company in the amount of $4,000 (80 percent times $5,000). Sue Mulligan, a billing and collection person in the office, steals the check and deposits it into her bank account by turning over the check and writing on it "Pay to the Order of Sue Mulligan." She then forges the doctor's signature (Many banks still allow third party endorsements).

After stealing the money, Sue must now eliminate Ms. Granberry's account receivable. She then goes into the computer and writes off the entire amount as a "contractual adjustment." Practices with large amounts of contractual adjustments rarely catch this type of embezzlement activity. Obviously the way you prevent this situation is to make sure the person who posts payments into the computer system never touches checks and currency.

2. To assess whether or not the payer mix is shifting on the practice.

If contractual adjustments are increasing, it could be because the practice's payer mix is shifting to more fixed-fee payment arrangements. This is common when managed care penetration continues to grow in a particular service area. When this occurs, the practice is usually seeing the same patients or type of clinical situations as before, but is just getting reimbursed less for the services. By identifying this early on, a practice can develop strategies to address the situation and as such, hopefully prevent or lessen the expected impact on cash flow.

As mentioned before in the definition of a contractual adjustment, you will want to know what the practice included in their contractual adjustment numbers. If wrong figures are included, the amount and related contractual adjustment percentage could be artificially inflated. Contractual adjustments include the difference between what a doctor billed and what was approved for payment. The most common category incorrectly included in contractual adjustments is bad debts. However, for most medical practices, bad debts should not be included because most practices have made their own decision to write off a particular balance as uncollectible. There are usually two exceptions to this: academic medical centers and nonprofit community health centers. Both of these entities have a commitment to treating the indigent patients. Generally, they represent a significant portion of the entities' patient base. Therefore, their bad-debt write-offs will be recurring on a daily and monthly basis. In this type of situation, bad debts might be included in the contractual adjustment category.

The practice also does not want to see contractual adjustments fluctuating wildly since this might be an indication that EOBs (Explanation of

Benefits) are not getting posted on a timely basis. Failure to post EOBs timely could be an indication of embezzlement and could impair the receivables management process because patient statements cannot be sent until these postings occur for the month. How many times have you heard of the situation where a person quits, goes on vacation, or someone looks in their desk drawer and finds a huge stack of checks and EOBs that have not been posted? This is a situation all medical practices need to avoid.

Exhibit 1.7 shows what could be arguably the most important benchmark statistic on the whole worksheet. It shows the practice just how well its billing, collection, and receivables management processes are working, as well as showing practice management how well the related personnel are performing. This statistic shows the practice how much of its "collectible dollar" it is really collecting. This percentage should always be 90 percent or higher. If the percentage is below 90 percent, there is usually some problem in the billing and collection system that needs to be corrected (See chapter 4 on billing and collection processes).

This percentage sometimes will dip below 90 percent with the addition of new providers. So if you discover a low net collection percentage, investigate the possibility of new physicians in their first year with the practice. You may also sometimes see this percentage exceed 100 percent when a practice institutes revised or new collection efforts, and they begin to collect some of the other past due accounts. This will temporarily inflate the collection percentage. Rarely, would this level of collection be maintained over six to twelve months.

Exhibit 1.7
Net Collections Worksheet

Month	Production	Collections	Gross Coll %	Adjustments	Adjustment %	Net Coll %
Month 1						
Month 2						
Month 3						
Month 4						
Month 5						
Month 6						
Month 7						
Month 8						
Month 9						
Month 10						
Month 11						
Month 12						
Total						
Monthly Avg						

THE INITIAL ANALYSIS OF ACCOUNTS RECEIVABLE

After the financial analysis worksheet is prepared and analyzed, the next step is to prepare a similar worksheet for accounts receivable. You will need to obtain an aging of the practice's accounts receivable, preferably for each of the immediate prior twelve-month periods. Exhibit 1.8 (📖 CH0108.DOC) is a sample worksheet.

As you can see, you will want to insert the age of the receivables into the worksheet. You will also want to calculate the percentage of the receivables for the most recent month. In other words, what percentage of the total receivables are current, 30 days old, 60 days old, and so on. You might also want to include comparison figures from medical practice financial surveys, such as Medical Group Management Association's annual Cost Survey.

Once the worksheet is prepared, you should be able to see very quickly how well the office is collecting its receivables. First, scan the "over 90 days" column; Does it appear reasonable or does it appear too high? Has it been increasing from month to month? What percentage of the current total are the 90 and over 90 days columns? A reasonable benchmark for most medical practices is 18 to 22 percent of total accounts receivable 90 days old and older.

Next scan the worksheet to see if practice receivables are growing over time. Visually start at the upper left of the worksheet and scan your way down to the lower right part of the worksheet. This is often called "bracket creep" and is another indication that there may be problems with the billing and collection processes within the practice.

In addition to an initial analysis of overall receivables, you might also want to analyze the receivables further by breaking them down by payer

Exhibit 1.8
Initial Accounts Receivable Analysis

Month	Total A/R	Current	30 days	60 days	90 days	Over 90 days
Month 1						
Month 2						
Month 3						
Month 4						
Month 5						
Month 6						
Month 7						
Month 8						
Month 9						
Month 10						
Month 11						
Month 12						
Current %						
Survey Compare						

class and even by specific payer. Completing the two worksheets shown in Exhibit 1.9 (□ CH0109.DOC) can accomplish this task.

This information shows you which payer-related areas the practice is having the most difficulties with. These could be problems with either billing and/or collections. For example, the practice could be experiencing continued charge denials by a specific payer or within a specific payer class, or it could be experiencing continuous payment delays by a specific payer or within a specific payer class. Again, this will allow you to assess whether or not problems exist within the practice's billing and collection processes and possibly its personnel.

One of the practices we monitor on a semiannual basis began to experience this "bracket creep" and develop some serious accounts receivable problems. After we broke the analysis of accounts receivable down into more detail, it was very easy to see that 90 percent of the change was the result of problems with the Medicaid carrier. This allowed us to zero in immediately to where the reimbursement problems were.

The final part of your receivables analysis is to review the calculation of the current accounts receivable ratio. This ratio was shown and calculated on the financial analysis worksheet:

Accounts Receivable Balance: $ _____ (As of _____)

Accounts Receivable Ratio: _____

Exhibit 1.9
Overall Receivables Worksheet

Month	Total A/R	Current	30 days	60 days	90 days	Over 90 days
Medicare						
Medicaid						
Indemnity						
PPO plans						
HMO plans						
Workers compensation						
Self pay						
Other						

Receivables Aging by Payer Class

Month	Total A/R	Current	30 days	60 days	90 days	Over 90 days
Aetna US Healthcare						
Cigna						
Pacificare						
Kaiser						
Healthsource						
Beechstreet						
Blue Cross/Blue Shield						
Prudential						

Receivables Aging by Specific Insurance Company

This ratio tells you whether or not the practice's current receivables balance is an acceptable amount. In other words, the accounts receivable ratio is used as a tool to assess the reasonableness of the current accounts receivable balance. For primary care medical practices in which revenue is mainly derived from office work, the ratio should be between 1.0 and 2.0. For surgical practices or others with a heavy concentration of hospital services, the ratio should be between 2.0 and 3.0. Under no circumstances should the accounts receivable ratio exceed three times the average monthly gross production. A ratio that exceeds this benchmark almost always indicates a problem with the practice's collection processes.

One exception to this would be an ob/gyn clinic, which books the delivery/maternity care at the start of the patient's prenatal visits. This tends to inflate accounts receivable for the practice. Likewise, an ob/gyn clinic which records payments of the patient's co-pay amount for the delivery without recording any relative accounts receivable will show accounts receivable at a discounted amount.

ANALYZING THE COMPARATIVE WORKSHEET

As previously mentioned, you should also prepare a comparative financial worksheet (Exhibit 1.10, ▣ CH0110.DOC) in addition to the financial analysis worksheet.

Look for declining production and declining collections from that of the previous year. Reasons why must be found and corrected. These will be discussed throughout this book. Also look for increasing production but a lag in corresponding collections. If production increases, related collections probably should increase accordingly. If not, look for possible embezzlement and/or a problem with accounts receivable management.

Exhibit 1.10
Production/Collections Comparative Worksheet

Month	Production- Current Year	Production – Prior Year	Variance	Collections- Current Year	Collections- Prior Year	Variance
Month 1						
Month 2						
Month 3						
Month 4						
Month 5						
Month 6						
Month 7						
Month 8						
Month 9						
Month 10						
Month 11						
Month 12						

This comparative analysis also helps identify seasonal trends in the practice. Cash flow management is enhanced with this knowledge. This information is very valuable in strategic planning, marketing, and overall staff management. How do you increase the low periods or smooth out the busy cycle?

SUMMARY OF FINANCIAL BENCHMARKS

The following is a summary of the specific financial benchmarks discussed in the chapter and that should be a part of your initial financial analysis of the practice. These benchmarks hold true for all medical practices, large ones as well as the solo practitioner.

Gross Collection Percentage:

	Primary Care	*Specialty*
Concentrated fixed-fee environment	*60–80%*	*45–60%*
Moderate fixed-fee environment	*65–80%*	*55–70%*
Indemnity insurance dominates	*75–90%*	*70–85%*

Net Collection Percentage: — *Always greater than 90%*

Accounts Receivable 90 + days: — *No more than 18% of total receivables balance*

Accounts Receivable Ratio:

Primary care	*Between 1.0 and 2.0*
Specialist	*Between 2.0 and 3.0*
Any medical practice	*Never above 3.0*

CONCLUSION

As mentioned very early on in this chapter, numbers really do not lie. They tell you a lot about the practice: how well it is operating, how good its people are, how well it is being managed, and how good its processes are. This is the first step because it gives you a road map planning your additional analysis. We always perform this analysis prior to doing any on-site work at the practice. Valuable time and possibly identifying operational problems can be lost by not preparing the financial analysis first. This initial step of the process should have alerted you to potential problem areas; in other words it should have "pointed you in the right direction."

The next step is to look further for potential practice problems by performing a detailed review of accounts receivable and reviewing explanation of benefits (EOBs). You are still in the process of identifying problems that warrant further investigation.

CHAPTER TWO

Accounts Receivable Review

The lifeblood of any practice is its accounts receivable. Accounts receivable represents the practice's uncollected work efforts. The management of accounts receivable will directly affect the cash flow of the medical practice and ultimately the income of the physicians. A thorough practice assessment will involve many of the components which directly affect accounts receivable. This includes fee schedule analysis, evaluation and management coding or CPT coding, billing, and collection procedures, as well as EOB analysis. All of these components of a practice assessment will ultimately tell you how well accounts receivable is being managed by the practice as well as help you identify where there are related problem areas that deserve immediate attention.

ESTABLISHING ACCOUNTS RECEIVABLE RATIO

The first step in this analysis is to review the total amount of the practice's accounts receivable. This is usually evaluated in terms of how many months of work are contained in the accounts receivable balance. This is commonly referred to as the accounts receivable ratio, explained in detail in chapter 1. An example of the financial analysis worksheet and how it can be used to assess the receivables balance is shown in Exhibit 2.1. This ratio is calculated by dividing the current accounts receivable balance by the average of the prior twelve months of the practice's gross production.

Exhibit 2.1
ASSAF OB/GYN Clinic
Accounts Receivable Analysis

Month	Production	Collections	Gross Coll. %	Adjustments	Adjust.%	Net Coll.%
Jan-97	$143,975	$85,944	59.69%	$49,854	34.63%	91.31%
Feb-97	$172,660	$86,879	50.32%	$58,934	34.13%	76.39%
Mar-97	$117,605	$65,693	55.86%	$40,561	34.49%	85.27%
Apr-97	$164,915	$83,282	50.50%	$38,601	23.41%	65.93%
May-97	$178,020	$102,562	57.61%	$44,430	24.96%	76.77%
Jun-97	$84,310	$83,722	99.30%	$55,707	66.07%	292.70%
Jul-97	$162,043	$80,466	49.66%	$51,048	31.50%	72.50%
Aug-97	$167,740	$83,242	49.63%	$63,971	38.14%	80.22%
Sep-97	$178,654	$90,165	50.47%	$68,168	38.16%	81.61%
Oct-97	$163,935	$112,419	68.58%	$78,736	48.03%	131.95%
Nov-97	$127,980	$71,456	55.83%	$33,596	26.25%	75.71%
Dec-97	$95,654	$79,456	83.07%	$46,153	48.25%	160.52%
Total	$1,757,491	$1,025,286		$629,759		
Monthly Avg.	$146,458	$85,441	58.34%	$52,480	35.83%	90.92%

Accounts Receivable Balance: $258,772 (as of 12/31/97)
Accounts Receivable Ratio: 1.77 (see below for computation)

Computation of Accounts Receivable Ratio:

Accounts Receivable Balance (as of 12/31/97):	$258,772
Average Production from Worksheet Above:	$146,458
A/R Ratio (A/R divided by Average Production):	**1.77**

BENCHMARKING

For this practice, what should this ratio have been? As shown in Exhibit 2.2, we have included what we consider to be industry accepted accounts receivable ratio benchmarks:

Exhibit 2.2
Accounts Receivable Ratio Benchmarks

Primary Care	1.75–2.00
Specialty	2.00–3.00

The Ratio Should Never Exceed 3.0

For primary care, you do not want to exceed two months of production in accounts receivable at any one time. For specialty practices, you would expect a ratio between two and three times average monthly production. Never would we expect a practice to have an accounts receivable ratio over three. This is a definite indication that the practice has some significant accounts receivable management problems that must be analyzed immediately. This analysis will determine how lowering the accounts receivable ratio to an acceptable benchmark can increase the cash flow of the clinic. High accounts receivable ratios can indicate problems with staff turnover, claims processing, collection procedures, insurance follow-up, payer problems, unprocessed contractual adjustments, as well as other operational issues. This is why the financial analysis discussed in chapter 1 is performed, as well as the EOB review discussed in chapter 3 and the analysis of the billing and collection processes in chapter 4.

As mentioned previously, adding new physicians will usually inflate the accounts receivable ratio during their first year of practice. This, however, could be another indicator that problems exist with claims processing. Whatever the case may be, if the accounts receivable ratio is above the accepted norms, a priority of the practice assessment should be to determine why.

Caution: For medical practices that have prepayment revenues (capitation), these revenues and related production information can distort the analysis efforts. Capitation-related services are never included in the accounts receivable balances, since these services are prepaid. Your calculation of the accounts receivable ratio should only include fee-for-service production. However, your initial financial analysis as described in chapter 1 should include capitation production and payments.

Survey Comparisons

Once the accounts receivable ratio has been calculated, the next step is to make a comparison to accepted industry benchmarks (i.e., Medical Group Management Association or others). Exhibit 2.3 shows medical practice accounts receivable ratios by specialty compared to MGMA benchmarks.

Graphing to benchmarks and industry surveys is an excellent way to communicate information to physicians and medical practices re-

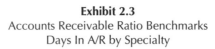

Exhibit 2.3
Accounts Receivable Ratio Benchmarks
Days In A/R by Specialty

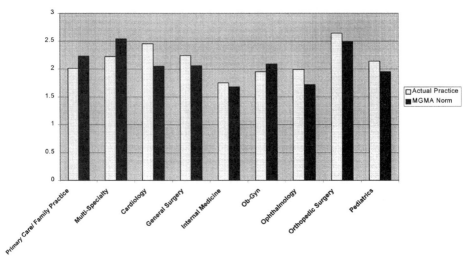

garding their accounts receivable management and calculation of their accounts receivable ratios. This benchmarking is an extremely important part of medical practice management and these efforts will be intensified in the coming years as all medical practices will strive for better efficiencies.

PAYER CLASS ANALYSIS

The next step in the receivables analysis process is to obtain an accounts receivable aging report by payer class, which can provide valuable insight into specific accounts receivable accounts. Analyzing this report will allow you to evaluate the aging and collection activity of the accounts receivable based on the type of payer to determine whether or not there are collection problems with specific payers. For example, a practice may have trouble with Medicare receivables but does fine collecting other payer accounts. This could be because practice billing personnel are unfamiliar with Medicare billing rules.

The following is a sample accounts receivable aging report by payer:

Fry Multi-Specialty Clinic
Accounts Receivable Aging by Payer

	Current	31 to 60 Days	61 to 90 Days	91 to 120 Days	Over 120 Days	Totals
A/R Aging						
Medicare	$ 59,419	$ 2,745	$ 3,828	$ 3,256	$ 63,144	$ 132,392
Medicaid	26,872	7,195	2,333	3,502	85,428	125,330
Blue Cross/Blue Shield	48,465	10,952	1,602	3,850	161,400	226,269
Commercial and Other	17,116	7,440	4,356	3,049	23,660	55,621
Self-Pay	15,754	13,957	11,680	11,647	180,909	233,947
Gross Accounts Receivable	**$ 167,626**	**$ 42,289**	**$ 23,799**	**$ 25,304**	**$ 514,541**	**$ 773,559**
Percent of Total A/R	21.67%	5.47%	3.08%	3.27%	66.52%	100%

As part of the accounts receivable analysis, it is important to understand how some of the other components of a practice assessment directly affect accounts receivable. For example, as we discussed in the financial analysis chapter 1, you must determine how the medical practice records gross charges for each payer. Some practices actually record accounts receivable as production less contractual adjustments, so that their accounts receivable more accurately reflects what they expect to collect. We also noted in chapter 1 that there are advantages and disadvantages to recording accounts receivable at gross versus net expected realizable amounts. It is our opinion that a medical practice is better off recording accounts receivable at gross for analysis and comparative purposes. This is because you and the practice can easily generate a worksheet which would calculate an estimated net realizable value of accounts receivable to be used for cash flow planning, buy-sell agreements, or other purposes where the medical practice might need to know expected cash flow.

COLLECTIBILITY ANALYSIS

Shown in Exhibit 2.4 is a worksheet that can be used to calculate the net realizable value of a medical practice's accounts receivable. The collection ratios are established using the practice's own gross collection percentage. You can use the current year's collection ratio or a two- or three-year average as we have done in Exhibit 2.4.

Exhibit 2.4
Calculation of Collectibility Ratio

Date	Charges	Payments	Collection Rate
Total 1996	$1,570,645	$1,191,764	75.88%
Total 1997	$1,212,245	$909,410	75.02%
Total 1996–1997	$2,782,890	$2,101,174	75.50%
Collectibility Factor Used			**75.50%**

ACCOUNTS RECEIVABLE AGING

Once you have determined the practice's collectibility ratio, you can then establish collectibility based on the age of the accounts receivable. The following worksheet establishes collectibility by payer based on aging of the balance. This was developed based on our experience with medical practice collections and valuation work. It is a conservative way to estimate future collections. This grid may need to be adjusted for your own experience or the experience of an individual clinic.

Collectibility by Payer

Payer	Current	31–60 Days	61–90 Days	91–120 Days	Over 120 Days
Medicare	95%	90%	80%	65%	40%
Medicaid	95%	90%	80%	65%	40%
Blue Cross/Blue Shield	90%	85%	75%	50%	30%
Other	90%	80%	65%	50%	25%
Self-Pay	90%	80%	60%	30%	20%

By applying all of these payer factors, you can now calculate an expected collectibility percentage for each aging category of accounts receivable. These percentages are shown in Exhibit 2.5.

Using the accounts receivable aging report, you apply the factors to arrive at an estimated net realizable collection amount for accounts receivable by payer (bottom section of above worksheet). While not a part of a normal practice assessment, it is used in a due diligence assessment in anticipation of a practice acquisition or in situations where a practice is having severe cash flow problems.

For purposes of analyzing the reasonableness of overall accounts re-

Exhibit 2.5
Fry Multi-Specialty Clinic
Accounts Receivable Estimated Net Collectible Amount

	Current	31 to 60 Days	61 to 90 Days	91 to 120 Days	Over 120 Days	Totals
A/R Aging						
Medicare	$ 59,419	$ 2,745	$ 3,828	$ 3,256	$ 63,144	$ 132,392
Medicaid	26,872	7,195	2,333	3,502	85,428	125,330
Blue Cross/Blue Shield	48,465	10,952	1,602	3,850	161,400	226,269
Commercial and Other	17,116	7,440	4,356	3,049	23,660	55,621
Self-Pay	15,754	13,957	11,680	11,647	180,909	233,947
Gross Accounts Receivable	$ 167,626	$ 42,289	$ 23,799	$ 25,304	$ 514,541	$ 773,559
Percent of Total A/R	21.67%	5.47%	3.08%	3.27%	66.52%	100%
Collectibility Factors	71.7%	68.0%	60.4%	49.1%	30.2%	
Medicare	71.7%	68.0%	60.4%	49.1%	30.2%	
Medicaid	68.0%	64.2%	56.6%	37.8%	22.7%	
Blue Cross/Blue Shield	68.0%	60.4%	49.1%	37.8%	18.9%	
Commercial and Other	68.0%	60.4%	45.3%	22.7%	15.1%	
Self-Pay						
Expected Collections						
Medicare	$ 42,603	$ 1,867	$ 2,312	$ 1,599	$ 19,069	$ 67,450
Medicaid	19,267	4,893	1,409	1,719	25,799	53,087
Blue Cross/Blue Shield	32,956	7,031	907	1,455	36,538	78,987
Commercial and Other	11,639	4,494	2,139	1,153	4,472	23,897
Self-Pay	10,713	8,430	5,291	2,644	27,317	54,395
Net Collectible Amount	**$ 117,178**	**$ 26,715**	**$ 12,058**	**$ 8,570**	**$ 113,295**	**$ 277,816**
Average Collectibility Factor	69.9%	63.2%	50.7%	33.9%	22.0%	35.9%

ceivable, you will only review a summary accounts receivable aging report. Generally, it is not necessary to review a detailed accounts receivable aging unless you find problems within a certain payer class. This aging can help you immediately identify delays in claims processing and collection cycles for certain payers. We referred to this earlier in chapter 1 as "bracket creep." However, keep in mind you will at some point in the assessment process review a detailed aging of the accounts receivable (refer to chapter 4 on analyzing the billing and collection processes).

Is the Receivables Report Accurate?

When performing your analysis, however, always be aware of the fact that you cannot take medical practice management reports at face value. First, you must understand exactly how the management information system ages the accounts. When we review medical practice management information systems, we find out that there are numerous ways that the systems can and will age accounts receivable. Obviously, the most common aging is by service date. The system begins to age the account based on the date that the service was delivered to the patient; however, there are numerous systems which age the account by the posting date.

Hopefully this would not generate a significant difference in aging if the medical practice is current and timely with its posting of services. Unfortunately this is not always the situation, and aging by post date can make a significant difference in the aging. Another common loophole in the aging analysis is that some systems will actually start the aging over if you generate a rebill on a claim. For example, let's assume the practice has an outstanding claim to Blue Cross/Blue Shield of Texas on a Mr. Steve Napier; this claim has not paid within 45 days. The system is set up to automatically generate a rebill on that claim to the insurance company. Some systems will then show that account as current because of the rebill date.

Another common option for aging accounts receivable is to base the aging on patient responsibility date. This can in fact be extremely beneficial if the system can move an account from insurance responsibility to patient responsibility, and then age the account based on the time that the patient has actually been responsible for the bill. One of the additional surprises we have seen is the situation where the system ages the account based on date of last transaction. Let's assume Mr. Steve Napier has a large outstanding surgery deductible of $600 and he has been paying $5 every other month for the last year. Based on this aging concept, Mr. Napier's account will never show aging past the 30 day column. Accounts like Mr. Napier's do not receive collection efforts because they are never shown as past due. Many patients like Mr. Napier quickly learn how to keep their account balances current without significant reductions in the amount owed. So when you request and receive your accounts receivable aging analysis by payer, you must also understand explicitly how the medical practice's MIS system ages accounts; how rebills affect that aging; how moving it to patient responsibility or changing payers affects the aging; and how payments on the account affect the aging.

An Example of Problem Detection

During one of our practice assessments, we received the aging analysis and gave it a cursory review noting that the aging looked extremely good. However, when we completed our financial analysis, we noted that the accounts receivable ratio was not as low as we had anticipated it would be. Also, the general collection ratio was not as high as we had expected it to be. When we started researching and analyzing what was really happening with the accounts receivable, we began to look in depth at the accounts receivable aging analysis and talking to the collectors about their procedures to follow up on accounts. What we quickly learned from an alphabetical detail of accounts receivable aging was that the patients listed alphabetically A through M had been extremely well-worked (i.e., managed); most had current balances or payment plans on their accounts.

However, when we looked further into the aging detail past the M accounts, we noted that many more of these accounts had past due balances. Our inquiries into this situation revealed some interesting things: Each month the collectors would begin working the past due accounts and would always start at the beginning of the report, which alphabetically started with an A. Without exception, each month they were unable to complete the cycle A through Z before it was time to do month-end close again and run new accounts receivable reports. What had developed was great follow-up and collection on accounts from A through M and mostly inadequate follow-up on the N through Z accounts. Our recommendation to that medical practice and its management was to work the past due accounts receivable aging analysis by size of claim rather than alphabetically. In other words, we want to work the accounts that have the potential for generating the most cash flow for the medical practice. Any limited time should be spent on the higher balances. Some systems even have the capability to run the accounts receivable aging detail by account size.

Graphing the Results

Once you have obtained the aging of accounts, we suggest comparing the aging to additional industry benchmarks in addition to the accounts receivable ratio. The following are sample graphs you should prepare and analyze; this example used the Medical Group Management Association survey.

Looking at Exhibit 2.6, it is evident that the clinic has problems collecting its accounts receivable. This is evidenced by the significant amount of accounts receivable in excess of 120 days.

You need to also analyze accounts receivable by benchmarking the ac-

Exhibit 2.6
Fry Multi-Specialty Clinic
Accounts Receivable Aging Compared to Industry Benchmarks

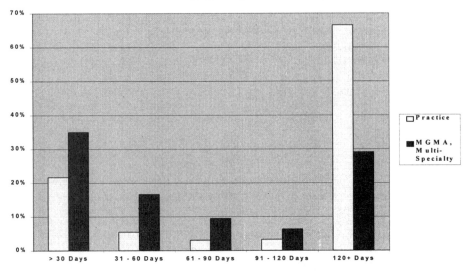

counts receivable with prior years. This analysis should be performed by payer type; this allows you to perform a quick comparison with a related trend analysis to see if problems are developing within certain payer classes. Exhibit 2.7 is a sample graph you can prepare.

Other Factors Impacting Accounts Receivables

It goes without saying that the collectibility of an account diminishes significantly when the patient walks out the office door without making a payment, and collectibility diminishes as these accounts age from current to 30, 60, 90, and 120 days. Therefore, it is imperative, as you will see in Chapter 4, that a practice must do a good job of patient education and collection at the time of service. If practices cannot collect patient-responsible amounts up front, not only does the practice have to deal with the diminishing chances of collection, but it is also quite expensive and time consuming to generate related patient account statements. This is especially true in primary care practices where the copays and deductibles can be extremely small. As we mentioned in chapter one, a practice never wants to see more than 18 percent of its total receivables over 90 days old.

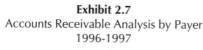

Exhibit 2.7
Accounts Receivable Analysis by Payer
1996-1997

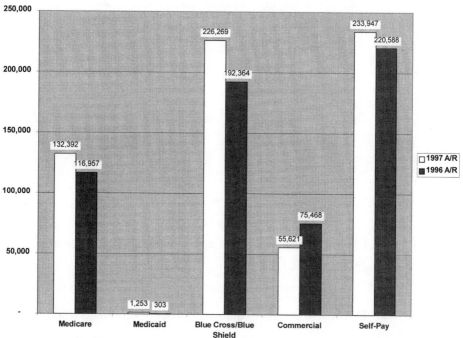

Management Information System (MIS) Evaluation

As we stated, the practice's medical billing software has a major impact on your ability to analyze accounts receivable. As such, you should add a related assessment of the software as part of your overall practice assessment. Practices need to know whether or not they have an adequate software system to properly manage accounts receivable. The following is a series of questions you can ask of the practice administrator or billing personnel. Answers to these questions should allow you to make comments in your assessment report about the software system as it relates to accounts receivable.

1. How does the management information system age accounts?

2. What management information reports are available on accounts receivable balances?

3. Can reports, including aging reports, be run for insurance responsibility only?

4. Can reports be run for patient responsibility only?

5. Does the system re-age once an account moves from insurance responsibility to patient responsibility?

6. Does the system re-age the account when a rebill is generated to the insurance company?

7. Does the system provide the ability to age the accounts by:

   Type of payer?

   Provider?

   Location?

   Practice?

8. Can the system run a management report on outstanding claims sorted by size of claim?

9. Can specific accounts be put on hold status for various reasons?

10. Does the system provide a report of all accounts on hold status?

11. Can promises to pay be tracked or payment budget established?

12. Can the system automatically rebill outstanding claims after a user-specified number of days?

13. Does the system have "no activity" reports for statement generation, payments, or collection activity?

14. How are accounts sent for collection maintained on the system?

15. Can the system track information by managed care plan (co-pays, deductibles, etc.)?

Monthly trends are extremely important in accounts receivable management. When reporting the results of a practice assessment, it can be very beneficial to graphically display the accounts receivable monthly trends with the related charges, collections, and adjustments. The graph in Exhibit 2.8 is from a recent practice assessment for a twelve-month period where accounts receivable, charges, payments, and adjustments are

Exhibit 2.8
Lowery Cardiology Associates
1997 Charges, Payments, Adjustments

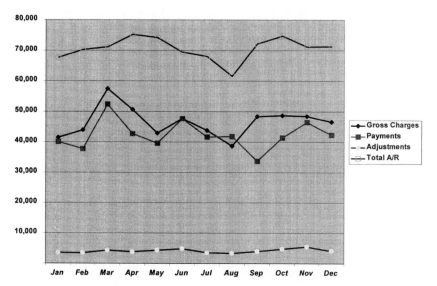

trended to provide the medical practice with a graphical analysis of what is occurring with the accounts receivable balance.

In summary, every practice assessment has to take a close look at accounts receivable and the management thereof. Remember that accounts receivable is the lifeblood of the medical practice and will directly affect cash flow and ultimately the profitability of the medical practice. Good accounts receivable management is the centerpiece of any successful medical practice.

CHAPTER THREE

Reviewing Explanation of Benefits (EOBs)

Now that you have calculated and analyzed the financial performance of the practice, the next step in the assessment process is to review explanation of benefits. An EOB is the document that accompanies the reimbursement check from the insurance company, Medicare, or any other third-party payer. This piece of paper shows the practice what it billed, what the payer will pay for the service, and whether or not there is any deductible and copayment due from the patient.

The financial assessment should show you where potential problems might lie within the practice. It will indicate to you either standard or substandard financial performance, and as such, has a direct bearing on the physician(s), practice personnel, and practice operations. We suggest a review of EOBs as the next step in the assessment process because this review will confirm some of your suspicions resulting from your review of the practice's financial data and related practice management statistics. A review of the EOBs, along with the financial analysis, will allow you to specifically pinpoint potential problem areas within the operations of the practice and its office(s). From here you will be able to concentrate this part of your assessment on these likely problem areas. EOBs are arguably the most important documents within a medical practice. This is because it provides a wealth of information about the practice. By inspecting closely EOBs, you will be able to tell if:

1. The practice is coding properly;

2. The practice is filing its charges correctly;

3. The practice is having problems in the billing process;

4. The practice's personnel are competent;

5. The practice's fee schedule is adequate; and

6. The receivables management process is working or not.

You should inspect enough EOBs necessary for you to formulate an opinion about the six issues just mentioned. Once you do so, the assessment process can proceed to a detailed analysis of the practice's billing and collection process and other specific practice areas.

Gaining access to EOBs is sometimes difficult however. Some smaller offices will place them in the patients' medical records. Larger practices store them off the premises or even throw them away once the reimbursement check is posted to the patient's account. This is such an important part of the assessment process, you must get your hands on these documents. Once you have gained access to the EOBs, you need to do the following procedures with them.

LOOK FOR DENIED CHARGES

The first step is to scan the EOBs for denied charges. If a billed charge is denied, it is usually indicated by a zero in the column on the EOB entitled "Amount Allowed." A third-party payer can deny a billed charge for a variety of reasons; the following are just a few:

1. An improper CPT code and/or diagnosis code was used.

2. The charge conflicted with the patient's insurance coverage.

3. The claim form was submitted too late to the payer.

As you scan the EOBs for denied charges, complete the worksheet in Exhibit 3.1 (⊟ CH0301.DOC). The information list here should provide you with insights on the six practice issues mentioned earlier and might answer certain of your questions that were raised during your initial analysis of the practice's financial performance. On the worksheet you will list the patient's last name, the date of the service, the amount that was billed the payer, and the reason the charge was denied. The reason you want to list the date of the service shown on the EOB is because you want to document that you have reviewed the most recent EOBs and their related charges and services. The

Exhibit 3.1
Listing of Denied Charges

Practice Name: _____
Worksheet Preparation Date: _____

Patient Last Name	Date of Service	Amount Billed	Reason for Denial of Charge

problem with reviewing old EOBs is that either the practice might have already addressed any related problems that you might find or the payer may have changed billing policy, which led to the old denial of the charge in the first place. You want to work with as many recent EOBs that you can.

As stated, third-party payers deny claims for a variety of reasons. The following are common ones, along with an explanation of what might be occuring within the practice causing the denial; specific solutions to these and other problems will be discussed in the next chapter on the analysis of the billing and collection processes:

"Coverage not in effect at the time the service was provided." This means the patient did not have the indicated insurance when he or she was treated. This is a common situation in many medical offices. The patient could have switched jobs and failed to inform the practice of the new health insurance coverage or lost coverage altogether and failed to inform the practice of such occurrence. In most cases, the patient's insurance coverage was not verified before the service was performed.

"Our records indicate this client is enrolled with Medicaid; Please bill Medicaid first." In this instance, the patient had insurance coverage but the prac-

tice billed the wrong payer first. The office failed to verify coverage first or got the wrong insurance information from the patient at the time of the initial appointment.

"*Client is covered by other insurance which must be billed prior to this program.*" Practice failed to obtain the patient's primary health insurance coverage program.

"*These charges were incurred after the patient's cancellation date with the Plan.*" Practice failed to either obtain correct insurance information at the initial new patient visit, verify coverage, or get the patient's new insurance coverage at a subsequent visit.

"*This charge is not covered by the subscriber's benefit plan.*" The practice rendered a service that was not covered by the patient's health plan. One example is a yearly physical—some plans cover it, some don't. Here the practice is not aware of all the coverage requirements of the plan. The practice also probably did not verify coverage before the service was rendered.

"*Your claim lacks information which is needed for adjudication.*"; "*Your claim contains incomplete and/or invalid information, and no appeal rights are afforded because the claim is unprocessable.*" The practice failed to file a "clean claim." This means there was missing information on the insurance claim form necessary to allow the payer to process and pay for the service that was rendered. For example, the patient's social security number could be missing, the health plan's identification number is missing, or information directly related to the service is missing (e.g., A missing diagnosis code).

"*Incomplete/invalid patient's diagnosis (es) and condition (s).*" The practice used the wrong diagnosis code on the insurance claim form.

"*Duplicate claim/service.*" This means the practice has already filed a previous claim to be paid for the service. This is a common occurrence in practices that refile the claim if the original one has not been paid by a certain number of days, such as in 60 days.

"*Physician/supplier signature missing or not in correct block on claim.*" The practice failed to file a clean claim.

"*Services provided outside your office require facility name and address or 9-digit facility provider number.*" The practice failed to file a clean claim.

"*Denied. Incomplete claim beyond 90 day deadline.*" The practice failed to initially file a clean claim form, and failed to detect and correct the problem within the required time filing deadline. Repeated occurrences usually mean there is a problem with the insurance receivable follow-up process.

"*Visit part of global surgical fee.*" Practice either failed to include a CPT modifier on the visit code or is unaware of postoperative global periods.

Obviously the more denied charges that you find, the greater the likelihood that there is a problem with either the billing and collection processes within the practice, the competency of the billing and collection personnel, or a combination of both. As you can see, by finding and analyzing the reasons for the denials, you will be able to go directly to the potential practice problem area and correct it (or provide specific recommendations for correction).

ANALYZE HOW QUICKLY CLAIMS ARE BEING PAID

Every medical practice needs to get paid on a timely basis by insurance plans and third-party payers. Practice cash flow depends on it. EOBs can provide an indication of how quickly the practice on average is getting paid by its payers. On the EOB document is what is commonly called a "control date." This is the date the EOB and related reimbursement check was printed by the insurance company or payer. This is the date you will compare to the last date of service indicated on the EOB. Count the number of days between the control date and the last service date to arrive at an estimate of when the practice received reimbursement from the payer. This is an estimate because there should be a small lag between when the EOB was printed and when it was actually mailed.

You will want to calculate an average payment for a sample of EOBs. This will give you some idea how quickly the practice is getting paid by its payers. *On average, a medical practice should be getting paid between 30 and 45 days from the date the service was rendered.* This is an industry accepted benchmark. If the average exceeds 45 days, this is usually an indication of some problem in the billing and collection process.

Complete the worksheets in Exhibits 3.2 through 3.4(🖫 CH0302.DOC, 🖫 CH0303.DOC, 🖫 CH0304.DOC) to calculate the average payment turnaround. Be sure to investigate EOBs that show a significant number of days before payment was made—you may need to eliminate these from the worksheet because if included, they might skew the average by artificially increasing it. For example, do not include EOBs from a Medicare secondary payer. This applies to patients who have an additional insurance policy to supplement their Medicare coverage. These policies usually pay for amounts that the Medicare patient would normally have to pay out of their own pocket (i.e., deductibles and copayments). A practice cannot file a claim with a Medicare secondary payer until it first receives payment from Medicare; so including these EOBs on the worksheet would increase the payment average.

You might also want to complete the worksheet for individual payers and/or specific medical services. These types of worksheets are also included on the pages that follow. For example, you may want to calculate

Exhibit 3.2
Documentation of Insurance Turnaround by Service

Practice Name: _____
Worksheet Preparation Date: _____

Patient Last Name	Name of Payer	EOB Control Date	Last Date of Service on EOB	Number of Days	Comments

Total Number of Days per Worksheet: _____
Average Payment Turnaround: _____

Exhibit 3.3

Documentation of Insurance Turnaround by Service

Practice Name: _____

Payer Name: _____

Worksheet Preparation Date: _____

Patient Last Name	EOB Control Date	Last Date of Service on EOB	Number of Days	Comments

Total Number of Days per Worksheet: _____

Average Payment Turnaround: _____

Exhibit 3.4
Documentation of Insurance Turnaround by Service

Practice Name: _____
Service: ( ) Procedures ( ) Visits ( ) Radiology ( ) Lab ( ) Other: _____
Worksheet Preparation Date: _____

Patient Last Name	Name of Payer	EOB Control Date	Last Date of Service on EOB	Number of Days	Comments

Total Number of Days per Worksheet: _____
Average Payment Turnaround: _____

how quickly Aetna, Prudential, or Blue Cross/Blue Shield is paying the practice on average. You may want to calculate how quickly the practice is getting paid for surgical procedures only for instance.

INITIAL REVIEW OF THE PRACTICE'S FEE SCHEDULE

The EOBs can be used to initially assess whether or not the practice's fee schedule needs an adjustment, either upward or downward. The objective of every medical practice should be to establish a fee schedule insurance companies consider to be "usual, customary, and reasonable" for the practice's particular service area. You can get an idea what might be usual, customary, and reasonable fees by reviewing a large sample of recent EOBs. If different payers are all approving the billed charge for a particular service for payment, this is an indication the practice's fee schedule might need to be reviewed for specific fee increases.

Exhibit 3.5 is an example of a line item from an EOB indicating full approval of the billed charge:

Exhibit 3.5
EOB Line Item

Service	Billed Charge	Approved Amt	Deductible	Copayment	Payment to Practice
Surgical	2,500	2,500	500	500	1,500

A major indicator that the fee schedule needs adjustment is when you find managed care EOBs where the entire billed charge is approved for payment. Remember what a managed care plan approves for payment is a contractually agreed to *discounted fee*. So if the practice is billing its normal charge *and* the EOB shows the entire charge was approved for payment, then you know there are problems with the fee schedule and a further detailed analysis is warranted. There may be cases where certain practice fees need a reduction. This usually occurs when payers are reducing the fees by indicating on the EOB *"Billed charge exceeds a reasonable, usual, and customary level."* Do not confuse this with fee reductions based on contracts with managed care plans.

To formulate an initial opinion about the practice fee schedule, use the worksheets in Exhibits 3.6 through 3.11 (📄 CH0306.DOC, 📄 CH0307.DOC, 📄 CH0308.DOC, 📄 CH0309.DOC, 📄 CH0310.DOC, 📄 CHO311.DOC) to document billed charges that were approved for payment in full. These

Exhibit 3.6
Documentation of Visit Fees Approved at 100% of Billed Charge

Practice Name: _____

Worksheet Preparation Date: _____

Patient Last Name	Name of Payer	CPT Code	Billed Charge	Comments

Exhibit 3.7
Documentation of Surgical Fees Approved at 100% of Billed Charge

Practice Name: _____
Worksheet Preparation Date: _____

Patient Last Name	Name of Payer	CPT Code	Billed Charge	Comments

Exhibit 3.8

Documentation of Medicine Fees Approved at 100% of Billed Charge

Practice Name: _____

Worksheet Preparation Date: _____

Patient Last Name	Name of Payer	CPT Code	Billed Charge	Comments

Exhibit 3.9

Documentation of Radiology Fees Approved at 100% of Billed Charge

Practice Name: _____

Worksheet Preparation Date: _____

Patient Last Name	Name of Payer	CPT Code	Billed Charge	Comments

Exhibit 3.10

Documentation of Lab/Pathology Fees Approved at 100% of Billed Charge

Practice Name: _____

Worksheet Preparation Date: _____

Patient Last Name	Name of Payer	CPT Code	Billed Charge	Comments

Exhibit 3.11
Summary of Managed Care Reimbursement

Practice Name: _____

Worksheet Preparation Date: _____

CPT Code	Current Fee	Plan __ Reimb	% Discount	Plan __ Reimb	% Discount	Plan __ Reimb	% Discount	Plan __ Reimb	% Discount	Plan __ Reimb

worksheets are separated by the following service lines: visit services, procedures, medicine service, radiology, and laboratory. After completion of these worksheets, as stated above, you may need to perform a more detailed analysis of the fee schedule as part of your assessment process.

CURSORY REVIEW OF MANAGED CARE REIMBURSEMENTS

The next step in the review of EOBs is to perform a cursory review of managed care reimbursements. The purpose of this review is to determine what percentage discount the practice receives on its most commonly performed procedures. Since many managed care plans are continuing their reduction of what they pay physicians for their services, one form of revenue enhancement is the negotiation, or even termination, of managed care contracts. Unfortunately many practices do not closely monitor changes in managed care reimbursements. The movement toward an RBRVS payment methodology has reduced reimbursement substantially in some specialties and in some areas of the country.

A medical practice assessment needs to identify substandard reimbursement and provide solutions on how to either (1) increase reimbursement or (2) diversify the practice's revenue mix. Scan the EOBs to assess which managed care plans are reimbursing the practice at a level that is below an acceptable standard. In other words, the discount off the practice's current fee schedule is unacceptable.

Exhibit 3.11 is a worksheet you can complete that summarizes managed care reimbursement for the practice's 20 most commonly utilized services from its top 4 managed care plans. These four plans generate the majority of the practice's production related to managed care enrollees. If there are more than four plans, make copies of the worksheet to document reimbursement for the additional managed care plans.

CONCLUSION

The intent of the EOB review is to confirm your initial impressions and findings resulting from the analysis of practice financial performance. If the statistical information you calculated during the financial performance analysis appears substandard or not what you think it should be, then a review of the EOBs will confirm some of your suspicions.

If collections are lagging or inconsistent, it might be the result of poor receivables management or a problem with filing the claims in the first place. If receivables are too high or the percentage of old receivables is unacceptable, again it could be the result of poor receivables management or a problem with the billing process. As stated at the beginning of this chapter, the EOB review will detect the following problems, which in turn will have a DIRECT impact on the financial performance of the practice:

The practice is coding properly;

The practice is filing its charges correctly;

The practice is having problems in the billing process;

The practice's personnel is competent;

The practice's fee schedule is adequate; and

The receivables management process is working or not.

Once you have calculated and analyzed practice statistics, and once you have reviewed and analyzed EOBs and performed a detailed analysis of the accounts receivable, the next step in the assessment process is to perform a detailed analysis and review of the practice's billing and collection processes. Most of the problems associated with the practice's financial performance can be traced directly to them.

CHAPTER FOUR

Analysis of the Billing and Collection Processes

The next step in the assessment of the medical practice is to perform a detailed analysis of the medical practice's billing and collection processes. Your analysis of the practice's past financial performance, along with the accounts receivable and EOB analyses, should have provided insight into these processes. In particular, potential problem areas could have, and most likely should have, been identified.

A detailed analysis of the billing and collection processes is a critical component of any medical practice assessment. The assessment should target these processes early on because of the significant impact they have on the practice's earnings and cash flow. Bettering these processes usually creates a positive impact on the cash flow of the practice.

The following is a detailed breakdown of the billing and collection processes in the form of a questionnaire. As part of the assessment engagement, you should provide an answer to each question in each section. Generally this can be completed by the practice's billing and collection personnel or by the practice administrator. You may want to conduct a formal interview with these individuals using the questionnaire. The complete checklist is included in the appendix.

Included in this chapter will be a discussion of potential problem areas, how to detect each during the financial analysis and EOB analysis, and possible solutions for each problem by analyzing the practice's billing and collection processes. To make this analysis make sense, the processes have been broken down as if you are walking a patient through the practice's billing and collection system from start to finish. In other words, from the patient's visit to the office, to the related billing, and to the resulting final collection.

PATIENT SCHEDULING

What are patients instructed when they call into the office for an appointment?:

_____

_____

_____

The answer to this question is vital for most medical practices simply because it has the initial direct impact on the practice's billing and collection processes. For example, new patients need to be instructed to bring in their insurance card or established patients need to be asked if their insurance has changed since the last visit so they can be asked to bring in their new insurance card. Failing to obtain certain information off the card could result in filing an incomplete insurance claim form; in other words, a "clean claim" is not filed. It could also delay the filing of the claims because the billing personnel are trying to get the patient's insurance information after he or she visits the office.

Patients should also be instructed of the practice's visit payment policy. For example, *Mrs. Taylor, your appointment is set for this Friday at 11 a.m. As a reminder, our office policy is that you will need to pay your copayment at the time of your visit.* One reason offices have problems collecting for visit related charges is because patients are not informed beforehand of the policies. Did you ever wonder why dentists do a much better job at collecting monies from patients as they checkout of the office than doctor offices do? It is because they rely on these payments and as such, place greater emphasis on this part of the billing and collection process. Physician offices need to do the same. As you will see later on in this chapter, attempting to collect these monies as part of the receivables process is not very efficient.

The EOB analysis should detect these problems as well as the analysis of front desk collections and the analysis of how quickly insurance claim forms are getting filed, each of which will be discussed later on in this chapter. Production moving up and down on the financial analysis worksheet could also be an indicator.

What is the office visit payment policy:

_____

_____

_____

There should be one policy and one policy only for all medical practices: To collect monies owed by patients at the time of their office visit. This policy needs to be communicated to patients on a regular basis, as for example at the time of their appointment as just discussed above. Any breakdown in this part of the billing and collection process will have a direct impact on the cash flow of the practice. Any breakdown also has a direct impact on the receivables management process in that it is costly and a waste of the staff's time to try to collect small deductibles and copayments. Not having this policy at all has a direct impact on the billing process in that more claims will have to be filed than is ordinarily necessary. This takes up valuable staff time and will obviously delay cash flow.

Your financial analysis of the accounts receivable is usually a good indicator of whether or not the office has a visit collection policy and whether or not it is being followed. As will be discussed later on in this chapter, the analysis of front desk collections could also be an indicator (refer to section on patient checkout) of visit collection policy. To further the receivables analysis, obtain a current detailed aged accounts receivable listing by patient name. Scan the report for all balances $200 or less; are there many? Couldn't these amounts have been collected by front desk personnel as they checked out the patients?

To further the investigation, complete the simple worksheet shown in Exhibit 4.1 (📄 CH0401.DOC), to detect possible collection problems related to office visits.

This should be a small percentage of the total accounts receivable balance. If not, look for two problems:

- A lack of a front desk collection policy, and

- A failure by the front desk to collect monies at the time of patient visits. You will then complete the front desk collection analysis worksheet as described later on in this chapter.

Exhibit 4.1
Analysis of Small Receivable Balances

Practice Name: _____

Worksheet Preparation Date: _____

Accounts receivable balance as of _____	$	
Total of balances that are $200 or less (small balances)	$	
% of small balances to total accounts receivable		%

When is the patient's insurance information first obtained?:

_____

_____

_____

    This applies to new patients. Is the insurance information obtained before the visit, or as is usually the case, at the time of the patient's visit to the office? Some offices will attempt to secure patient insurance information over the telephone; this way the patient's coverage and coverage benefits can be verified before the patient's visit. It is becoming a common practice for medical offices to mail new patient packets prior to the patient visit for completion of this vital information. Most offices, however, have the patient complete a New Patient Registration Form when they arrive at the office. A sample form is shown in Exhibit 4.2.

    This is where many offices have problems—when they fail to obtain all insurance information or accurate information from the patient or the patient's family. Front desk personnel must make sure all line items on the form are completed. This is also why it is so important to obtain a copy of the patient's insurance card so that what is written down on the registration form can be confirmed by the information on the card itself. One of the most common billing problems is filing claims without accurate information on them, which in turn leads to a denial of payment or at the very least, a delay in payment. This situation is usually detected during the analysis

Exhibit 4.2
New Patient Registration Form

AUS   ⏌ PERINATAL ASSOCIATES, . ..
DAVID L. BERRY, M. D.

PATIENT DEMOGRAPHICS SHEET
PLEASE PRINT ✎   Date: _____

Name: _____   Date of birth: _____ / _____ / _____
       (Last)   (First)   (Middle)   (Month) (Day) (Year)

Address: _____ Age _____
        (Street Number & Name)   (City)   (State)   (Zip)

Phone (_____) - _____ Marital status: ▢ Married ▢ Single ▢ Divorced

Patient's employer: _____ Work phone (_____) - _____

Spouse's name: _____

Spouse's employer: _____ Work phone (_____) - _____

Person responsible for bill (if other than above) _____ Relationship to patient _____

Address: _____ Phone (_____) - _____
      (Street Number & Name)   (City)   State)   (Zip)

Nearest relative (Not living with patient) _____ Relationship to patient _____

Address: _____ Phone (_____) - _____
      (Street Number & Name)   (City)   State)   (Zip)

Were you referred by another physician? If so, whom? _____ Phone (_____) _____

Address: _____
      (Street Number & Name)   (City)   (State)   (Zip)

Primary Insurance Company (#1)

Insurance name _____

Member name _____

Employer _____

Address for mailing claims: _____
     (Street Number & Name)   (City)   (State)   (Zip)

Policy #, Certificate #, or ID #: _____ Group # _____ Phone (_____) - _____

Reason for visit _____ **Last menstrual period** _____ / _____ / _____

AUTHORIZATION TO RELEASE INFORMATION AND TO PAY BENEFITS
I hereby authorize any physician who has treated or attended me or my dependent to furnish any medical information requested In consideration of services rendered, I hereby transfer and assign to David Berry, M.D., who has treated me or my dependent. any benefits of insurance that I may have A photocopy of this authorization shall be considered as effective and valid as the original

Patient's Social Security #: _____ / _____ / _____   Spouse's Social Security # _____ / _____ / _____

Drivers License #: _____ (State) _____   Medicare # _____

Signature _____   Medicaid # _____

Please check insurance type   ▢ **STANDARD**   ▢ **HMO**   ▢ **PPO**   ▢ **MEDICAID**   ▢ **OTHER** of EOBs. Denial messages indicate that accurate patient insurance information was not obtained by the practice.

Payment analysis will also detect a problem with obtaining accurate insurance information (refer to the section below on collections). If a practice is having problems getting paid on a timely basis, one reason might be that they send the insurance claim to a wrong address for the carrier. The carrier's billing address is almost always indicated on the patient's insurance card.

Overall, it is preferable to obtain patient insurance information at the time the appointment is made. This way, the practice can verify the patient's coverage and coverage benefits before they walk in the door. This allows the practice to address coverage problems immediately with the patient and also to be able to collect copayments and deductibles at the time of patient checkout. For example, if the patient has not met their deductible, the practice must attempt collection at the time of visit; otherwise, the claim form will be filed and a portion of the allowed payment will get allocated to the unmet deductible. This means the practice will now have to try to get payment from the patient; in other words, getting paid for the service will take longer than what it should have if the practice had just collected the deductible at the time of the visit.

Securing patient insurance information will admittedly be difficult for smaller offices or for any office with an inadequate amount of front desk-related personnel. An office with an unusually high number of daily phone calls will also have problems; it is hard to obtain insurance information after making the appointment when the phone is ringing off the hook! If this is the case, analyze front office job duties to determine if these individuals are being as efficient as they can be and to make sure valuable time is not being wasted. As part of the assessment, you might want to even spend time in the front desk area to just observe what is going on and to assess employee efficiency.

When is insurance verified:

_____

_____

_____

As just mentioned above, preferably insurance should be verified before the patient's appointment or inpatient service. For example, the practice will want to verify the patient's coverage before surgery is performed. However, as you will see below, insurance verification ideally should be performed before the patient's appointment. Exhibit 4.3 is a sample insurance verification form.

Exhibit 4.3
Sample Insurance Verification Form

TODAY'S DATE_____
INITIAL'S   _____

INSURANCE PRECERTIFICATION INFORMATION

PATIENT INFO

NAME _____   ADDRESS _____

PHONE _____   _____

DOB _____   _____

SS# _____   _____

NEAREST RELATIVE NOT LIVING WITH PATIENT (NAME)_____RELATION_____

                               ADDRESS _____
                               PHONE   _____

EMPLOYER_____   INSURANCE_____

ADDRESS _____   ADDRESS _____

        _____   _____

PHONE _____ CONTACT_____   PHONE _____CONTACT_____

REF. PHYSICIAN _____   GROUP# _____

SYMPTONS _____   POLICY# _____

        _____   PRE-CERT# _____

        _____   CONTACT(s)_____

TYPE SURGERY _____   COVERAGE _____

        _____   _____

        _____   OTHER NOTES:_____

PROPOSED DATE OF SURG. _____   _____

PHYSICIAN _____   _____

_____

_____

_____

_____

_____

_____

_____

_____

The following is why insurance should be verified before the patient's appointment:

1. In order to know what the practice should collect from the patient when the patient checks out—deductibles, copayments, or full payment for the services that were rendered.

2. If the patient has to have surgery, to be able to know beforehand what the patient's financial responsibility will be and attempt to collect this amount before the surgery is performed. At the very least, the office should attempt to collect what is normally termed a "surgical deposit."

3. If the patient does not have insurance, or if the insurance does not cover the service that is going to be performed, the office will want to make payment arrangements with the patient before the service is actually performed.

4. To determine if the physician is a participating physician with the plan.

5. Pre-certification requirements.

6. Referral requirements.

7. Ancillary/facility participants and guidelines.

8. Patient eligibility.

The EOB analysis will usually detect problems with insurance verification issues. This is particularly true if one reason for charge denials is because the patient was no longer covered under the policy to which the service was billed. This means the office failed to verify coverage or find out that the patient's insurance coverage had changed and that he or she failed to inform the office of the change.

This is again why it is important for the front desk to inquire at the time of each patient appointment whether or not the patient's coverage has changed since their last appointment or at least have some signage in the waiting area or near the patient check in area prompting the patients to: *"Please inform the office if your insurance coverage has changed since your last visit."*

A question often arises as to how often an office should verify coverage for established patients. In our opinion, an office should verify coverage if the patient has not been treated within six months of the patient's last visit to the office. Some offices will make the patient complete another registration form if the patient has not been seen in the office for over a year.

A final word about verification and obtaining patient insurance information: offices should not rely on hospital face sheets for patient insurance information. Face sheets are computer generated sheets prepared by a hospital at the time of patient admittance. Physicians have access to these sheets and as such, many will bring a face sheet back to the office for the office's billing and collection personnel. These individuals will then use the face sheets to get the patient's insurance information in order to file a claim to the patient's insurance carrier. It has been our experience that many times the patient information on these sheets is either wrong or incomplete. Therefore, we always suggest a practice independently obtain and verify a patient's insurance coverage whenever practically possible.

PATIENT CHECK-IN

Are patients required to sign in: ___ yes ___ no; if yes, is the sign-in sheet maintained as a permanent office record: ___ yes ___ no

A sign-in sheet is exactly what it means: patients sign the sheet when they arrive for their appointment. For management purposes, there are only two reasons to maintain and keep a sign in sheet: (1) To make sure all charges are inputted into the computer on a timely basis (or at all) and (2) to check for embezzlement. One excellent checks-and-balances procedure is to periodically take a sample of the sign-in sheets and compare the names to when the charge was posted into the computer. The longer it takes charges to get posted to the computer, the longer it takes to file a claim form and the longer it takes the practice to get paid (Excluding, of course, payments that can and should be collected at the time of the patient's visit). Management will also, during this process, want to make sure all visit charges did get entered into the computer. Missing charges can be a problem for some practices, especially those with inexperienced personnel.

One other reason the sign-in sheets are used is as a checks and balances for employee embezzlement. When management compares the names on the sign in sheet to the charges that were entered into the computer, management should also look for names on the sign-in sheet that were not entered into the computer. The reason for the lack of posting is that an employee might have embezzled from the practice. Sometimes an employee will check a patient out, keep whatever monies were paid by the patient, and not post the charge to the computer. This is the simplest form of embezzlement in a medical office.

Of course, patient confidentiality should be maintained, and, as such, sign-in sheets should not be used for some medical practices. Sign-in sheets are not recommended for cancer and mental health offices. However, many doctors do not want to use sign-in sheets at all because of patient confidentiality issues.

The financial analysis may lead you to investigate embezzlement issues. These are situations where cash flow and the related financial statistics just do not agree with how hard the physician or physicians are working. In this situation, an employee might be stealing money but not posting the related charge into the computer. In other situations, the amount the office is collecting does not seem to agree to its payer mix; in other words, based on the practice's payer mix, it should be collecting more on its production that it presently is. In this case, an employee could be embezzling by stealing money and covering their tracks by writing off the patient's entire receivable as a contractual adjustment.

How does the office find out if a patient's insurance coverage has changed since the last visit:

_____

_____

_____

This issue was previously discussed in this chapter. A common reason for charge denials is when the patient's insurance coverage has changed and the practice bills the patient's old insurance carrier for reimbursement. To avoid this situation, we recommend the following:

1. Have signage in the waiting area or near the reception desk asking the patient to inform the office if their coverage has changed since their last visit;

2. Make the patient complete another registration form if the patient has not visited the office within the past twelve months; and

3. Make sure the office verifies insurance coverage when appropriate, especially for new patients and inpatient services.

Does the office make a copy of the patient's insurance card: _____ *yes* _____ *no*

Does the office make a copy of the patient's driver's license: _____ *yes* _____ *no*

The need to obtain a copy of the patient's insurance card has already been discussed in this chapter. Many offices like to also make a copy of a new patient's driver's license in case there is a problem collecting that patient's account sometime in the future. The driver's license can be used to track down patients who have moved without your knowledge and can be used in other collection efforts.

Does the office document and track where new patients come from: ___ *yes* ___ *no. If yes, how:*

_____

_____

_____

The financial analysis may indicate an immediate drop in production or a steady decline in production over time. One reason production for some doctors has slowed is because their referrals from other physicians or sources have decreased. This is why it is so very important that any office track where their new patients are coming from. This applies to primary care practices as well as specialty practices.

If the financial analysis indicates production declines for a specialty physician or practice, the first place you should investigate is the referring physician report; this report can be printed out of most medical billing software systems. Ideally the practice has printed and maintained these reports for at least the previous two years or, hopefully, you can reprint these reports from the practice's computer system. The objective is to compare current referral patterns to those of the past, especially by individual physician or source referral. If referrals have, in fact, declined, you will need to investigate why.

Consider it a red flag if the practice cannot provide referring doctor/source reports; this usually means the practice has not been tracking this information. Specifically, the front desk has not been making sure new patients are completing the referral/source section on the new patient registration form. You should look to make sure the new patient registration form even has this line item on it; there are some practices that do not have a "where were you referred from" line item on their new patient registration form!

For example, a general surgeon could be experiencing a decline in production. You investigate the referring doctor report and find that referrals have declined from the doctor's top two referrers. The next step is to find out why this has occurred; maybe the doctors are on managed care plans that the practice is not, thereby resulting in a situation where the doctors cannot refer to the practice. Maybe the referrals have declined because the doctor or practice has done something to upset the referring physicians. In any event, find out why the referrals have declined by documenting the worksheet in Exhibit 4.4 (⊟ CH0404.DOC).

If a primary care practice has experienced a decline in new patient encounters (i.e., production), look not only to the lack of participation in managed care plans for an answer, but a decrease in new patients as a result of reducing marketing efforts. Keep in mind that most primary care practices in reality are somewhat similar to "retail" businesses. In other words, new

Exhibit 4.4
Analysis of Physician Referral Patterns

Referring Doctor/Source	Referrals Current Year	Referrals Last Year	Referrals for Year _____	Reason for Decline in Referrals

patients come to a primary care practice "off the street." This means that patients needing treatment must be aware of the practice, the doctors, and/or the practice location. These must be marketed to the patient community on an ongoing, almost continuous, basis. As a result, some practices actually do lose new patients simply because they have decreased or eliminated their marketing efforts. These include advertising, direct mail, public participation activities, and so on. Again, the financial analysis portion of the assessment process should identify a decline in new patient encounters.

Is new patient demographic information inputted into the computer before a patient is escorted to the exam room? _____ yes _____ no. If no, please explain:

_____

_____

_____

The financial analysis may indicate inconsistent production and inconsistent collections. One reason might be that insurance claims forms are not being prepared and filed on a timely basis. Obviously when a claim is filed late, the time it takes to get paid by the third-party carrier will be extended also. One common reason why claims do not get filed on time is because new patient demographic information is not inputted into the computer at the time of the patient's first visit to the office. Specifically, this information should be inputted before the patient is escorted to the exam room. Why? Mainly because after the patient is checked out and leaves the office, a claim form for the office service can be prepared immediately.

If billing personnel have to wait for this information, for example when not all information is obtained from the patient, they cannot prepare a claim form. To reiterate, this delay affects the timing of the practice's cash flow. Demographic information is obtained from the New Patient Registration Form. Once this form is given back to the front desk, the personnel should first make sure all line items are completed. The next step is to input the information into the practice's computer system. After this is accomplished, the billing personnel will be ready to file the insurance claim.

PATIENT CHECKOUT

Does the doctor complete all information on the charge ticket? _____ yes _____ no

When a doctor treats a patient, a charge ticket (often called a superbill) is placed on top of the patient's medical chart. This form is used by the doctor and the office to record the services that were rendered and to record the related diagnoses. Exhibit 4.5 shows an example of an office charge ticket.

If the physician does not complete the charge ticket, the patient will not be able to be checked on properly. In other words, the people at the checkout desk will not know what services were rendered (the CPT code) and/or why they were rendered (the diagnosis code). In this situation, the office cannot tell the patient what they owe for the services that were rendered and even more important, cannot collect the payment, copayment, or sometimes even the deductible. Also, if applicable, a claim form cannot be prepared because the billing staff is waiting for someone to enter into the computer the services that were rendered along with their related diagnosis codes.

The issue here again is cash flow. If a practice cannot collect monies at the time of the patient's visit, it will have to bill an insurance company and/or the patient for these services. This results in delayed cash flow and in some cases, bad debts. If the practice must bill an insurance company, the claim cannot get prepared in a timely manner.

This issue is best illustrated by a real life example. There was a cardiologist who refused (for reasons nobody could figure out!) to fill out the charge ticket when treating patients in the office. As such, when a patient checked out, he or she did not receive any kind of paper showing the patient what services were rendered and what amounts are owed. The office personnel then had to go directly to the patient's medical chart, figure out what the doctor did, and record this information on the patient's charge ticket. You should be able to see the problems all of this caused in the office.

First, the patient was given no information when he or she left the office. If a patient is totally unaware of what it cost to be treated, he or she might be in store for a surprise when the office finally gets around to billing the patient for their ultimate financial responsibility for these services. This can lead to delayed collection and often a bad debt situation because the patient is balking at paying the amount billed. Secondly, the office was unable to collect any monies from the patient at the time of the visit. This too delayed cash flow because the services were placed in the practice's billing cycle.

The office used up a tremendous amount of time resources by causing employees to search through medical charts just to complete the charge tickets. This obviously caused the employees to get behind on all of their other job duties. This created numerous inefficiencies and bottlenecks in small offices since employees only have so much time to complete all of

Exhibit 4.5
Sample Office Charge Ticket

MARION HILLS MEDICAL CLINIC RICHARD L. ROSS, MD 967 Medical Drive, Marion Hills, MS 32095 (228) 394-2905 Tax ID# 73-0195863	Patient Name		DATE ENCOUNTER FORM NO.
	Acct #	Pt's DOB	Appointment Time
	Address		**Previous Balance**
Referring Doctor	City, State, Zip		**Today's Charge**
Primary Insurance	Phone #		**Today's Payment**
Secondary Insurance	Payment:___ Cash ___Credit Card		**New Balance**
RETURN APPOINTMENT:	Check No.		

OFFICE VISIT / LABORATORY / INJECTIONS

X	NEW PATIENT	CODE	AMT	X	DESCRIPTION	CODE	AMT	X	DESCRIPTION	CODE	AMT
	Focused / Straightforward	99201			CBC, Partial diff	85024			Allergy Injection	95115	
	Expanded / Straightforward	99202			Cholesterol	82465			Bicillin 1.2ml	J0540	
	Detailed / Low Complexity	99203			CULTURE, Throat	87060			Celestone	J0702	
	Comprehensive / Moderate Comp	99204			CULTURE, Urine	87088			Decadron 4mg/ml	J1100	
	Comprehensive / High Complexity	99205			Glucose, strip	82948			Decadron LA	J1095	
	Initial OV for * Procedure	99025			H. Pylori Kit	87082			DepoMedrol 40mg	J1030	
X	ESTABLISHED	CODE	AMT		Hemoccult	82270					
	Minimal / May not require physicia	99211			Mono Spot Test	86310			Phenergan 50mg	J2550	
	Focused / Straightforward	99212			PPD, TB	86585			Rocephin 250mg	J0696	
	Expanded / Low Complexity	99213			Pregnancy, serum	84702					
	Detailed / Moderate Complexity	99214			Specimen transfer	99000			Tetanus Toxoid	90703	
	Comprehensive / High Complexity	99215			Strep ID	83518			Toradol 15mg	J1885	
X	PREVENTIVE OFFICE VISIT	CODE	AMT		UA Pregnancy	81025			Vitamin B-12	J3420	
	New Patient/12-17 years	99384			Urinalysis, w/o microsc	81003			OTHER:		
	New Patient/18-39 years	99385			Venipuncture	36415					
	New Patient/40-64 years	99386			OTHER:						

X-RAYS

X	Est Patient/12-17 years	99394		X	DESCRIPTION	CODE	AMT
	Est Patient/18-39 years	99395			Ankle	73600	
	Est Patient/40-64 years	99396			Chest 1-view	71010	
					Chest 2-views	71020	

OFFICE PROCEDURES / SUPPLIES

X	DESCRIPTION	CODE	AMT	X	DESCRIPTIONS	CODE	AMT	X	DESCRIPTION	CODE	AMT
	Biopsy Skin (Cytology)	11100			Ace S M L	A4460			Elbow 2-views	73070	
	Cryotherapy, Warts	17340*			Crutches	EO112			Femur 2-views	73550	
	Ear Irrigation	69210			Dressing S M L				Fingers 2-views	73140	
	EKG, Complete	93000			Eye Tray/Patch				Foot 2-views	73620	
	Excision Lesion/Site (Size)	113 *			Knee Imobilizer	L2999			Forearm 2-views	73090	
	I & D Abscess, simple	10060			Rib Belt	A4572			Hand 2-views	73120	
	Removal Foreign Body, eye	65220*			Sling	A4565			Humerus 2-views	73060	
	Simple Repair, Superficial	12002*			Splint	A4570			Knee 2-views	73560	
	OTHER:				Steri Strip	A4454			Ribs 2-views	71100	
					Surgical Tray	A4550			Spine, CX, 2 views	72040	
					Tennis Elbow Sleeve	L6100			Spine, LS, 2 views	72100	
					OTHER:				OTHER:		

DIAGNOSES

X	DESCRIPTION	CODE		DESCRIPTION	CODE		DESCRIPTION	CODE
	Abdominal Pain, Unsp.	789.0		Edema, unspecified cause	782.3		Upper Respiratory Infection	465.9
	Adenitis, cervical	289.3		Esophageal Reflux	530.81		Urinary Tract Infection	599.0
	Allergic Reaction	995.2		Fatigue	780.7		Urethritis	597.80
	Allergy	995.3		Foreign Body, Eye	930.		Vaginitis	616.10
	Amenorrhea	256.8		Gastritis	535.5		Verneral Disease	099.9
	Anemia, Iron Deficiency	280.9		Headache	784.0		Vertigo	780.4
	Angina, unstable	411.1		Hernia, Hiatal	553.3		Wart, common	078.10
	Anxiety	300.00		Herpes, Simplex	054.9		OTHER:	
	Arthritis,_____,_____			Hypercholesterolemia	272.0			
	Asthma, unspecified	493.9_		Hypertension	401.1			
	Bleeding, rectal	569.3		Lower back pain	724.2			
	Bronchitis, acute	466.0		Influenza with resp manifest	487.1			
	Bursitis, unspecified	727.3						
	Cellulitis, leg	682.6		Menopause Syndrome	627.2			
	Chest pain, unspecified	786.59		Migraine	346.9_			
	Cholelithiasis	574.1_		Nausea and Vomiting	787.01			
	Congestive heart failure	428.0		Otitis Media	382.9			
	Conjunctivitis	372.03		Pap Smear	V72.3			
	Constipation	564.0		Pelvic Inflammatory Dis—P.I.D.	614._			
	Contact Dermatitis, unspecified cause	692.9		Pharyngitis	462			
	Cyst, Sebaceous	706.2		Phlebitis, unspecified site	451.9			
	Cystitis, unspecified	595.9		Physical Exam, General	V70.0			
	Dehydration	276.5		Pneumonia	486			
	Depression, major	296.30		Prostatitis	601.9		Outpatient Tests:	
	Diabetes Mellitus, Insulin Dep	250.01		Sinusitis, maxillary	473.0			
	Diabetes Mellitus, Non-Insulin Dep	250.00					Referrals:	
	Diarrhea	787.91		Strep Throat	034.0			
	Dysfunctional/func uterine hemorrhage	626.8		Stye	373.11		Remarks:	
	Dyspepsia	536.8		Tendonitis	726.90			
	Eczema	692.9		Tonsilitis	474.0			

their duties during the day. Finally, the employees were actually recording what the doctor did based on his documentation in the chart. What if the employees recorded the wrong information, using the wrong CPT codes, or used the wrong diagnosis codes? This type of situation could eventually lead to an insurance audit, especially one by a government agency.

If the patient is on a managed care plan, how does the front desk know how much to collect as a copayment from each patient?

   The receivables analysis may indicate numerous small balances owed by patients to the practice. Most often than not this has occurred because the front desk has failed to collect managed care copayments from these individuals. We all should know the time and effort it takes a practice to collect these small amounts; sometimes the cost of collection actually exceeds the amount to be collected. If managed care copayments (or any other type of copayment for that matter) are not collected by the front desk at the time of patient checkout, it means that the practice has delayed its cash flow and most likely, valuable staff time is spent trying to collect these small amounts rather than concentrating on collecting larger amounts.

   The way to detect whether or not an office is doing a good job at front desk collections is to complete the Front Desk Collection Analysis Worksheet (Exhibit 4.6, ▤ CH0406.DOC) mentioned later on in this chapter. If a practice ever does have a problem collecting copayments, it is usually because the front desk did not know what to collect from the patient. This situation obviously occurs as a result of a lack of knowledge of what copayment to collect from the patients. Attempt to find out how the front desk identifies how much a person should pay as their copayment at the time of service. If the office is having problems with this, you may suggest the development of a managed care cheat sheet, one that lists what a person owes as their copayment.

   However, there is no problem guessing at the copayment amount and collecting it for most managed care contracts. For example, many offices have the policy to collect $10 from a patient if the copayment amount is unknown. While this may result in an overpayment situation in some instances, keep in mind the practice still has received its money. This is much more cost effective than sending out numerous patient statements trying to collect these small amounts (and spending valuable staff time), even if a refund check may have to be sent out for the overpayment.

When the patient checks out, is all the charge and payment information entered into the computer before the patient leaves the office? ____ yes ____ no. If no, explain why not:

_____

_____

_____

When a patient checks out after his or her office exam or services, it is best if the related charge and payment data is entered into the computer before the patient leaves the office. This allows the office to bill the patient's insurance immediately, hopefully the next day. This speeds up cash flow if the charge can get billed to the carrier quickly. If the insurance claim turnaround analysis (discussed later on in this chapter) indicates that claim forms are not being filed quickly, this could be one of the reasons why.

By inputting the charge information into the computer at time of checkout, collections of copays and deductibles goes up. Having the computer calculate this and inform the patient adds credibility to the process. Don't underestimate the benefits of this checkout policy.

If the patient has an overdue balance, is there an attempt to collect this amount from the patient while the patient is in the office? ____ yes ____ no. If no, explain why not:

_____

_____

_____

The financial analysis may indicate a problem with accounts receivable collections. As such, one way to improve these collections is to make sure the office is attempting to collect overdue balances while the patient is in the office. If monies can be collected on overdue accounts when the patient is in the office, then the office does not have to incur the cost of sending out patient statements and hopefully eliminate related staff time.

Most practices will have the front desk personnel discuss with the patient about their overdue balance. Others will give the patient a statement while they are in the office with a note attached asking the patient if a payment can be made toward the account. This avoids the situation where other patient may accidentally hear the front desk conversation regarding overdue balances. For larger receivable balances, the office manager or a collection clerk will personally speak with the patient in private before the patient is escorted to the exam room. This is often done in a separate room in the office. As noted under patient scheduling, many clinics make these collection efforts at the time the patient calls in for an appointment.

If the patient is scheduled for surgery, does the office attempt to collect a surgical deposit? ____ *yes* ____ *no*

Do patients receive any type of financial counseling before the procedure is performed? ____ *yes* ____ *no*

Most offices operate backwards. What we mean by this is that a doctor will render a service, the office will bill the patient's insurance, and only then bill the patient for his or her ultimate financial responsibility. This only has the effect of delaying cash flow, which should be indicated by the gross collection percentage and the related receivable analysis. Just look at the small balances in the detailed accounts receivable aging report; ask yourself, why couldn't these amounts have been collected before the service was rendered?

If a patient has to have surgery, hopefully the office will have verified the coverage and related benefits before the surgery is rendered. Preferably this is done before or at the time of the patient's visit to the office. This way, if a patient has to be scheduled for surgery, the office manager or a collection clerk can counsel the patient on what his or her personal responsibility is for the service to be rendered. At this time, a surgical deposit or at least a request for payment of patient's ultimate copayment and/or deductible can be made.

The objective of this duty should be clear: If monies are collected up front, they do not become receivables, which in turn improves practice cash flow, saves personnel time, and decreases the practice's cost of collection. In other words, from a financial analysis viewpoint, this activity will improve collections, the gross collection percentage, the net collection percentage, the percent of receivables over 90 days old, and the accounts receivable ratio.

When a patient checks out after the office visit is complete, does the front desk (or checkout desk) attempt to collect full payment, deductibles, and/or copayments? ____ *yes* ____ *no*

As just mentioned, the more a practice can do to obtain monies for services rendered before these related charges enter the receivables cycle, the better the practice's cash flow and financial position will be. One reason receivables are too high and related collection poor is because the office does an inadequate job of collecting monies from patients when they check out after their appointment is finished. This is a chronic problem especially for very busy offices (i.e., offices that see a large number of patient visits each day) and offices that are understaffed.

Problems with front desk collections should show up in your analysis of accounts receivable; a simple review of a detail aging report could reveal numerous small account balances, most of which probably could have been collected at the front desk. Unfortunately, many offices actually believe they do a good job of collecting monies from patients at the front desk. To find out exactly how good the office is at collecting, you should complete a Front Desk Collection Analysis Worksheet. An example of this worksheet is shown in Exhibit 4.6. This worksheet calculates the percent of visits where some payment was received at time of check out.

We think it is unrealistic to believe a front desk is going to collect all the monies they can collect all the time. We think a better analysis approach is to see of all the patients that came into the office for a particular time period, how many made a payment on their account, even if it was only a dollar. The objective should be to obtain some payment from each patient who comes into the office for care. Don't forget, any monies the front desk collects do not end up in accounts receivable!

On the worksheet, select a sample of patient visits. Generally, this sample is a full day of patient visits. For example, analyze all patient visits for November 24 and possibly other specific days; you will want to make sure your sample size is large enough to be able to form an opinion on how well the front desk does at collection. On the worksheet, it is important to point out that you will only include those patients who can make a payment at the time of their visit, even if it is only one dollar. Do not include patients that are precluded by law or some other reason from making a payment at the time of their appointment. Good examples are Medicaid and workers' compensation payments; offices cannot collect monies from these patients at the time of their visit.

This is why it is important to complete the column indicating "type of insurance." If you do not know if a particular type of insurance precludes payment by a patient at the time of the office visit, ask the office manager or a member of the billing staff. If in doubt, assume the monies could have been collected from the patient. Once the worksheet is complete, count the number of visits on the worksheet and then count up the number of visits where some payment was collected, even if it was only one dollar. Then calculate the percent of visits where a collection occurred.

Exhibit 4.6

Front Desk Collection Analysis Worksheet

Practice Name: _____

Worksheet Preparation Date: _____

Date	Patient Name	Type of Insurance	Office Charge	Amount Collected

Total visits per worksheet _____
Total visits where collection occurred _____
Percent of visits collected _____%

A practice should be able to collect at least 90 percent or more of patient visits applicable to patients that are able to pay some amount at the time of their visit. If the percent shown in Exhibit 4.6 is below this benchmark, obviously you need to investigate why and provide recommendations to improve it. Any improvement in this percentage will improve the cash flow and receivables position of the practice. Generally front desk people do a poor job of collecting because of two reasons: A lack of training and a lack of oversight. Never assume someone "likes" to collect money from people and they know "how" to collect money from people. Sometimes the wrong person is in the front desk position or their job duty is unclear. In any event, practice management must oversee the front desk just as much as it oversees other areas of the practice, such as patient insurance billing.

BILLING

Explain how the office communicates inpatient (generally hospital) charges to the office so that the office can bill these services to the patient's insurance carrier.

_____

_____

_____

During the financial analysis, if production and even collections are uneven (i.e., inconsistent) from month to month, one explanation could be because the office is having trouble capturing and billing inpatient services. Keep in mind a practice's billing personnel has absolutely no idea what a doctor is doing when he or she visits patients in an inpatient facility, such as a hospital. It should be up to the doctor to communicate what he or she did at this facility so that the billing personnel can properly and timely file for payment on the patient's insurance. Any breakdown in this communication will cause a delay in filing claims and a resulting delay in cash flow.

A problem here, and other problems with the claims filing process, can usually be identified by completing the Insurance Filing Worksheet, an example of which is shown in Exhibit 4.7. Using the worksheet, take a sample of claim forms for a particular service; do not mix, for example, office visits with hospital visits, with surgical procedures, and so on. You want to analyze specific service lines because you want to assess whether or not the office is having trouble billing one particular type of service as opposed to other services. Mixing services will distort the analysis; for example an office may do a good job at billing office visits but a poor job at billing surg-

Exhibit 4.7
Insurance Filing Worksheet

Type of Service: _____ Inpatient _____ Office _____ Surgical _____ Other _____

Practice Name: _____

Worksheet Preparation Date: _____

Patient Last Name	Type of Insurance	Date Claim Prepared	Date of Last Service	Number of Days

Total number of days _____
Total number of claims _____
Average time to file a claim form _____

eries. Mixing the two will distort this because the calculated average will look better than what it is.

On the worksheet, for each claim form insert when the form was prepared; this is shown in the lower left hand column of the HCFA-1500 insurance claim form. Next, insert the last date of service shown on the same claim form. Then just count the number of days between the two dates. At the bottom of the worksheet, total up the number of days and divide by the number of claims shown on the worksheet to calculate an average time it took the practice to prepare (and assuming filed) an insurance claim. For hospital services, the average should not exceed seven days. If it does, then most likely the practice has a problem getting information from the doctor or other sources necessary to file the claim on a timely basis.

If the average for inpatient services exceeds seven days, investigate how the physician communicates the inpatient charges to the office and whether or not the office has any problems interpreting this information. In most cases, the doctor will carry a piece of paper or card so he or she can record the inpatient services as they occur. Some practices will actually give the doctor a list of his or her patients in the hospital that day and this is used to record services when the doctor visits the patient.

Other offices and physicians will use a hospital charge card to record inpatient services. Exhibit 4.8 is an example of this card.

How are surgical or procedural charges captured so they may be billed properly and timely?

_____

_____

_____

Like inpatient services, surgical production and related collections can become inconsistent if these charges are not captured properly and communicated to the billing staff. Complete the Insurance Filing Analysis Worksheet for surgical/procedural charges only. Like inpatient services, it should take no more than seven days to prepare and file the claim form. Reasons for delay will be identified and explained later on in this chapter. However, like inpatient services, a lack of communication can cause delays. To improve communication and allow a timely, accurate filing of a surgical claim, many practices utilize a surgical charge ticket to capture these services.

Some physicians like to take responsibility for coding their services and others do not. For maximum efficiency, doctors should code their own services; this saves staff time and should improve accuracy since the doctor knows what he or she did. A surgical charge ticket can aid in the capturing and billing of surgical services. A sample surgical charge ticket is shown in Exhibit 4.9. If a surgical charge ticket is used, the doctor will complete it as soon as possible after the procedure and give it to the billing staff for preparation and filing. If a surgical charge ticket is not used, the billing staff will have to use dictation notes, operative reports, or some other form of documentation to bill these services; as you will see below, this often leads to a delay in filing the claim form.

Exhibit 4.8
Hospital Charge Card

✓	CODE	DIAGNOSIS (cont.)
	6584	Infection of Amniotic Cavity
	65623	Isoimmunization, Oth. Bld. Grp. Incompat.
	65613	Isoimmunization, Rhesus
	65113	Multiple Gestation, Triplets
	65103	Multiple Gestation, Twins
		Multiple Gestation, Unspecified
	6, .ᴗ_	Obstetrical Pulmonary Embolism
	6580_	Oligohydramnios
	V288	Other Specified Antenatal Screening
	67133	Phlebothrombosis, Deep, Antepartum
	64103	Placenta Previa, without Hemorrhage
	64113	Placenta Previa, with Hemorrhage
	64243	Pre-eclampsia, Mild
	64253	Pre-eclampsia, Severe (HELLP)
	64273	Pre-eclampsia, Superimposed
	64421	Premature Delivery
	64403	Premature Labor, Threatened
	6581	Premature Rupture of Membranes
	6542_	Previous Cesarean Section
	V234	Previous Poor Obstetric History
	64503	Prolonged Pregnancy
	6582	Prolonged Rupture of Membranes
	67002	Puerperal Infection, Major
	4633	Recurrent Pregnancy Loss
	64623	Renal Disease without Hypertension
	V	Elevated MSAFP
		Supervision of Normal Pregnancy
	65553	Suspected Damage to Fetus from Drugs
	65533	Suspected Damage to Fetus from Viral Dis.
	7100	Systemic Lupus Erythematosus
	64813	Thyroid Dysfunction
	65233	Transverse or Oblique Presentation

Patient Name: _____   Patient No.: _____

Physician: _____   Date: _____

HOSPITAL VISIT & CONSULTATION									
	✓	CONSULT	✓	FOLLOW UP	✓	ADMISSION	✓	ROUNDS	✓	OBSERV.
Level I		99251		99261		99221		99231		
Level II		99252		99262		99222		99232		
Level III		99253		99263		99223		99233		99218
Level IV		99254								99219
Level V		99255								99220
					✓	DISCHARGE				
						99238				
ADMISSION DATE			ROUNDS DATE				DISCHARGE DATE			

Exhibit 4.9
Example of Surgery ••.

UVALDE
BONE & JOINT
CLINIC, P.A.

Gloria G. Box, M.D.
1025 Garner Field Road
P.O. Drawer 1340
Uvalde, TX 78802
Phone: 210/278-2292
Fax: 210-278-1409

$\mathcal{S}$ 419
SURGERY FEE SLIP

☐ Gloria G Box, M.D.
☐ _____

Patient's Name _____   ☐ Place of Service:

Date of Service _____ Diagnosis No. _____   _____

Surgery Assistant _____   ☐ Right   ☐ Left

CODE	TREATMENT	FEE	CODE	TREATMENT	FEE	CODE	TREATMENT	FEE	CODE	TREATMENT	FEE	CODE	TREATMENT	FEE
	GENERAL			**SPINE** (cont'd)			**FOREARM-WRIST** (cont'd)			**PELVIS-HIP JOINT** (cont'd)			**TIB/FIB-ANKLE** (cont'd)	
20000	Incision Abscess		63035	Add Lami Level		25240	Darrach Procedu		27176	SCFE in situ pin		27696	Rpr Both Coll Ligam	
20005	Deep/Com		63042	Laminotomy/Re-Do		25260	Rpr Flexor Each		27177	SCFE ORIF		27698	Sec Rpr Rup Ligament	
20200	Biopsy Muscle		63047	Laminectomy/Decom		25270	Rpr Extensor Ea		27187	Prophyla Tr Fem		27705	Osteotomy Tibia	
20205	Deep		63048	Add Lami Level		25300	Rpr NoUn Rad/Ul		27284	Arthrodesis Hip		27707	Osteotomy Fibula	
20206	Biopsy Mus. Needle					25305	w/graft		27236	Gilberty/FX		27709	Osteotomy Tib/Fib	
20240	Biopsy Bone			**SHOULDER**		25440	Rpr NoUn Navicu					27870	Arthrodesis Ankle	
20245	Deep		23040	Arthrotomy G-H Jt		25800	Arthrodesis, Wr			**FEMUR KNEE JOINT**		27880	BK Amputation	
			23044	Arth A-C, S-C Jt		25820	Intercarpal Fus		27310	Arthrotomy Knee		27888	Amputation Syme	
	INTRODUCT REMOVAL		23120	Claviculectomy, Pt		25900	Amp Forearm		27332	Meniscectomy One		27889	Ankle Disartic	
20650	Insert/Skel Tx		23130	Acromioplasty		64719	Ulnar Nerve Wri		27333	Meniscectomy Both		29894	M-A Loose Body	
20680	Rem of Implant		23160	Saucerize Clavicle		64721	Carpal Tunnel		27334	Arth Synovectomy		29895	M-A Synovec-Partial	
20690	External Fixation		23182	Saucerize Scapula					27340	Exe Prepat Bursa		29897	M-A Debride-Limited	
			23184	Saucerize Prox Hum			**HAND-FINGERS**		27345	Exe Baker's Cyst		29898	M-A Debride-Extensi	
	I&D ABSCESS HEMATOMA		23410	Rep Rot Cuff/Acute		26055	Rel Trig Finger		27350	Patellectomy		27892	Fasciotomy-Ant &/or Lat	
10060	SO Abscess		23412	Chronic		26123	Fasciectomy Pal		27380	Rpt Infrapatel Ten		27893	Fasciotomy-Post Comp.	
10140	SO Hematoma		23415	Rel Cor-Acro Lig		26123	Fasciectomy Fin		27385	Rpt Quad/Ham Rup		27894	Fasciotomy Ant &/or Post	
23030	Shoulder, deep		23420	Rep Cuff Avulsion		26125	add finger		27403	Meniscal Repair				
23930	Upper Arm/Elbow		23430	Tenodesis Bicep		26135	Synovectomy M-P		27405	Repari MCL, LCL			**FOOT**	
25028	Forearm/Wrist		23450	Magnuson/Put Plat		26450	1° Flexor Repair		27418	Maguel Epip Arr		28003	I&D Subiascial	
26011	Finger		23455	Bankart		26356	1° Flex RepNoMan		27425	Lateral Relcase		28005	I&D/Osteomyelitis	
26990	Pelvis/Hips		23462	Bristow		26410	Ext Ten Rep Hand		27427	X-Art Rpr ACL		28008	Fasciotomy	
27301	Thigh/Knee		23470	Neer Implant		26418	Ext Ten Rep Fing		27428	intr-art open		28035	Tarsal Tunnel	
27603	Leg/Ankle		23472	Total Shoulder		26432	Mallet Fin Perc		27447	TKA		28060	Fasciectomy Plantar	
28001	Foot		23332	Rom Total Shoulder		26433	Mallet Fin Open		27486	Rev TKA 1 comp		28080	Morton Neuroma	
			23700	Manipulation		26450	Tenotomy FiPalm		27487	Rev TKA all		28090	Exc Ganglion/Oysil	
	FOREIGN BODY REMOVAL		29619	M-A Loose Body		26455	Tenotomy FiRing		27457	High Tibial Oste		28110	Bunionette	
10120	SO		29820	M-A Synovec-Partial		26460	Tenotomy Extens		27475	Dis Fem Epip Arr		28111	Exc 1st Metatarsal	
20520	Mus/Ten Sheath		29822	M-A Debride-Limited			Hand/Finger		27477	Prox Tib Epip Arr		28112	Exc 2-4th Metatarsal	
20525	deep/com		29823	M-A Debride-Extens		26500	Pulley Repair		27570	Manipulation		28113	Exc 5th Metatarsal	
23330	Shoulder, SQ		29826	M-A Decom/Acromio		26525	Capsulotomy I-P		27590	AK Amputation		28285	Hammertoe	
23331	deep		29821	M-A Synovec - Comp.		26527	Arthroplasty C-M		27598	Disartic Knee		28288	Ostectomy	
24200	Up Arm/Elb, SQ		29825	M-A Debride-w-w/o Man		26530	Arthroplasty M-P		29874	M-A Loose Body		28290	Silver Procedure	
24201	deep					26531	w/implant		29875	M-A Synovec-Limit		28292	Keller Prcedure	
26070	C-M Jt			**HUMERUS-ELBOW**		26535	Arthroplasty 11-P		29876	M-A Synovec-Major		28293	w/implant	
27086	Pel/Hip, SQ		24000	Arthrotomy/Drainage		26536	w/implant		29877	M-A Debrid/Shaving		28294	w/tendon transfer	
27087	deep		24101	Arthrotomy Loose Bod		26540	Col Lig Rpt M-P		29879	M-A Abras Arthropl		28296	1st Metatarsal Osteotomy	
27372	Th/Knee, Deep		24105	Exc Olecranon Bursa		26565	Osteotomy Metaca		29880	M-A Menisc Both		28299	Double Osteotomy	
28190	Foot, Sq		24130	Exc Radial Head		26567	Osteotomy Phal		29881	M-A Menisc One		28715	Triple Arthrodesis	
28192	deep		24342	Reinsert Bicep Ton		26820	Fusion Thumb		29882	M-A Men Repair One		28725	Subtalar Arthrodesis	
			24351	Tennis Elbow Relsa		26541	Fusion C-M Thumb		29883	M-A Men Rapr Both		28750	Fusion Gr Toe M-P	
	SKIN DEBRIDEMENT		24356	w/ostectomy		26843	Fusion Q-M Other		29888	M-A ACL Repair		28755	Fusion Gr Toe 1-P	
11040	Partial Thickness		24400	Osteotomy, Humerus		26850	Fusion M-P		29889	M-A PCL Repair		28810	Amp Metatarsal	
11041	Full Thickness		29534	M-A Loose Body		26860	Fusion L-P		29850	Knee FX-w-w/o Man		28820	Amp M-P	
11042	Skin & SQ		29835	M-A Synovec-Partial		26851	Amp Fin/Thumb		29851	KneeFX-w-w/o I or E Fix		28825	Amp 1-P	
11043	Skin, SQ, Muscle		29837	M-A Debride-Limited					29855	Tib FX-w-w/o I or E Fix				
11044	Skin, SQ, Musc, Bone		29838	M-A Debride-Extens			**PELVIS-HIP JOINT**		29856	CondyleFX-w-w/o I or E				
			64718	Ulnar Nerve Transfer		27001	Tenotomy Adduc							
	SPINE					27030	Arthrotomy/Sep.			**TIB/FIB-ANKLE**				
22625	Fusion-Lumbar			**FOREARM-WRIST**		27030	Coecygectomy		27600	Decom Fascietomy Ant				
22520	Harvest Bone Gr.		25000	Release DeQuervains		27130	THA		27601	Posterior Compart				
22840	Harrington Rod		25101	Arthrotomy Wrist		27132	THA Conversion		27602	Both Compartments				
22842	Segmental Fixation		25111	Exc Ganglion		27134	Revision THA		27610	Arthr Ankle/Sepsis				
22852	Rem Post Seg Inst.		25115	Synovec Rheums		27137	Acetabulum Only		27620	Arthr Ank/Loose Body				
62292	Chemonucleolvsis		25118	Synovectomy, Wri		27138	Femural Only		27650	Repair Achilles				
63010	Gill Type Opera								27652	w/graft		PAYMENT		_____
63030	Laminotomy/l-1								27695	1 Rpr Rup Ligament		TYPE		_____

NOTES/COMMENTS

Finally, complete the worksheet for office services. It should take no more than two to three days to prepare and file a claim form for office services.

How often are insurance claim forms filed each week?

_____

_____

Knowing what the benchmarks should be for filing an insurance claim (two to three days for office services; seven days for all other services), another way to speed up the filing process is to assess how often claims are actually filed each week. Obviously the more days allocated to when claims are filed, the more claims that will get filed, and the quicker a practice will get paid for these services. The best practices file claims every day. At a minimum, claims should be filed at least twice a week to maintain production consistency.

Are operative notes attached to claim forms when they are filed with an insurance company? ____ *yes* ____ *no; If yes, detail situations when operative notes are attached:*

_____

_____

When filing surgical charges to an insurance company, some practices have the policy of attaching an operative report to the claim form. An operative report is a document that basically details the surgical procedure performed; it becomes a part of the patient's hospital record. Many offices use this report to determine what the doctor did and bill the services. Unfortunately, it often takes time to get the report and as a result, claims are not filed on a timely basis. This is a common reason why surgical claims forms get filed late.

If during your financial analysis you find high receivables and/or poor or inconsistent cash flow, one reason might be the practice is attaching operative notes to most of its surgical claim forms. This also will be identified when you analyze how quickly the practice gets paid for its services during the EOB analysis. In most cases, an operative note should be attached to a claim form in the following cases:

1. When the -22 modifier is billed with the surgical procedure;

2. When an unlisted procedure is billed; and

3. When an insurance carrier consistently asks for the operative notes for specific services.

When an operative note is attached, most insurance companies will want to review the claim form and the accompanying report. As a matter of fact, many carriers like operative report attachments because it is one more reason for them to delay paying the claim. In most situations, if a clean claim is filed, an operative report does not have to be attached to a surgical claim in order to get paid. If billing personnel are ever skeptical about this, just try sending in a claim a few times without the report and see what happens; most end up surprised to find out insurance companies really do pay the claim without it.

Does the doctor dictate notes on a timely basis? _____ yes _____ no; If no, how long does it take and explain why.

_____

_____

_____

One reason why claims get filed late is because the doctor does not produce his or her medical notes on a timely basis, resulting again in inconsistent production and cash flow. Billing personnel often use these notes to bill the doctor's services. Note production could include dictating the operative report, hospital records, and office medical chart notes. The largest concern generally is the dictation of the operative report since, as mentioned, many offices use this document to bill surgical charges. However, implementation and completion of a surgical charge ticket, hospital charge ticket, and office charge ticket should eliminate the need to rely on dictated notes to bill physician services.

If a physician uses a surgical charge ticket, it is suggested at periodic times that the billing staff compare what was recorded on the ticket to the operative report. This is a checks-and-balances procedure to make sure the services recorded on the ticket are correct.

Does the practice utilize electronic billing? _____ yes _____ no; If no, explain why.

_____

_____

If during the EOB analysis and the financial analysis it appears the office is getting paid slowly by insurance companies and other third-party payers, one way to speed up collection is to electronically bill the physician's services instead of preparing and mailing a paper claim form. If a practice is not utilizing electronic billing to bill its services it is important to find out why and whether or not implementation will help the practice. There are numerous clearinghouses on the market that can implement electronic billing systems for a practice. The practice's medical billing software vendor should be able to provide you with a list of clearinghouse vendors.

If the practice's cash flow is good, if it gets paid on average 45 days by insurance companies, and the collection percentages look good, then implementing electronic billing may not help the practice that much. However, one good reason to implement electronic billing is that it is harder not to file a clean claim. Most electronic billing systems have billing edits that prevent the filing of a claim electronically unless it is correct (i.e., a clean claim). For example, missing information will be identified along with billing errors, such as using an incorrect CPT code. Electronic billing will prevent errors and reduce the staff's burden of having to deal with claim denials as a result of billing mistakes.

Are insurance claim forms held for any reason? ____ *yes* ____ *no; If yes, explain situations when this occurs.*

_____

_____

_____

One reason the EOB analysis will show an extended time period before the practice is getting paid by its insurance companies and other third-party payers is because the practice is holding its claims. Inconsistent production per the financial analysis may also indicate this pattern of billing behavior. The most common reason practices hold claims is so that another healthcare provider will get allocated the patient's deductible; when this occurs, the practice does not have to worry about collecting the deductible from the patient—someone else has to. For example, a surgeon may hold the claim awhile so that the hospital will get hit with the patient's deductible.

This practice occurs frequently at the beginning of the year when patient deductible amounts start anew. While holding claims might sound good in practice, we really see no reason to implement such a policy. If the practice does a good job at insurance verification before the service is performed, it should be able to find out the amount of the deductible still in force and collect such amount from the patient. Holding claim forms only delays cash flow in the long run.

How accurate is the front desk or other personnel in obtaining the patient's insurance information?

_____

_____

_____

The search for service denials during the EOB analysis may indicate problems because there was incorrect or missing information on the claim form. When this occurs, the office has to refile the claim using the correct information. The result is another delay in cash flow. The EOB analysis may indicate this problem when the analysis detects a difficulty getting paid on time by insurance carriers. If the office is collecting the wrong insurance information from the patient or not all the information, research to find out why. As previously mentioned earlier in this chapter, the front desk must make sure to make a copy of the patient's insurance card at the time of their new patient visit as well as making sure all insurance related line items on the patient registration form are complete. Errors can also be made when the correct information is obtained but it is miskeyed into the computer system.

How are charge denials handled in the office?

_____

_____

_____

If a large enough sample of EOBs are looked at during the EOB analysis, denials of services rendered should be detected. If so, the next step is to find out how the office handles these situations. It should be the policy of every office to review, investigate, and dispose of charge denials on a timely basis. If it was truly a billing error, the denial should be written off and the office and doctor(s) need to be educated to make sure the same mistake does not reoccur. If it was not a billing error, the office should appeal the denial so it can receive payment.

As part of the assessment process, you need to make sure charge denials are in fact being appealed by the practice. There are many instances where a practice will not appeal a denial and just write it off as uncollectible or as a contractual adjustment. Ask the billing staff for examples of appeal letters. Review these to make sure the appeal was drafted properly. Even better, if you have identified charge denials during your EOB analysis that could have been appealed, ask the practice for the appeal letters that apply to these specific denials. If the practice cannot produce them, more than likely it does an inadequate job of the appeals process and even more important, there is the likelihood cash flow has been lost due to this inadequacy.

COLLECTIONS

When does the practice begin following up on unpaid insurance claim forms?

_____

_____

_____

There are two forms of receivables in a medical practice: insurance receivables and patient receivables. Insurance receivables are those accounts where an insurance company or related third-party carrier owes the practice a balance. This occurs when the practice files a claim with the carrier. Patient receivables are accounts owed by patients individually. For most medical practices, insurance receivables will comprise the largest percentage of the overall total accounts receivable balance.

If the EOB analysis indicates an inconsistency and delay in payment from insurance companies, and if the practice's collection statistics are unacceptable, one reason why might be the practice is not managing the insurance receivables properly. Specifically, the practice is not following up with unpaid insurance accounts on a consistent, timely basis (or at all in some cases!).

The quicker an office can follow up on unpaid insurance accounts, the quicker it will find out why the claim has not been paid, and the quicker the problem can be resolved so the practice can receive payment. We believe an office should begin following up on unpaid claims when they become 28 to 30 days old. However, many practices do not begin the follow up process for at least 60 days. This longer period only hinders the practice's cash flow because it will take longer to get paid for its services.

We also recommend starting early on the follow-up process because unless the patient has made some type of prepayment on the account, he or she will still owe the practice a balance after the insurance has reimbursed the practice. Only then can a patient statement be sent out showing how much the patient owes after his or her insurance has made payment. The longer it takes to get this statement in the patients' hands, the greater the likelihood problems could be encountered collecting some of these patient receivable balances.

What is the practice's follow-up procedure for unpaid insurance accounts?

_____

_____

_____

To improve practice cash flow, every medical practice should have a defined follow-up policy for unpaid insurance accounts. If a policy is in place, it must be adhered to on a consistent basis; you don't want to hear follow up occurs "when we can get to it." Preferably, each week unpaid claims 28 to 30 days old should be identified. Once identified, assigned personnel should begin the follow-up process. This usually involves contacting the payer and documenting the conversation. The office should document the following:

1. Name of the person spoken to;

2. Was the claim received by the payer;

3. Has the claim been approved for payment;

4. If yes, when is an estimated time for payment; and

5. If no, why was payment denied.

Documentation is usually done directly into the medical software billing system. There is usually a section entitled "billing notes" where this can be done. If the software does not allow this type of documentation to be entered, follow-up can be documented on paper. Some practices prefer paper documentation to computer input, even though this seems impractical. Exhibit 4.10 shows a sample paper insurance follow-up form.

Once a reason has been determined why payment was denied, the office can correct the claim, usually by resubmitting a corrected claim or sub-

Exhibit 4.10

Patients Name:_____Date of call:_____

Account number:_____

Insurance company:_____Phone #:_____

Spoke with:_____Fax #:_____
        (get first and last name)

1)   Status on claim for date of service;_____

2)   Was claim received:_____
      a. if NO–always check to see if claim was mailed to correct address.
      b. if address is incorrect---MAKE SURE YOU CORRECT THE COMPUTER!!

3)   Claim being processed:_____

4)   When will payment be mailed:_____Amount:_____

5)   Was claim denied: yes_____   no_____
      a. reason for denial or delay:_____
      _____

ADDITIONAL COMMENTS:

_____

_____

_____

_____

Follow up date:_____by_____

mitting additional information needed by the payer in order to get the
claim paid. If the payer has not received the claim, the practice can immediately refile it, usually by faxing it to the carrier in care of the person spoken to on the phone. If follow-up procedures are not in place or are not
being followed, the only way a practice will know if there was a problem
with the claim is if it never has received payment or has received an EOB
indicating a denial of the charge.

Larger practices have numerous unpaid insurance accounts and as
such, it is unrealistic to think that all balances can be followed up on. This
is why practices with this number of accounts will identify the larger balances first each week and work those; follow-up on other balances will be
performed if additional time is available.

As part of your assessment, always ask to see samples of the practice's documentation of their follow-up. You might want to even take a sample of unpaid insurance accounts that are at least 60 days old and review what follow-up work has been done (and documented) on these balances. Your objective is to make sure a follow-up policy is in place, that it is being implemented efficiently, and it is being performed correctly. Mistakes in any one of these areas will likely result in problem receivables and delayed or impaired cash flow.

How does the office follow up on unpaid patient receivables and how often?

_____

_____

_____

As mentioned, most practices will concentrate their follow-up on unpaid insurance accounts because these represent a larger portion of the total accounts receivable and because these unpaid accounts usually have larger balances. However, patient receivables must not be overlooked. As a matter of fact, your receivables analysis will probably show that most of the older accounts are in fact monies owed by patients individually. This is why a follow-up policy for these accounts is important too. Follow-up will usually follow the same methodology as that for insurance accounts; patients are contacted directly, usually by phone or correspondence, about their unpaid account. Since emphasis is placed on collecting insurance receivables, the most practical approach is to concentrate follow-up efforts on patients with large overdue balances. Follow up on other balances is usually limited to collection letters.

Like insurance receivables, make sure a policy is in place and that it is being followed. More importantly however is to make sure the practice has and follows appropriate front desk collection procedures, like those discussed earlier in this chapter. Receivables don't occur or are minimized if payments are received at the time of an office visit, if overdue balances are discussed with patients at the time of their office visits, and surgical deposits are collected.

When are patient account statements mailed out?

_____

_____

_____

One way accounts receivables can be minimized is to make sure patient account statements are mailed out each month, even if the patient's insurance has yet to pay. Patients cannot make a payment on their account unless they know what they owe; a patient account statement informs them of this. It is a good idea to send a statement even if the patient's insurance has yet to pay because it lets the patient know the overall charge and some will know what they will ultimately have to pay; in these situations, many patients will go ahead and make a payment on the account even though their insurance has yet to pay (e.g., When a patient knows they will owe a deductible).

For most practices, patient statements are mailed at the end of each month. Large practices send them out each week in cycles, usually taking the alphabet and dividing the related patients into each week. Never assume patient statements do get sent out consistently. Some practices just do not put the necessary emphasis on this important part of the collection process. Therefore, ask to see an example of the statements; hopefully your assessment will be timed in a way to be in the office when they are planning to send out the statements. Review the form of the statement to be sure it communicates receivable information correctly to the patient and that the patient will understand their personal financial responsibility for the balance.

Are collection letters used by the practice? ____ yes ____ no; If yes, how often are they sent out and what types of collection letters are sent.

_____

_____

_____

To improve collections and reduce the receivables balance, the practice should be sending out collection letters to patients with overdue accounts. This is extremely important for those cases where an office does not have the manpower or time to personally contact patients about their overdue balance; in these situations, collection letters are the primary collection activity. The letters should be sent separately from the patient account statements. Collection messages on the account statements, while somewhat helpful, do not replace the issuance of collection letters tied directly to the age of the overdue balance.

Generally collection letters start off mild in their wording and become more serious as the account grows older. Three letters are usually sent to a patient, the first one beginning 30 days after the patient receives their first

Exhibit 4.11
Sample Collection letter

_____

_____
_____
_____

Dear _____:

Our records indicate the following outstanding balance with our practice:

Account Balance: $_____
Account Number: _____

According to our records, this account is over 60 days past due. We are asking that you send full payment as soon as possible. If for some reason you can not send full payment, please contact our office immediately to arrange alternate payment terms.

Failure to contact our office or remit full payment will result in more severe collection efforts.

If your payment has already been mailed to our office, please disregard this notice. Thank you, in advance, for taking the time to resolve this account.

Sincerely,

_____
Office Manager

notice of how much they personally owe the practice. Exhibits 4.11 and 4.12 are sample collection letters. After the last collection is mailed, a decision is then usually made by the practice to write off the account as a bad debt if it is not paid or send the account to a collection agency. Just be sure the practice is not wasting personnel time and money continually sending out statements to individuals who obviously are not going to pay their account.

Does the practice use a collection agency? ____ yes ____ no; If yes, how often are accounts sent to the collection agency?

_____
_____
_____

Exhibit 4.12
Final Notice

_____

_____
_____
_____

FINAL NOTICE

Dear _____:

The following account balance is outstanding:

Account Balance: $_____
Account Number: _____

We have tried to contact you concerning this account. The account is not current and we need to receive a payment immediately.

You must contact our office within ten (10) days from the date of this letter to make payment arrangements. If you do not contact our office or submit payment in full within ten (10) days, we will consider our records to be accurate and turn your account over to our collection agency.

Please contact us as soon as possible, we would like to resolve this issue. Please disregard this notice if your payment has already been mailed to our office.

Sincerely,

_____
Office Manager

Some practices use a collection agency to collect overdue accounts and some do not. Those that do not think that a patient may sue the doctor for malpractice if their account is ever turned over to collection. The decision to use a collection agency depends on how well the office is collecting their receivables by themselves. Most offices, however, should not be spending their valuable time trying to collect old accounts. It is much more efficient to turn these accounts over to an independent party for collection, even though it means paying a collection fee. It is much wiser to have the staff concentrating its efforts on collecting current accounts so that they don't have to be sent to the collection agency!

The practice should be consistent in turning accounts over to collection. Preferably, each month the receivables aging report should be reviewed and problem accounts turned over to collection. Once turned over, write the accounts off as uncollectible so that when the practice looks at a detailed aging of the receivables, they are looking at accounts that are in fact collectible. Monies received from the collection agency can be recorded as a "bad debt recovery" in the practice's computer system.

Once you have satisfied yourself during the assessment process that accounts are being sent consistently to the collection agency, the next step is to make sure the collection agency is doing a good job at collection (TAB03.DOC). Why turn accounts over to collection if it will never get collected? This does nothing for the cash flow of the practice. There are two ways to analyze the success of the collection agency:

Total balances turned over to collection: _____
Total amount collected by the agency: _____
Percent collected: _____%

Total individual accounts turned over to collection: _____
Total individual accounts where collection occurred: _____
Percent collected: _____%

We suggest performing both of these analyses. This analysis cannot be performed if the practice has not received collection information from the agency; otherwise, you will have to contact the agency directly to get this data. If the agency is doing a poor job, let the practice know so whether or not a change is necessary can be evaluated by the management of the practice.

Does the practice routinely review a detailed aging of the accounts receivable?
_____ *yes* _____ *no*

Management should review an aging of the accounts receivable each and every month. This includes the physician; he or she must review their own aging reports. This review is an excellent form of checks and balances that lets management know how well the billing and collection process is working. The review will also identify problem accounts, that will then allow management to ask why these accounts have not been collected to date. It will also identify accounts that must be sent to collection and/or written off as a bad debt. One way to tell if management is reviewing the aging report is to see how much is written off as bad debt each month and in total. Practices with small bad debt write-offs usually do not consistently review their accounts receivable.

CONCLUSION

Once the financial analysis and EOB analysis are performed, the logical next step is to perform an analysis of the practice's billing and collection process. Remember that the financial and EOB analysis identifies potential practice problems and issues that require further investigation. Many of these will be found during the billing and collection analysis and will form a major portion of your recommendations to practice management for areas of improvement. The entire billing and collection questionnaire, along with the forms, is included in the appendix.

CHAPTER FIVE

Fee Schedule Analysis

A fee schedule analysis is a significant element of every practice assessment. Too many practices lose money every year as a result of an inadequate and/or inconsistent fee schedule. This is the result of not establishing a good fee schedule to begin with and not monitoring payer reimbursements on an ongoing basis to see if additional fee adjustments are warranted. The practices objective is to maximize payer reimbursement as much as it can. Generally, a practice will generate approximately 80 percent of its revenues from 20 to 25 percent of its CPT codes, depending on the specialty. In orthopedics, for example, it might take upwards of 50 CPT codes to capture 80 percent of those revenues. Concentrate your work efforts during the practice assessment on reviewing the fees for the CPT codes that represent the most revenues for the practice.

The fee schedule analysis for a practice assessment does not warrant a full-scale fee schedule analysis. A complete fee analysis would include evaluating the propriety of the CPT codes being utilized, analyzing the market data, analyzing the fees in reference to a relative value scale, and making recommended fee changes for each CPT code utilized by the practice. The intent of a fee schedule analysis during the practice assessment process is to simply highlight any inconsistencies or problems in the medical practice's pricing structure and to communicate that to the medical practice. In other words, a quick snapshot of the key CPT codes is performed. The analysis is not intended to be sufficient to make actual pricing recommendations for all of the practice's services, even though you will want to suggest fees to practice management for the codes that are reviewed. This will give management specific information that its fee schedule is inadequate. If it is determined that there are problems in the fee schedule, then a recommendation to perform a full-scale fee schedule analysis should be made for completion at a later date. The scope of the fee schedule analysis for the practice assessment should center on those top 20 to 25 codes.

METHODOLOGY

This fee analysis process begins with one simple question. "When was the last time the medical practice revised the current fee schedule?" The second question is "At the time of the fee schedule's last revision, what methodology was utilized to revise the fees?" These two questions will immediately let the evaluator know if significant problems can be expected with the practice's fee schedule. Obviously, if it has been over a year or if some random methodology of pricing was used, then you can anticipate some pricing inconsistencies and problems. Many medical practices are in the habit of systematically raising all fees a certain percentage. This does not address the appropriateness of the price of individual CPT codes which might be either overpriced or underpriced. Too often, fee schedule changes come from information obtained from other practitioners which certainly creates some legal risk. In addition, many times the information obtained from other providers is just as "unfounded" as the medical practice's own fee schedule. All of these methodologies are signals of a poor fee schedule.

As part of the analysis, the next step is to review a sample of commercial (sometimes referred to as indemnity) explanation of benefits (EOBs) and EOBs received from managed care companies. An EOB is the document that is remitted by the insurance company with its payment for the services delivered. This document basically states how much the doctor billed, how much was approved by the insurance company and any amounts which are related to copays or deductibles. Select EOBs of managed care payers that represent a significant amount of revenues to the practice.

Insurance companies establish what is commonly referred to as usual, customary, and reasonable (UCR) fee profiles. These profiles are developed using Medicare's Resource Based Relative Value Scale (RBRVS) payment system, fees accumulated by the Health Insurance Association of America (HIAA) and many times developed with internal methodologies developed by that specific insurance company. The review of commercial EOBs and managed care EOBs provides you with a comparison of what is being charged by the practice for a particular service or CPT code versus what has been established as the UCR by the third-party payer. Obviously, any situation where the practice is being reimbursed close to or at 100 percent of charges indicates that the fee for that CPT is priced too conservatively.

EOB REVIEW

This is particularly true when you review managed care EOBs. Keep in mind that most managed care payers who reimburse on a fee-for-service basis discount their rates, oftentimes 20 to 50 percent less than what indemnity payers will pay. Managed care payers will pay a practice the lesser of this discounted rate or what they actually bill. If the actual billed amount is less than the payer's allowable rate, the EOB will show the entire billing as approved for payment. This is a major indicator the fee schedule has problems since the practice's normal fee is less than the payer's discounted fee.

Exhibit 5.1 displays an example of the selected CPT codes and the practice's usual and customary fee as compared to the EOBs from the leading practice payers, as well as Medicare.

Of course you can add as many payers as you wish to this worksheet; try to concentrate on the private payers that generate a majority of the practice's revenues. Any CPT codes that are noted during this review as being reimbursed at or close to 100 percent should be noted in the practice assessment report for future follow-up by the medical practice. If this seems

Exhibit 5.1
Fry Urology Specialists
EOB Review

CPT	Description	Practice List Fee	Medicare	Private Payer 1	Private Payer 2	Private Payer 3	Private Payer 4
50230	REMOVAL OF KIDNEY	3,075	1,329.85	2,829.00	2,829.00	2,727.53	3,000.00
50590	LITHOTRIPSY	6,375	628.43	2,346.00	2,346.00	2,261.85	2,550.00
50780	REIMPLANT URETER IN BLADDER	2,500	1,057.08	2,300.00	2,300.00	2,217.50	2,400.00
51726	COMPLEX CYSTOMETROGRAM	240	98.50	220.80	220.80	212.88	235.00
51772	URETHRA PRESSURE PROFILE	175	83.90	161.00	161.00	155.23	170.00
51785	ANAL/URINARY MUSCLE STUDY	200	84.42	184.00	184.00	177.40	189.00
51845	REPAIR BLADDER NECK	1,925	673.92	1,771.00	1,771.00	1,707.48	1,800.00
52000	CYSTOSCOPY	315	109.66	289.80	289.80	279.41	300.00
52336	CYSTOSCOPY, STONE REMOVAL	1,880	482.48	1,729.60	1,729.60	1,667.56	1,850.00
52337	CYSTOSCOPY, STONE REMOVAL	2,300	557.16	2,116.00	2,116.00	2,040.10	2,000.00
52601	PROSTATECTOMY (TURP)	2,000	797.05	1,840.00	1,840.00	1,774.00	2,000.00
99201	OFFICE/OUTPATIENT VISIT, NEW	50	28.57	46.00	46.00	44.35	48.00
99202	OFFICE/OUTPATIENT VISIT, NEW	55	45.47	40.00	42.55	44.62	38.00
99203	OFFICE/OUTPATIENT VISIT, NEW	60	63.03	63.48	70.00	59.00	58.65
99211	OFFICE/OUTPATIENT VISIT, EST	25	12.51	18.55	20.00	19.00	11.60
99212	OFFICE/OUTPATIENT VISIT, EST	35	24.94	32.54	29.00	21.00	29.00
99213	OFFICE/OUTPATIENT VISIT, EST	45	35.70	41.00	50.00	38.11	35.00
99221	INITIAL HOSPITAL CARE	90	63.57	60.00	60.00	55.00	52.00
99222	INITIAL HOSPITAL CARE	125	103.53	116.60	104.50	81.00	110.00
99223	INITIAL HOSPITAL CARE	150	133.42	120.00	140.00	138.00	138.00

to be more than an isolated CPT code or two, then generally the recommendation would be for the practice to consider a full-scale fee schedule analysis as a follow-up to the practice assessment.

As part of the fee schedule analysis, you may want to conduct an additional analysis utilizing a relative value scale. Relative value scales (RVS) were popularized initially by the California Relative Value Scale and developed as early as the 1960s. The present Medicare fee schedule is based on a relative value scale called Resource Based Relative Value Scale (RBRVS) which was developed by Harvard University and is managed by Cambridge Health Economics Group (CHEG). This was developed exclusively for use by the Health Care Finance Administration (HCFA) and is used to determine the reimbursement to physicians under the present Medicare fee schedule system. Another popular relative value scale is St. Anthony Publishing Company's Relative Values for Physicians (RVP, formerly McGraw-Hill).

What is a relative value? A relative value is determined by factoring in certain specific components of work, including time and skill required to perform the procedure, risk of the procedure, as well as the expenses related directly to the procedure. The system of relative values then simply ranks these procedures, comparing one CPT code to another. The higher the relative value unit (RVU), the greater the payment amount for that procedure. For example, CPT Code 99213 (mid-level established office visit) might receive a relative value unit of 1, while an appendectomy has a relative value unit of 12. The point is the more complex or costly the procedure, the higher relative value a CPT code will have.

Once you have decided which relative value system will be utilized in the fee schedule analysis, the next component to understand is the conversion factor. The conversion factor is utilized to calculate a fee based on the relative value units. For example, with respect to Medicare, the conversion factor for the 1998 fiscal year is set at $36.6873. So, if a CPT code has a relative value of 4, then the RBRVS system would pay approximately $146.75 (4 × 36.6873) as reimbursement for that service. This system enables you to derive fees for the CPT codes by multiplying the adopted conversion factor by the relative value units to establish fees for individual CPT codes. Inversely, if you have the practice's fee and the relative value unit for the CPT code, then you can determine what the practice's internal conversion factor is by dividing the fee by the relative value unit. Before selecting which relative value scale you will utilize for your fee schedule analysis, it should be noted that the two most common are, as mentioned above, the Medicare RBRVS and the St. Anthony RVP relative values. The RBRVS relative value scale uses one conversion factor for all areas of the fee schedule. The RVP relative value scale utilizes a range of conversion factors for evaluation and management, medicine, surgery, pathology, radiology, and anesthesiology.

Exhibit 5.2 is a worksheet showing a quick analysis of a practice's fee schedule for its evaluation and management codes and selected surgery codes utilizing the St. Anthony RVP relative value units. As previously noted, the RVP study divides the services and procedures into several sections, each with its own unique conversion factor. Therefore, in the worksheet the evaluation and management codes have a significantly different conversion factor than the surgery codes. Conversion factors for evaluation and management codes usually range from a low of $4 to a high of $7.50. Surgery codes might have conversion factors ranging from $80 to $200 depending on the specialty and market. The evaluator must be proficient in their knowledge of market pricing, relative value scales, and related conversion factors to successfully analyze the fee schedule.

Let's assume we are doing a medical practice assessment for Dr. Matt Fry that includes a fee schedule analysis. Dr. Fry has been in practice for a

Exhibit 5.2
Fry Urology Specialists
Relative Value Analysis

CPT	Description	Practice Fee	St. Anthony RVP	Practice CF
50230	REMOVAL OF KIDNEY	3,075	32.50	94.62
50590	LITHOTRIPSY	6,375	37.50	170.00
50780	REIMPLANT URETER IN BLADDER	2,500	22.30	112.11
51726	COMPLEX CYSTOMETROGRAM	240	1.60	150.00
51772	URETHRA PRESSURE PROFILE	175	1.50	116.67
51785	ANAL/URINARY MUSCLE STUDY	200	2.10	95.24
51845	REPAIR BLADDER NECK	1,925	20.00	96.25
52000	CYSTOSCOPY	315	2.00	157.50
52336	CYSTOSCOPY, STONE REMOVAL	1,880	16.00	117.50
52337	CYSTOSCOPY, STONE REMOVAL	2,300	18.00	127.78
52601	PROSTATECTOMY (TURP)	2,000	20.00	100.00
99201	OFFICE/OUTPATIENT VISIT, NEW	50	6.50	7.69
99202	OFFICE/OUTPATIENT VISIT, NEW	55	9.50	5.79
99203	OFFICE/OUTPATIENT VISIT, NEW	60	14.00	4.29
99211	OFFICE/OUTPATIENT VISIT, EST	25	3.50	7.14
99212	OFFICE/OUTPATIENT VISIT, EST	35	6.00	5.83
99213	OFFICE/OUTPATIENT VISIT, EST	45	9.00	5.00
99221	INITIAL HOSPITAL CARE	90	12.50	7.20
99222	INITIAL HOSPITAL CARE	125	22.00	5.68
99223	INITIAL HOSPITAL CARE	150	28.50	5.26

short period of time and like so many other practitioners, he inherited his fee schedule without ever performing an actual fee schedule analysis with a relative value unit comparison to market data.

As you can see from the above analysis, Dr. Fry's evaluation and management codes are fairly consistently priced. However, on his surgery codes, his lithotripsy procedure (CF of $170) is priced extremely high as compared to his other surgical procedures. In addition, there are some inconsistencies throughout the pricing of these surgical procedures. It is possible for significant variations in the conversion factors to be beneficial if the market data supports such pricing. This is where the evaluator will have to weigh consistent pricing and actual market data. But remember, for most fees, you will usually want a consistent conversion for each class of services; that is, a consistent conversion factor for surgical procedures, a consistent conversion factor for radiology services, and so on. Fee schedules that optimize revenues are usually customized to not only have some consistent pricing but to also have some flexibility for market trends.

Another possible fee analysis methodology utilizes the RBRVS relative value scale to evaluate CPT pricing. Exhibit 5.3 is an example using the same procedures shown in Exhibit 5.2. First, you must calculate the RBRVS

Exhibit 5.3
Computation of Practice's RBRVS Conversion Factors

CPT	Description	Practice Fee	RBRVS RVU	Practice CF
50230	REMOVAL OF KIDNEY	3,075	40.80	75.37
50590	LITHOTRIPSY	6,375	19.87	320.84
50780	REIMPLANT URETER IN BLADDER	2,500	32.36	77.26
51726	COMPLEX CYSTOMETROGRAM	240	3.13	76.68
51772	URETHRA PRESSURE PROFILE	175	2.66	65.79
51785	ANAL/URINARY MUSCLE STUDY	200	2.68	74.63
51845	REPAIR BLADDER NECK	1,925	20.86	92.28
52000	CYSTOSCOPY	315	3.48	90.52
52336	CYSTOSCOPY, STONE REMOVAL	1,880	16.68	112.71
52337	CYSTOSCOPY, STONE REMOVAL	2,300	19.26	119.42
52601	PROSTATECTOMY (TURP)	2,000	24.54	81.50
99201	OFFICE/OUTPATIENT VISIT, NEW	50	0.86	58.14
99202	OFFICE/OUTPATIENT VISIT, NEW	55	0.86	63.95
99203	OFFICE/OUTPATIENT VISIT, NEW	60	1.92	31.25
99211	OFFICE/OUTPATIENT VISIT, EST	25	0.38	65.79
99212	OFFICE/OUTPATIENT VISIT, EST	35	0.75	46.67
99213	OFFICE/OUTPATIENT VISIT, EST	45	1.38	32.61
99221	INITIAL HOSPITAL CARE	90	2.01	44.78
99222	INITIAL HOSPITAL CARE	125	3.27	38.23
99223	INITIAL HOSPITAL CARE	150	4.20	35.71

conversion factor for each CPT code. This is done by dividing the practice's fee by the Medicare RVUs. Since most payers use total RVUs to set reimbursement rates, they are usually not adjusted for the local Geographical Practice Cost Index (GPCI) component. The GPCI is Medicare's way to adjust rates for a particular locality. GPCIs could be included in the RBRVS RVUs if you know the payers are also using it in their rate setting methodology; if not or if you are unsure, just use total RVUs.

This analysis also shows significant variances in the pricing of Dr. Fry's services based on RBRVS units. Once you have determined the respective conversion factors, the next part of the fee schedule analysis includes comparing these conversion factors to the leading payers in Dr. Fry's market. The worksheet shown in Exhibit 5.4 can be completed for each leading payer to determine a local RBRVS rate (Note: you should complete the same worksheet using St. Anthony's RVPs. Review a sample of recent EOBs from each payer and determine the allowable rate for each CPT code you are analyzing. Then divide the rate by each related RBRVS RVU to arrive at a conversion factor for each significant payer.

Compare the practice's conversion factor to those of the practice's major payers. With this quick analysis, we can see which CPT codes have been priced high or low in reference to the market and make recommendations to the medical practice as to the pricing of these procedures. Exhibit 5.5 is an example comparison.

Exhibit 5.4
Payer 1
Conversion Factor Calculation

CPT CODE	SERVICE DESCRIPTION	PAYER #1 ALLOWABLE PER EOB	RBRVS RVU	PAYER'S CONVERSION FACTOR

Exhibit 5.5
Fry Urology Specialists
RBRVS Conversion Factor Analysis

CPT	Description	Practice CF	CF for Payer #1	CF for Payer #2
50230	REMOVAL OF KIDNEY	75.37	69.34	69.34
50590	LITHOTRIPSY	320.84	118.07	118.07
50780	REIMPLANT URETER IN BLADDER	77.26	71.08	71.08
51726	COMPLEX CYSTOMETROGRAM	76.68	70.54	70.54
51772	URETHRA PRESSURE PROFILE	65.79	60.53	60.53
51785	ANAL/URINARY MUSCLE STUDY	74.63	68.66	68.66
51845	REPAIR BLADDER NECK	92.28	84.90	84.90
52000	CYSTOSCOPY	90.52	83.28	83.28
52336	CYSTOSCOPY, STONE REMOVAL	112.71	103.69	103.69
52337	CYSTOSCOPY, STONE REMOVAL	119.42	109.87	109.87
52601	PROSTATECTOMY (TURP)	81.50	74.98	74.98
99201	OFFICE/OUTPATIENT VISIT, NEW	58.14	53.49	53.49
99202	OFFICE/OUTPATIENT VISIT, NEW	63.95	46.51	49.48
99203	OFFICE/OUTPATIENT VISIT, NEW	31.25	33.06	36.46
99211	OFFICE/OUTPATIENT VISIT, EST	65.79	48.82	52.63
99212	OFFICE/OUTPATIENT VISIT, EST	46.67	43.39	38.67
99213	OFFICE/OUTPATIENT VISIT, EST	32.61	29.71	36.23
99221	INITIAL HOSPITAL CARE	44.78	29.85	29.85
99222	INITIAL HOSPITAL CARE	38.23	35.66	31.96
99223	INITIAL HOSPITAL CARE	35.71	28.57	33.33

Using these worksheets, you should be able to identify CPT codes that are priced too high or too low by reviewing the conversion factors for consistency in pricing. After evaluating the targeted fees using both St. Anthony and Medicare RBRVS, the next step is to determine whether or not the medical practice would benefit from an in-depth fee schedule analysis. If you find numerous inconsistencies that are not justified, one should be recommended. However, keep in mind there will be times where high conversion factors for certain fees will be justified, such as those for subspecialty services. The point to be made here is not to jump to the conclusion that a practice should reduce fees for certain specific services just because the fee looks too high from a relative value analysis standpoint.

Also keep in mind a relative value analysis should also be used to assess rates before executing a discounted fee-for-service managed care contract. What are the contract's conversion rates? How do they compare to the practice's conversion rates and to those of the practice's other payers?

Regardless of how a medical practice has obtained or developed its existing fee schedule, the goal of every medical practice is to set fees for its services which are fair and reasonable for its medical specialty, fair and reasonable according to community standards, and as close as possible to what insurance companies have deemed to be reasonable and customary.

The objectives of the fee schedule analysis are to make sure the practice is not losing revenues as a result of an inadequate fee schedule and to ensure that the fee schedule is consistently priced and in line with usual, customary, and reasonable standards within its market area. Since the fee schedule has a significant impact on the profitability of a medical practice, this analysis should always be included in the practice assessment.

Reviewing Charge Tickets

One part of the assessment process is to perform a review of the charge tickets the office uses. This includes the office charge ticket (which almost all practices have) and if applicable, the hospital charge ticket, and the surgical charge ticket. As stated in the chapter on analyzing the practice's billing and collection processes, these tickets are used to record what services are rendered to patients and are then used as a tool to bill the physician's services. Therefore, it is important to review these charge tickets since any mistakes on them could result in a billing error or missed billing opportunities.

When errors occur, the staff will have to spend time determining why the error was made and then either refile or appeal the denial for payment if the opportunity presents itself to do so. Some errors are in fact true errors and a payer will not reimburse the billing. In this situation, however, at least there will be documentation of the error. When an inadequate charge ticket results in missed billing opportunities, most of the time the practice is totally unaware of when this happens; there is nobody saying to the practice "Hey, you just missed some revenue!" This is why charge tickets must capture all services that can be rendered and related billing opportunities identified on it.

THE OFFICE CHARGE TICKET

A sample of an office charge ticket was shown previously of a practice's billing and collection processes. As also mentioned was an office charge ticket is commonly referred to in the physician community as a "superbill." You should obtain a copy of the office charge ticket and do or look for the following:

1. First, ask how long it has been since the superbill was updated. It should be updated at least once a year since CPT and ICD-9 codes change each year. If the answer is something other than "annually," you can most likely assume there might be errors to be found on the charge ticket.

2. Take current office charge ticket and trace all CPT (service) and ICD-9 (diagnosis) Codes listed to the CPT and ICD-9 Books.

These codes are listed directly on the charge ticket. A doctor usually circles or checkmarks them after he or she has performed the service. This tells the office staff what the doctor did to the patient and this information is used to check the patient out of the office and bill the insurance company (Refer to chapter 5 for more explanation on how the charge ticket impacts a practice's billing and collection process). Therefore, the codes listed on the superbill must be correct.

As you trace the codes to a CPT book and an ICD-9 book, circle or highlight the errors you found directly on the charge ticket. Most commonly found during this step are deleted CPT codes that are still on the superbill, descriptions are incorrect, and an ICD-9 code now has an extra digit. Trying to bill a deleted code will almost always result in a charge denial. Incorrect descriptions might cause the doctor to miscode a particular service, resulting in a missed revenue opportunity. Billing an ICD-9 code without using the code that goes out to the farthest digit might also result in a charge denial or a delay in the payment of the claim by the insurance company.

To document errors you find for presentation to the practice, you might want to set up a worksheet like the one below; errors found could be documented in Exhibits 6.1 and 6.2 (CH0601.DOC, CH0602.DOC).

1. Make sure all CPT codes and ICD-9 codes are included on the charge ticket.

Not only must a charge ticket be correct, but it also must be efficient. Inefficient superbills hinder the billing and collection process; efficient ones help it tremendously. An efficient office charge ticket is one that includes both CPT and ICD-9 codes on it. When a doctor has the ability to indicate what service was performed (the CPT code) and why the service was

Exhibit 6.1
Analysis of Office Charge Ticket—CPT Codes

Practice Name: _____
Worksheet Preparation Date: _____

CPT Code	Code Description	Error Found

performed (the ICD-9 code), the office should be able to immediately bill the service.

There are many, many offices that only include CPT codes on their superbill. On these office tickets there is usually only a line item where the doctor will write in what the diagnosis was. When this happens, someone in the office is going to have to waste their time looking up the related ICD-9 code; this person might even select the wrong code, maybe resulting in a delay in payment by the insurance company. As mentioned in the chapter on billing and collection processes, a practice wants to bill its services as quickly as possible in order to speed up its cash flow and to be able to send

Exhibit 6.2
Analysis of Office Charge Ticket—ICD-9 Codes

Practice Name: _____
Worksheet Preparation Date: _____

CPT Code	Code Description	Error Found

a statement to a patient for their personal financial responsibility for the service. Office services should be billed no more than two to three days after the patient visited the office. If someone has to look up ICD-9 codes, this may delay the filing of the insurance claim.

The top half of the charge ticket could be used for CPT codes and the bottom half used for the diagnosis codes. However, you want to make it as easy as possible for the physician to record his or her office services; therefore, you will want as many codes as possible on the ticket. This is why some offices prefer to have the CPT codes on the front of the office charge ticket and the ICD-9 codes on the back.

2. Make sure all levels of service are included on the office charge ticket.

All levels of service must be included on the charge ticket, including those for new patient visits, established patient visits, and office consultations. The following are the codes that should be included; keep in mind some medical specialties might not need these codes (e.g., Pathology) and that some practices might not perform consultative visits (e.g., Family practice):

New patient office visit codes: 99201, 99202, 99203, 99204, 99205

Established patient office visit codes: 99211, 99212, 99213, 99214, 99215

Office consultation codes: 99241, 99242, 99243, 99244, 99245

There are two reasons why all of the levels of service should be included on the office charge tickets. The first is to make sure the doctor is not accidentally miscoding his or her services simply because all of the levels of service are not on the charge ticket. Specifically, you want to make sure the doctor is not accidentally "upcoding" his or her services. Upcoding means the doctor is recording a higher level of service than what was actually performed. Upcoding can result in the following:

- Denial of the billed charge by an insurance company;

- Downcoding of the service to a lower CPT code by an insurance company; or

- An audit by an insurance company (or any other third-party payer, such as Medicare).

The denial or downcoding of an "upcoded" charge are usually tied together in that usually the CPT code that was billed does not agree with the ICD-9 code that was billed with it. In these situations, the diagnosis code explains a condition or symptom that is much less than the CPT code that was billed. A real simple example is the patient who has the flu and the doctor bills code 99214 for the minor treatment (keep in mind as the levels go up, the patients are suppose to be sicker and sicker; i.e., have more complicated problems).

When upcoding occurs, the doctor could be risking an insurance audit as well, especially one from a governmental agency such as Medicare and Medicaid. This often occurs when a doctor utilizes one or two codes time after time again *and is usually the result of having too few number of codes on the charge ticket (the ones actually on the charge ticket are the higher levels of service).*

The level of service must always be supported by appropriate chart documentation. For evaluation and management services, for example, medical records must include documentation of the following:

- The patient's chief complaint;

- The patient's history;

- The physical examination and review of systems;

- Medical decision making;

- The treatment or management plan; and

- The consultation/coordination of care.

If the CPT code billed does not agree with the documentation in the patient's medical record, the practice will usually owe monies back to the payer because he or she has been overpaid (i.e., a lower level of service should have been billed that supported the chart documentation). Civil penalties may also be assessed; a criminal investigation could occur if there was a deliberate attempt by the doctor to upcode the services.

The point should be clear: *a good superbill helps avoid an insurance audit!*

The second reason why all of the levels of service should be included on the office charge ticket is basically the opposite of the insurance audit discussion above: the practice wants to make sure it is not losing revenue because the higher levels of services are not included on the superbill. For example, many practices do not include code 99211 on their charge ticket because they feel they do not render this type of service; however, upon further investigation, they find that they do perform services at this level (e.g., blood pressure checks). At the opposite end, some practices in certain medical specialties will treat sicker patients more often than others. No matter, every practice wants the higher levels of service on the charge ticket in the event this type of treatment is ever rendered. One of the worst things that could happen is the situation where a doctor treats a very sick patient but checks only code 99213 because that is as high as the codes go on the charge ticket; codes 99214 and 99215 were left off.

A great indicator of these types of problems with the charge ticket is tied to your review of the practice's service frequency. By paying close attention to how often these office codes are billed, you can get an idea if there might be a problem with how the office charge ticket is designed. The following is a good example:

CPT Code	Frequency	Percent Used
99211	55	5
99212	92	9
99213	761	73
99214	111	11
99215	22	2
Total	1,041	100%

In this example, the doctor uses the established patient visit code 99213 73 percent of the time. Normally you will want to see a bell-shape curve when first analyzing coding patterns for office visits. When you see this type of example, you want to make sure that the medical record documentation is supporting the code billed. On the other hand, if you see that certain of the codes were not billed at all, it is likely that not all of the codes are included on the charge ticket. Remember that the doctor is in the exam room and recording only those services that are on the ticket. This type of situation might be causing the practice to lose revenues and/or cause an audit.

A real life example was a urology practice. The doctors billed CPT code 99214 100 percent of the time when the CPT frequency report was looked at. When a doctor bills all his established patient visits at one CPT code, this was obviously incorrect. When the office charge ticket was looked at, guess what was listed as the only service for an established patient office visit: 99214!

1. Search for missing services.

To reiterate, the doctor will only record services that are included on the charge ticket. As such, you want to make sure *all* office services that can be billed are on the charge ticket. If you are not experienced at CPT coding, we suggest you have the physician or an office nurse go through the entire CPT book and identify the procedures and services that can be performed in the office. This may identify additional procedures that will need to be added to the charge ticket. Examples include supply and injection codes.

2. For specialty practices, make sure the office consultation codes are properly aligned on the charge ticket.

Medical specialists are often asked by other doctors to consult on a patient. This often occurs when there is a suspected or unknown problem that needs the help of a medical specialist. In these situations, the doctor will send the patient to the specialist to find out what is really wrong with the patient. Under most of these circumstances, the specialist should bill a consultation code for the visit. However, many times a consultation code is not billed simply because the charge ticket is not designed properly.

First, make sure the consultation codes are listed first on the charge ticket. This will prompt the specialist to think whether or not the encounter should be billed as a consultation. When these codes are buried in the middle of the charge ticket, the doctor may not have a tendency to bill the appropriate code. Even more important, however, is to make sure the consultation codes are *even on the charge ticket* to begin with. If the doctor is a medical specialist, take a very close look at the usage of consultation services on the CPT frequency report. If the frequency report shows a lower amount of consultative services than the office visit codes, it might be because the codes are not aligned correctly on the charge ticket (or even included on the charge ticket in some cases). However, keep in mind it is usually the result of a lack of education about when a consultation code can be billed.

3. Make sure the office charge tickets are prenumbered and missing tickets (i.e., numbers) are accounted for.

Numbering charge tickets is a basic form of internal control. To prevent theft, all tickets should be numbered and accounted for. Evidence of missing tickets could be the result of employee embezzlement. Numbering and related accountability helps prevent the situation where an employee takes money from a patient, takes a superbill, and gives it to the patient as a receipt, and then pockets the money. The charge and payment are never entered into the practice's computer system.

HOSPITAL AND SURGICAL CHARGE TICKETS

You will perform all of the same review functions mentioned above for these tickets as you will for the office charge ticket. You need to make sure all of these tickets are accurate and contain the services that the doctor will need to bill, along with related diagnosis codes. Keep in mind, however, that most doctors do not want to be burdened with a lot of paper when they perform their hospital rounds. This is why the hospital charge ticket is usually much smaller in size, often the size of an index card. The challenge here is to make the card as efficient as possible; usually CPT codes are used and the doctor will write in the diagnosis code.

CHAPTER SEVEN

Overhead Analysis

Rising overhead, combined with lower revenues, is certainly bringing pressure to the net profit of medical practices everywhere. This declining profitability is leading to the demand for medical practice assessments as organizations strive for more efficiency and ways to lower their cost structure. Therefore, it is imperative that the practice assessment evaluates the overhead and staffing levels of the medical practice. Benchmarking these expenses is quickly becoming a standard practice in the industry as organizations try to evaluate their efficiency and cost structure in reference to other medical practices.

Historically, medical practices have evaluated their overhead as a percentage of overall collections. This percentage is calculated by taking total operating expenses before physician compensation and benefits and dividing it by gross collections. Calculate this percentage for the current year as the first step in the analysis of practice overhead. The next step is to calculate this percentage for each of the prior three years.

Shown below is an example of the overhead percentage calculation for a multi-specialty clinic.

Finley Multi-Specialty Clinic Overhead Analysis

Net Revenues	1,215,775
Total Operating Expenses	632,421
Operating Expenses as % of Net Revenue	52.02%

Exhibit 7.1

Overhead Benchmarks

Primary Care	50 to 60 percent
Specialty Practice	35 to 45 percent

As part of your analysis, this overhead percentage should be compared to national and specialty medians, compared to prior operating periods, and reviewed for reasonableness. Exhibit 7.1 shows general overhead benchmarks to keep in mind as you begin to analyze practice overhead:

As you may discover, actual practice overhead can vary significantly from these general benchmarks. This will depend on numerous factors, including level of capitation income, level of physician production, staffing, and front office collection problems. For example, adding new providers usually raises the overhead percentage as expenses are added to support the providers, while cash flow from the new physicians production is not collected for several months.

PRIOR YEAR COMPARISONS: A QUICK LOOK AT OVERHEAD

The next step in your analysis should be to compare practice overhead with prior years. This will provide you and practice management with an understanding of the trend line for the practice's overhead and will allow you to investigate any large variances. A sample worksheet is shown in Exhibit 7.2 which shows a practice overhead comparison year-to-year for a two-year period; you will need to prepare a similar worksheet for your own analysis.

Exhibit 7.2

Practice Overhead Year-to-Year Comparison

	Total Collections	Total Operating Overhead	Overhead %
1997	$ 3,595,800	$ 1,928,700	53.64%
1996	$ 3,930,700	$ 1,944,600	49.40%
Change	$ (334,900)	$ (15,900)	4.24%

Exhibit 7.3
Overhead Category Analysis

Expense	1997 $	1996 $	$ Change
Non-physician Payroll	$ 529,000	$ 541,800	$ (12,800)
Rent & Occupancy	$ 164,000	$ 140,600	$ 23,400
Medical Supplies/X-Ray	$ 185,800	$ 154,400	$ 31,400
Lab Supplies	$ 107,000	$ 139,000	$ (32,000)

As you can see in this example, even though expenses increased only approximately $16,000 on almost two million dollars worth of expenses, the overhead percentage rose over 4 percent. This was due to a significant decrease in collections. The point to emphasize here is that a rising overhead percentage does not always equate to escalating expenses. You must evaluate both collections and expenses to completely understand why the overhead percentage is rising.

In addition to comparing overhead percentage with prior years, you should also compare major operating overhead categories. Exhibit 7.3 is a sample worksheet that compares two years of selected overhead categories; you can use additional years for comparative purposes if you wish.

This quick comparison will allow you to identify specific overhead categories that require a more detailed analysis. The objective is to assess why the overhead increased so you can submit solutions on achieving reductions.

MGMA Comparison

In addition to performing year-to-year comparisons of practice operating overhead and related percentages, the overhead percentage should also be compared to industry norms. One industry accepted standard is to compare the practice's operating overhead to the Medical Group Management Association's cost survey. Shown in Exhibit 7.4 is a graph of the practice's last two years overhead percentage with matching specialty norms for the specialty by the MGMA cost survey.

The objective here is the same as the cursory comparison of major overhead categories: to see if the operating overhead appears out of line when compared to industry accepted norms. If so, further investigation is warranted and can be conducted.

Exhibit 7.4
West Multi-Specialty Clinic
Two-Year Overhead Comparison
with MGMA Norms

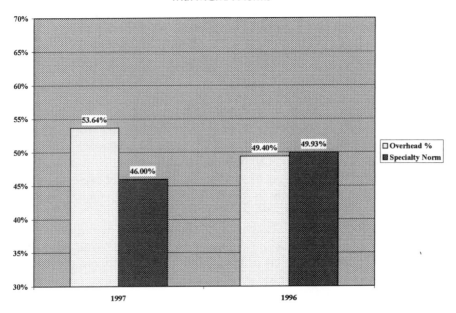

The same information can be presented in worksheet format, if the physicians relate better to numbers:

	Total Overhead	Overhead %	Specialty Norm	Difference
1997	$ 1,928,700	53.64%	46.00%	7.64%
1996	$ 1,944,600	49.40%	49.93%	-0.53%

You can also graph the MGMA comparison as shown in Exhibit 7.5

A word of caution: If the medical practice is large or one that has been acquired by a health system or practice management company, revenues and expenses may be reported on the accrual basis versus the cash basis. Whenever you are making comparisons of the overhead percentage to na-

Exhibit 7.5
Practice Performance Compared to MGMA Norms

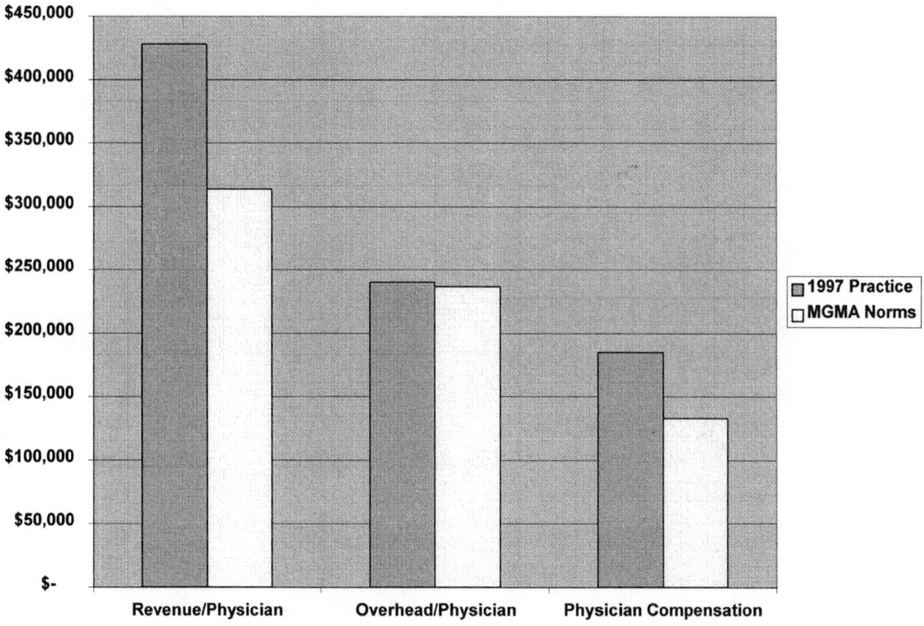

tional data or other surveys, understand that most of the reported data in these surveys is based upon a cash basis of recording revenues and expenses by the medical practice. Therefore, if you are working with a medical practice on the accrual basis, you will have to convert its statement of revenues and expenses to the cash basis in order to make an accurate comparison. The accrual basis of recording revenues is quite common in the physician practice management medical groups, as well as medical practices owned by health systems.

Graphing Overhead Trends

In addition to the analysis methods mentioned above, we recommend that you also graph the three-year history of revenues and practice expenses. This is just one more way to aid you in identifying potential problems with

Exhibit 7.6
Gibson Family Practice
Three-Year Trending of Revenues, Non-Physician and Physician Expenses

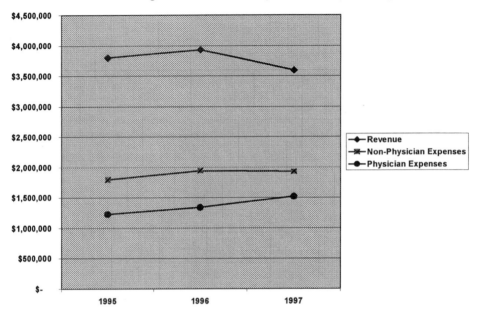

practice overhead. An example of this trend line graph is shown in Exhibit 7.6 to illustrate this comparison.

PERFORMING A DETAILED OVERHEAD COMPARATIVE

The next step in the overhead analysis is to perform a detailed review of practice overhead, comparing to both prior years and an industry survey. Your objective is to benchmark the clinic versus comparable clinics and understand at what level the clinic is operating. You will want to assess whether or not a problem exists on the revenue side, the expense side, or possibly both sides.

Your initial review of practice overhead was directed at the calculation of operating overhead percentages. Don't let overhead percentages fool you! Although the overall overhead percentage for a medical practice may be within what is considered to be a reasonable level, the practice could still have significant inefficiencies or high costs. Therefore, it is extremely important as part of the practice assessment and ongoing management to

Exhibit 7.7
West Family Practice Clinic
Income and Expenses Compared to MGMA Norms
(3 FTE Physicians)

	1997	1997 as % of Net Revenue	MGMA Norms*	Variance From Norm
INCOME				
Net Patient Revenue	1,217,167		** 961,044	**26.51%**
Interest Income	25			
Other Income	—			
Less Refunds	(1,417)			
Net Revenues	**1,215,775**			
EXPENSES				
Physician Expenses				
Compensation & Bonus	304,321	25.03%	38.10%	−13.07%
Payroll Tax and Pension	81,436	6.70%	4.04%	2.66%
Insurance	19,694	1.62%	1.45%	0.17%
Other Physician Discretionary Expenses	9,929	0.82%	0.72%	0.10%
Total Physician Expenses	**415,380**	**34.17%**	**44.46%**	**−10.29%**
Nonphysician Expenses:				
Nonphysician Payroll/Benefits	446,335	36.71%	31.97%	4.74%
Rent & Occupancy	39,595	3.26%	7.19%	−3.93%
Medical Supplies	77,700	6.39%	4.00%	2.39%
Medical Services	44,883	3.69%	4.28%	0.59%
Admin. Supplies/Services	39,727	3.27%	2.35%	0.92%
Promotion/Marketing Expenses	1,389	0.11%	0.41%	−0.30%
Insurance	37,451	3.08%	1.53%	1.55%
Interest	8	0.00%	0.24%	−0.24%
Outside Professional	21,687	1.78%	0.76%	1.02%
Informational Services	10,268	0.84%	1.80%	−0.96%
Furniture and Equipment	—	0.00%	1.23%	−1.23%
Other Operating Expenses	26,737	2.20%	1.17%	1.03%
Total Nonphysician (Operating) Expenses	**745,779**	**61.34%**	**59.53%**	**1.81%**

*MGMA reports statistics as median values; values will not add to totals.
**MGMA norms are calculated per FTE physician. This number is the MGMA norm multiplied times 3 FTE physicians.

Exhibit 7.8
West Family Practice Clinic
Income and Expense Historical Comparison

	1997	1996	Variance $ 1997-96	Variance % 1997-96
INCOME				
Net Patient Revenue	1,217,167	1,066,457	150,710	14.13%
Interest Income	25	2,102	(2,077)	−98.81%
Other Income	—	1,117	(1,117)	−100.00%
Less Refunds	(1,417)	(1,987)	570	−28.69%
Net Revenues	1,215,775	1,067,689	148,086	13.87%
EXPENSES				
Physician Expenses				
Compensation & Bonus	304,321	289,456	14,865	5.14%
Payroll Tax and Pension	81,436	72,275	9,161	12.68%
Insurance	19,694	18,423	1,271	6.90%
Other Physician Discretionary Expenses	9,929	18,490	(8,561)	−46.30%
Total Physician Expenses	415,380	398,644	16,736	4.20%
Nonphysician Expenses				
Nonphysician Payroll/Benefits	446,335	428,657	17,678	4.12%
Rent & Occupancy	39,595	37,875	1,720	4.54%
Medical Supplies	77,700	70,623	7,077	10.02%
Medical Services	44,883	62,107	(17,224)	−27.73%
Admin. Supplies/Services	39,727	35,573	4,154	11.68%
Promotion/Marketing Expenses	1,389	2,669	(1,280)	−47.95%
Insurance	37,451	41,979	(4,528)	−10.79%
Interest	8	264	(256)	−96.97%
Outside Professional	21,687	35,027	(13,340)	−38.09%
Information Services	10,268	15,831	(5,563)	−35.14%
Furniture and Equipment	—	12,253	(12,253)	−100.00%
Other Operating Expenses	26,737	14,159	12,578	88.84%
Total Operating Expenses	745,779	757,017	(11,238)	−1.48%
Operating Expenses as % of Net Revenue	61.34%	70.90%		−9.56%
Total Expenses	1,161,159	1,155,661	5,498	0.48%
Net Income (Loss)	54,616	(87,972)	142,588	162.08%

monitor the practice overhead expenses by category rather than just simply as a total and percentage of revenues.

An analysis of the overhead categories should be compared to national standards based on a percentage basis as shown in the worksheet below. This allows you and the practice's management to evaluate its own income statement in relation to industry norms, such as the norm created by the Medical Group Management Association (MGMA) cost survey. Exhibit 7.7 shows you a sample detailed comparative worksheet to MGMA norms.

In addition, the overhead category should be reviewed in detail based on a year-to-year comparison. Pay strict attention to the variance to identify overhead categories that might need further investigation. Exhibit 7.8 is a sample worksheet.

Any significant changes in overhead percentage or significant variances from year to year in various categories should be reviewed with the medical practice's management. While conducting the practice assessment, it may be necessary to make specific recommendations in reference to the overhead expenses.

TAKE A LOOK AT STAFFING

One area which always needs additional analysis, especially if there is any substantial increase in expenditures, is an analysis of nonphysician payroll and staffing. Typically, the largest single expense category will be nonphysician salary and benefits, which by definition excludes physician compensation and benefits. One of the most frequently asked questions during a practice assessment is "Are we staffed adequately or are we overstaffed?" This can be an extremely challenging question to answer because you must consider the efficiencies in the medical practice, the level of production and leverage generated for the physicians, level of capitation income, and other factors which might affect staffing levels.

To begin the process of analyzing staffing levels, prepare a worksheet comparing the practice's FTEs (full-time equivalents) to the MGMA median data. Exhibit 7.9 is a sample worksheet.

As you can see from this worksheet, the staffing comparison was completed by department or job description with an analysis at the bottom of the worksheet for total FTEs for the practice. Be very careful about informing a medical practice that it is over- or understaffed simply based upon this type of analysis. You must evaluate the efficiencies and overall production of the medical practice before drawing conclusions based on a simple headcount. For example, in the Medical Group Management

Association's *1997 Cost Survey Based on 1996 Data*, 15 multi-specialty practices were identified, which were out-performing all multi-specialty practices that had responded to the survey.

Those 15 practices actually carried total FTE support staff per FTE physician of 4.97, compared to an overall survey benchmark of 4.68. So these best performing practices in the survey actually had more staff per physician FTE than some of the other practices which were not as profitable. Also, in this same study, although these better performing practices had more staff per FTE physician, their operating costs as a percent of net medical revenue were almost five percent less than the median for the entire survey. This is an excellent example of how the evaluator of the medical practice must weigh all of the practice's operational performance indicators when making recommendations, especially concerning staffing.

Exhibit 7.9
Speights Multi-Specialty Clinic Support Staff FTE/Physician

Employee	Type	Title/Function	FTE	# FTE/ Physician	MGMA Norm
Joan Raines	Business Office	Data Entry Clerk	0.5		
Mary Beth Claudell	Business Office	Insurance Clerk	1		
Amy McGregor	Business Office	Bookkeeper	1		
	Business Office Count		**3**	**1.00**	**0.61**
Terrance Schmidt	Custodial	Custodian	0.5		
	Custodial Count		**1**	**0.33**	**0.15**
Juanita Lynley	General/Admin	Receptionist	1		
Janice Merle	General/Admin	Receptionist	1		
Darlene Rogers	General/Admin	Office Manager	1		
	General/Admin Count		**3**	**1.00**	**0.22**
Karen Smythe	Lab	Lab Tech	1		
	Lab Count		**1**	**0.33**	**0.32**
Pam Jones	LPN	LPN	1		
	LPN Count		**1**	**0.33**	**0.45**
Yancy Young	Medical Records	Transcriptionist	1		
	Medical Records Count		**1**	**0.33**	**0.39**
Maurice Keith	RN	RN	0.5		
Kasey Cartwright	RN	RN	1		
Louella Bounds	RN	RN	1		
	RN Count		**3**	**1.00**	**0.29**
	Grand Count		**13**	**4.33**	**3.94**

Exhibit 7.10
Speights Multi-Specialty Clinic Employee Salary Analysis

Employee	Type	Title/Function	Years of Service	FTE	Hourly Rate	Salary Survey Average	Range
Joan Raines	Business Office	Data Entry Clerk	1	0.5	6.00	9.66	6.93 - 19.00
Mary Beth Claudell	Business Office	Insurance Clerk	2	1	10.50	10.19	6.00 - 22.92
Amy McGregor	Business Office	Bookkeeper	6	1	12.00	14.52	8.00 - 25.16
Terrance Schmidt	Custodial	Custodian	1	0.5	6.00	9.18	5.25 - 18.00
Juanita Lynley	General/Admin	Receptionist	2	1	8.00	8.72	5.15 – 18.50
Janice Merle	General/Admin	Receptionist	4	1	8.50	9.38	5.25 – 16.00
Darlene Rogers	General/Admin	Office Manager	12	1	21.63	21.95	11.54 - 62.50
Karen Smythe	Lab	Lab Tech	5	1	12.50	13.79	9.00 - 21.57
Pam Jones	LPN	LPN	4	1	11.50	11.54	7.32 - 19.60
Yancy Young	Medical Records	Transcriptionist	2	1	12.00	10.90	6.00 - 20.00
Maurice Keith	RN	RN	1	0.5	15.75	14.79	8.00 - 31.00
Kasey Cartwright	RN	RN	4	1	18.00	15.95	9.00 - 35.95
Louella Bounds	RN	RN	8	1	19.00	16.57	8.51 - 30.00

Source: Staff Salary Survey, 1998, The Health Care Group

Other very common practice assessment questions regarding overhead and staffing levels are "Are we compensating our employees too much?" "Are our compensation levels reasonable?" Exhibit 7.10 is a sample worksheet listing employees by type, by function and title, years of service, and hourly rate compared to survey information as a range and average.

This analysis always provides insight into the reasonableness of employee compensation. However, keep in mind that superstar employees should be compensated as superstars. Survey information is simply data with no real verification ability or exact comparisons to job responsibilities and/or individual education and functionality to the practice you are evaluating. Therefore, recommendations or comments about employee compensation should be done cautiously. Any significant outliers must be closely analyzed before making final recommendations in the practice assessment report.

THE IMPORTANCE OF UNDERSTANDING PRACTICE REVENUE

Beginning an analysis of overhead also requires a good understanding of the revenue base of the practice. What percentage of the medical practice's income is from capitation? How much is pure indemnity business versus discounted fee-for-service? If there is a substantial amount of discounted fee-for-service business, what types of discounts are being negotiated? All of this information will help form the framework within which you will evaluate overhead and make conclusions on the various analyses.

For example, the *1997 MGMA Cost Survey: 1997 Report Based on 1996 Data* actually revealed that physician compensation was the highest in medical practices where over 50 percent of the income was from capitation. For clinics which have a high concentration of capitation income, the MGMA data also reveals some other significant variances in overhead compared to traditional operations based on fee-for-service business. Support costs per physician for practices that have over 50 percent capitation are significantly higher (over 50 percent higher) than practices with less than 50 percent capitation. Median operating costs are also higher under this comparison. The survey also shows staffing per FTE of 4.91 for clinics with over 50 percent capitation, compared to clinics with less capitation ranging from 3.75 to 3.92. So the staffing changes significantly as capitation revenues exceed 50 percent of the medical practice's revenues.

This is an indication that capitation does require more infrastructure than the traditional fee-for-service business. Physicians have to use every opportunity to leverage their time and resources. This additional cost per physician is another contributing factor to the fact that highly capitated groups tend to be larger than groups with less capitation. This allows the medical practice to spread this cost across more providers. Therefore, a medical practice assessment must consider the type of business that the practice is participating in and how it is set up to capitalize on that business. The amount of capitation income will affect the ultimate conclusions in reference to staffing and overhead.

A QUICK LOOK AT OTHER OVERHEAD CATEGORIES

While staffing represents a major portion of any medical practice's overhead, there might be other categories that require your attention. The following is a quick look at some of the important ones.

Health Insurance

Group health insurance premiums can rise dramatically from one year to the next. In some cases, we have seen the annual premium rise as much as

30 to 50 percent in one year. This can have a dramatic impact on practices with a large number of employees. Review the practice's current insurance coverage and determine when the insurance plan was last re-bid.

Overtime

This deserves separate attention from the overall review of practice staffing and related compensation. Many offices are so inefficient that employees spend an enormous amount of extra time completing their job duties. However, in other offices, the employees may be submitting overtime hours when in fact they are not necessary. Make sure employees are accountable for their overtime hours and that such hours are approved before they are incurred.

Supply Costs

Make sure the practice is paying a reasonable price for its supplies and also make sure supplies are not being wasted. Wastefulness results in an excess number of orders. Determine the last time supplies were re-bid with other supply vendors.

Rental Costs

Does the office have too much office space? Is rent increasing because of a large increase in building operating costs? Is the rental rate reasonable?

Advertising and Marketing

What is the rate of return on these expenses? Has the practice received new patients as a result? If not, maybe these costs can be reduced or eliminated. One of the largest cost items in this category is yellow page advertising, frequently mis-classified under the practice's telephone expense, since it is invoiced in the telephone bill.

Telephone Costs

Are long-distance calls managed? Does the office have phone lines it is paying for but not utilizing?

Maintenance Agreements

Are they necessary? Are there alternatives?

Professional Fees

Are they reasonable? We once found a CPA charging a practice $2,500 per month for regular compliance work for which most other CPAs would charge $800 per month.

SUMMARY

As medical practices begin to develop more sophisticated costing systems, information will become available to calculate cost per CPT code. As this data becomes available, it will be important for medical practices to benchmark their cost data against specialty and national norms. Information like cost per patient visit should be compared to prior year costs, as well as any benchmark data that becomes available as a national norm. As health care matures, it will be imperative that medical practices find new and better ways to evaluate overhead and to manage those dollars as efficiently as possible. The ratios and analysis that we have discussed in this chapter will provide tremendous insight into the overall performance of the medical practice.

The overhead analysis is a key component of any medical practice assessment. Always be sure to look at all of the components and to monitor individual categories before making assumptions concerning overhead and the practice's efficiency. Remember that sometimes higher costs can equate into more production and overall revenues and income for the medical practice. Declining revenues will raise the overhead percentage regardless of how well a medical practice manages its overhead from the previous year. The practice of discounting fees will continue to raise overhead percentages and lower profitability of medical practices until practices become more efficient at delivering health care. Utilizing these overhead analysis tools can be very beneficial in helping a medical practice achieve some of those efficiencies.

CHAPTER EIGHT

Coding and Compliance Plan Analysis

The coding of clinical services rendered is the critical link between a medical practice providing the services and getting paid for them. It is common knowledge that physicians do not receive adequate education in medical schools on how to code their services, how to bill their services, or the importance of medical record documentation. This fact alone highlights the need for diligent coding reviews, monitoring of coding levels, and compliance plan initiatives. A thorough practice assessment addresses these issues.

Physicians code their services utilizing a set of five-digit codes referred to as Current Procedural Terminology (CPT), which is copyrighted by the American Medical Association (AMA). Physicians use these codes to bill their services to insurance companies and other third-party payers. These codes cover services from office visits and consultations to brain surgery. Each year, the AMA issues updates to the CPT manual with new additions, deletions, and modifications. Since insurance companies adopt these changes, practices also might have to revise their chargemaster and charge tickets each year (Refer to chapter 6 on how to review charge tickets). Ignoring annual changes to CPT codes could result in billing errors.

As such, you begin this portion of the medical practice assessment by asking to see a copy of the most current edition of the CPT manual in the office. If the office presents an old copy, you can probably surmise that you are going to find billing errors. Many of these will be detected during your EOB analysis (See chapter 3). Which edition of CPT manual the practice has in the office or offices will tell you a lot about the practice's emphasis on coding. For example, we performed an assessment of a large hospital-owned primary care practice. During our assessment, we found out the hospital would not provide CPT manuals to the individual offices. As predicted, we found numerous billing errors because the office staff (which was responsible for physician coding) was unaware of what they could bill and did not have guidance on how to code the physicians' services.

In addition to CPT codes, medical practices must use another coding system to indicate the reason or the medical necessity for the procedure or service. These are the ICD-9 or diagnosis codes. Basically this coding system is utilized to show why the patient was treated (i.e., the diagnosis). For a practice to get paid for the services it renders, there has to be a proper matching of the CPT code(s) with an appropriate diagnosis or ICD-9 code.

In addition to coding, documentation of services is also important. When it comes to payment what is documented and reported rather than what was actually done often dictates actual reimbursement. This is why it is imperative that medical groups properly document and code their services. As far as the government and third-party payers are concerned, if is not documented, the service was not performed. There is a direct correlation between good documentation, proper coding, and medical practice profitability.

With the passage of the Health Insurance Portability and Accountability Act of 1996 (HIPAA) and the Balanced Budget Acts of 1997 and 1998, the federal government has promoted healthcare to the forefront for investigations and fraud auditing. The one very misunderstood concept about this new government oversight is the fact that HIPAA 1996 actually extends the fraud and abuse regulations to not only government programs (i.e., Medicare and Medicaid) but to all services provided to all insurance plans. In addition, the civil penalties have been increased significantly under the new laws. The reward system for whistleblowers has opened the floodgates for false claim cases; as a result, current or ex-employees, competitors, patients, or others have actually turned over or reported a false claim to the government.

The federal government has cast the spotlight on healthcare with an unparalleled allocation of money, manpower, and audit resources to rid the healthcare system of fraudulent and abusive coding and billing practices. This elevates the importance of a thorough coding and compliance analysis to a new level. Medical practice assessments have generally always included some review of evaluation and management coding as compared to specialty norms. This should still be done at a minimum. Depending upon the scope of the medical practice assessment, it may, however, also include an actual medical record chart review (usually a simple review versus a detailed Medicare compliance review). In addition to the coding analysis and medical chart review, the assessment needs some determination as to the medical practice's status of implementation of a compliance plan or its readiness to undergo a third-party investigation into its billing and coding records.

Also complicating this area is the fact that medical practices are also having to prepare to meet the newly published 1998 Evaluation and Management Documentation Guidelines, which feature significant changes in documenting the examination portion of these services. Although these new regulations have been postponed until January 1, 1999, they do present a significant compliance burden to medical practices; testing of compliance therewith might be a proactive way of heading off problems.

REVIEW PHYSICIAN PRODUCTION

After determining what version of the CPT manual the practice has, the next step of the coding and compliance analysis is a review of physician production by CPT code. You will need to obtain a report generally referred to as a CPT Productivity Report or CPT Utilization Report. This report can be printed by almost all medical billing software programs. This detailed report provides the evaluator with utilization information by CPT code for all of the evaluation and management codes. This report should contain at least twelve months of production.

After obtaining this report, the next step is to analyze the practice's coding for evaluation and management services related to patient visits. Complete the worksheet **on the following page** for each physician. If multiple physicians are involved, prepare a worksheet showing each doctor side by side (see sample worksheet for ABC Urology Practice in Exhibit 8.1).

Using a Limited Number of Levels of Service

It is quite common to find during this analysis that certain providers will have the habit of leaning to one particular code for their services. This could serve as a red flag to investigators and actually trigger an audit or review of the medical practice. In other words, the physician may be upcoding his or her services. In these instances, it is critical that the chart documentation agrees with the billing of these codes.

Evaluation & Management CPT Review

Practice Name: _____

Worksheet Preparation Date: _____

CPT Code:	Times Done	Percentage
99201	_____	_____
99202	_____	_____
99203	_____	_____
99204	_____	_____
99205	_____	_____
Total		100%
99211	_____	_____
99212	_____	_____
99213	_____	_____
99214	_____	_____
99215	_____	_____
Total		100%
99221	_____	_____
99222	_____	_____
99223	_____	_____
Total		100%
99231	_____	_____
99232	_____	_____
99233	_____	_____
Total		100%
99241	_____	_____
99242	_____	_____
99243	_____	_____
99244	_____	_____
99245	_____	_____
Total		100%
99251	_____	_____
99252	_____	_____
99253	_____	_____
99254	_____	_____
99255	_____	_____
Total		100%
99291	_____	_____
99292	_____	_____
Total		100%

There are numerous reasons for upcoding. These are the most common ones we find:

1. The physician is not educated on CPT coding;

2. The charge ticket is inadequate (see chapter 6); or

3. The physician is upset over what he or she gets paid by insurance companies and decides to make up the difference by upcoding.

The normal reaction when your assessment finds upcoding by the practice is "Our patients are sicker." This may very well be the case. However, quite often it is due to a lack of knowledge as to what is actually required to document the level of service or when the higher level of visit can be used. It can also be the result of a poorly designed charge ticket as we discussed in chapter 6. Unfortunately, but at least infrequently, it can be greed or "gaming" the system. This is a serious matter and should be approached with extreme caution. The significance of this upcoding is the greatly increased risk of a third-party audit that could result in significant penalties and repayments. Medical practices cannot and should not tolerate upcoding. If the analysis indicates this may be a problem, it should be noted in the assessment that the practice needs to follow up on this matter. You may even want to consider expanding the scope of the practice assessment to include a medical record chart review of these suspected upcoded services.

Downcoding

It is quite common to find a medical practice where there appears to be significant downcoding by the physician or physicians. This could be because the physicians fear a third-party audit or because they are not educated on which codes to use. In addition, a fee schedule which the physicians consider to be excessive will also trigger downcoding as physicians attempt to align the cost of the service with their perception of its value. This issue should be addressed during your fee schedule analysis (See chapter 5). Fee issues and related downcoding are particularly pervasive in small communities where many of the people have lower income levels.

Physicians will also downcode because they know they have done a poor job of documentation. Rather than make the effort to learn how to accurately document their services, they simply select a lower code hoping it will cover them in case of an audit. Numerous times physicians have communicated this activity to us during a practice assessment. This type of downcoding can be a serious threat to a medical practice's profitability and results in lost revenues! In addition, this type of downcoding eventually will hurt the practice should it ever move into capitation. Since the capitation rates are usually based on prior utilization, downcoding can lead to a lower capitation amount.

Missing Codes

Look at the worksheet to see if there are any missing services that you know the practice provides and should have billed for. The most common error found here is failure to bill for consultation services. This is most often found in specialty, as opposed to primary care, practices. In these instances, the service was probably recorded using a new patient or an established patient CPT code rather than the consultation code. Consultation codes pay on average $20 to $60 more than office visit codes, depending, of course, on the level of service billed. Missing codes could also indicate a possible upcoding situation.

Evaluation and Management Coding Analysis Example

The worksheet in Exhibit 8.1 shows a coding comparison for a urology practice. For example purposes, only new patient, established patient, and consultation codes are included; you will want to include all visit codes on your worksheet. All three urologists perform the same type of services. Now take a close look at the worksheet and note what you see. After the worksheet we document some of our observations.

These observations will require further investigation in order to answer the questions. Answers to these questions could improve practice revenues (downcoding) and determine if the practice is in coding compliance (chart documentation supporting codes billed). The answers might also highlight an overstatement of revenue (upcoding).

Observations:

1. Why is Dr. Ward recording 54 percent of his new patient visits as code 99202? Is he downcoding? If so, why?

2. Are Drs. Applewhite and Cutter using new patient code 99203 too much? Does the documentation in the medical record support this level of service?

3. Items 1 and 2 also apply to the established visit services.

Exhibit 8.1
ABC Urology Practice
Utilization for the Twelve-Month Period Ending December 31, 1997

CPT Code	Description	Dr. Ward # of Times	%	Dr. Applewhite # of Times	%	Dr. Cutter # of Times	%
99201	OV, New, Problem Focused	5	2.76%	-	0.00%	3	1.06%
99202	OV, New, Problem Expanded	98	54.14%	8	2.79%	17	5.99%
99203	OV, New, Low Complexity	72	39.78%	197	68.64%	255	89.79%
99204	OV, New, Mod. Complexity	6	3.31%	82	28.57%	6	2.11%
99205	OV, New, High Complexity	-	0.00%	-	0.00%	3	1.06%
Totals		**181**	**100.00%**	**287**	**100.00%**	**284**	**100.00%**
99211	OV, Est., Minimal	68	2.88%	116	4.35%	133	6.47%
99212	OV, Est., Problem Focused	1,655	70.16%	257	9.64%	226	10.99%
99213	OV, Est., Problem Expanded	475	20.14%	2,046	76.72%	1,542	74.96%
99214	OV, Est., Moderate Complexity	125	5.30%	224	8.40%	128	6.22%
99215	OV, Est., High Complexity	36	1.53%	24	0.90%	28	1.36%
Totals		**2,359**	**100.00%**	**2,667**	**100.00%**	**2,057**	**100.00%**
99241	Consult, Problem Focused	-	0.00%	1	3.33%	-	0.00%
99242	Consult, Problem Expanded	211	78.44%	4	13.33%	4	3.03%
99243	Consult. Low Complexity	47	17.47%	25	83.33%	126	95.45%
99244	Consult, Moderate Complexity	11	4.09%	-	0.00%	2	1.52%
99245	Consult, High Complexity	-	0.00%	-	0.00%	-	0.00%
Totals		**269**	**100.00%**	**30**	**100.00%**	**132**	**100.00%**

4. Why is Dr. Applewhite not billing consultations like the other two physicians are?

5. Is Dr. Ward undercoding his consultative visits?

REFER BACK TO THE EOB ANALYSIS

If you have performed a detailed analysis of the explanation of benefits (EOBs), you should have identified potential coding errors. These errors were detected when you found EOBs where billed services were denied payment. Some of these denials may have been the direct result of coding errors. Make a list of these coding errors and determine whether or not the problems are continuing. Sit down with the billing staff to determine why these problems occurred and what the practice has done to correct them.

The following are common coding errors that result in payment denials:

1. Missing CPT modifiers

2. Incorrect usage of CPT modifiers

3. The diagnosis code used did not agree with the CPT code that was billed

4. A visit code was billed for a regular postoperative checkup

5. A deleted CPT code was billed

6. An unlisted surgical procedure was billed.

SCAN THE CPT FREQUENCY REPORT

If you are experienced in CPT coding, you should scan the CPT Frequency Report to see whether or not coding problems are apparent. For example, you might find that starred surgical procedures were billed by the practice. This would lead you to find out whether or not an office visit could have been billed.

COMPARE CPT UTILIZATION TO OTHER PRACTICES

If an accountant or practice management consultant is conducting the assessment, compare the utilization per the CPT Frequency Report to other similar practice clients. You can place the utilization side by side to see where differences might exist in coding patterns. After making this comparison, prepare a list of questions for the billing staff to discuss the differences you found.

REVIEWING PRACTICE COMPLIANCE READINESS

As part of the coding analysis, you should also evaluate the medical practice's compliance plan readiness. The purpose of the compliance plan is to assure that all employees or other individuals associated with the medical practice are aware of and are making best efforts to comply with all the billing rules and regulations in order to avoid errors, fraud, and abuse. The compliance plan should provide everyone affiliated with the entity with timely information in regard to changes in the rules and regulations, as well as continuing education in how to comply with those rules and regulations. The compliance plan should put in place policies and procedures to help detect errors, omissions, or misconduct and should provide resources that would allow the identification of any such issue to be investigated and corrected. Finally, the compliance plan should provide a mechanism or communication channel for which anyone associated with the practice could report any suspicious activity or violations without any fear of consequences.

The objective of this portion of the assessment is to simply determine if the medical practice has performed due diligence in understanding the issues surrounding the new fraud and abuse initiatives and if it has made an assessment of its need for a compliance plan. A compliance plan questionnaire is shown below to assist in your inquiries to management. The questionnaire is not intended to evaluate the effectiveness or completeness of any such plan. As part of the medical practice assessment, again, the objective is to assess if the medical practice has addressed this, and if so, what stage its compliance plan is in.

COMPLIANCE PLAN QUESTIONS

1. Have you implemented an actual compliance plan, and if so, could you please provide a copy?

2. Has the medical practice passed a board resolution to adopt a compliance plan?

3. Have you conducted an internal risk assessment to establish an understanding of the risk areas in your operations for billing errors?

4. Have you performed an internal medical chart documentation review?

5. Have you identified a compliance plan officer?

6. Have you provided educational sessions for your employees in reference to your compliance plan?

7. Have you put in place continual monitoring to ensure ongoing adherence with your compliance plan and to identify coding and billing errors?

Medical practice assessments need to evaluate this phase of a practice's operations and make recommendations to the practice's management. In smaller medical practices, it is not necessary for them to have a compliance plan that rivals a hospital system. It should be developed based

Exhibit 8.2
Chart Audit Worksheet
Physician Name: Robert Simmons, MD

							Auditor Review							
Patient Number	Date of Service	Physician E & M Code	History	Exam	Medical Decision	Auditor E&M Code	Overcode 1 = Error	Undercode 1 = Error	Physician ICD Code	Auditor ICD Code	ICD Error 1= Error	Record Signed Y/N	Record Legible Y/N	Comments
1	22153	4/1/97	99211	F	F	S	99212		1	250.0	250.00	1	Y	Y	Transposition error, Missing 5th digit on Dx
2	35415	5/10/97	99214	E	E	L	99213	1		225.	225.0		Y	N	
3	44687	1/9/97	99201	F	F	S	99201			427.3	427.32	1	Y	Y	Missing 5th digit on Dx
4	34568	6/15/97	99242	E	E	S	99241	1		458.0	458.0		Y	Y	
5	25896	7/2/97	99213	E	E	L	99213			564.1	564.1		Y	Y	
6	74185	8/20/97	99215	C	C	H	99215			550.0	550.0		Y	Y	
7	39517	11/26/97	99214	F	F	S	99212	1		381.0	381.00		Y	Y	
8	75315	12/3/97	99211	F	F	S	99212		1	460	460		Y	N	
9	85248	3/3/97	99243	D	D	L	99243			255.0	255.0		Y	Y	
10	95235	1/8/97	99205	C	C	H	99203	1		842.01	842.00	1	Y	Y	

History and Exam	Key
Focused	F
Expanded	E
Detailed	D
Comprehensive	C

Medical Decision	Key
Straightforward	S
Low Complexity	L
Moderate Complexity	M
High Complexity	H

Provider Summary

	#	%
Total E/M Codes Reviewed	10	
Total E/M Overcoded	4	40%
Total E/M Undercoded	2	20%
E/M Coding Accuracy	40%	
Total ICD Codes Reviewed	10	
Total ICD Code Errors	4	40%
ICD Accuracy Rate	60%	
Records Signed	100%	
Records Legible	80%	

Documentation Strengths: All records signed; most records dictated
Documentation Weaknesses: Overcoding of 40% of cases presents high risk.

Overall Comments:
Overcoded cases and incorrect diagnosis codes create risk for this provider. Undercoding on some cases does not optimize reimbursement. Code 99211 does not require physician presence and should rarely be used when the physician sees the patient. Legibility would be at 100% if physician would dictate all notes.

on their risk assessment and may be very limited in comparison to larger entity plans. This assessment of compliance can be extremely important in the situation where the practice assessment is being performed in response to a possible merger or acquisition.

SHOULD THE ASSESSMENT INCLUDE A CHART REVIEW?

Sometimes the scope of the medical practice assessment will be expanded to include a third phase of the coding and compliance analysis. This includes an actual random sample and review of the medical charts. This will usually involve reviewing 5 to 10 charts per physician. Outpatient as well as inpatient services are usually included. Someone who is experienced in medical billing and coding should perform this medical chart documentation review. The reviewer should have extensive knowledge of Medicare, Medicaid, and State regulations and should also be well-versed in coding and documentation guidelines for the evaluation and management codes, as well as other CPT services.

In the evaluation of the medical records, the three review points are 1) medically necessary, 2) coded properly, and 3) documented properly. The level of care billed should comply with the evaluation and management coding guidelines. In addition, the review needs to determine that all the procedures performed were medically necessary with specific diagnosis codes which are also consistent with the CPT code selected. Shown in Exhibit 8.2 is an example of a summary coding sheet which can be utilized for each physician reviewed.

This is extremely important in documenting the actual review itself and assists in any subsequent questions from the providers or the medical practice management in reference to the findings during the medical chart review. By documenting the patient names, date of services, and so on, you can use the chart reviews to assist with physician questions and education.

As you can see, coding, compliance, and documentation play a significant role in medical practice operations. Consequently, a practice assessment should address these issues. Depending upon the scope and purpose of the medical practice assessment, you may need to do some analysis in all three areas. Specialty norms, historical trends, appropriate inquiry, and sometimes random medical chart reviews are all tools to assist you in accomplishing your assessment objectives.

CHAPTER NINE

Physician Analysis

The most valuable assets in any medical practice are the physicians and utilization of their time. Naturally, a complete practice assessment must analyze the physician component of the practice. The assessment should address such physician issues as productivity, compensation, clinical encounters, and governance. The assessment should review individual physician performance as well as the average physician performance for the entire practice.

By nature, physicians are competitive, and good analytical information on their performance and compensation generally leads to improvements in their production and an understanding of how they measure up to their peers. Well-managed medical practices, whether managed by the physician owners, a physician practice management company, or by a hospital system, tend to always ask how their practice physicians are doing and how they compare to their peers. Are they producing revenues at levels to justify their compensation? These questions and more can be resolved by completing a thorough physician analysis as part of the medical practice assessment.

PHYSICIAN FULL-TIME EQUIVALENTS

The first place to start the physician analysis is to gather information on each physician, including information by medical specialty and by availability during the working year. It is critical to compute the number of full-time equivalent (FTEs) for each physician and the medical practice in total. Utilizing national norms that are based on full-time equivalents (FTEs),

Exhibit 9.1
Physician FTE Calculation

Physician	Status	Hours/Week	FTE
Dr. Roberts	Full Time	50	1
Dr. Reid	Full Time	50	1
Dr.Pitts	Part Time	20	.4
Dr. McCloud	Part Time	25	.5
Total Physician FTEs			**2.9**

you must understand how the benchmark data defines an FTE. Then you must calculate comparable FTEs for the medical practice. Circumstances that will affect the calculation of a FTE include partially retired physicians, part-time physicians, leaves of absence, new physicians, retiring physicians, as well as others. Therefore, it is imperative that the evaluator understands the availability of each physician during the year and calculates an accurate FTE for each physician and the practice in total. A sample FTE calculation for a clinic is shown in Exhibit 9.1; using a normal work week of 50 hours.

PRODUCTION ANALYSIS

The most common analysis performed on physicians is a comparison of physician production by gross charges to national survey data. Shown in Exhibit 9.2 is a worksheet comparing physician production to various MGMA levels of production based on gross charges.

Exhibit 9.2
Ob-Gyn Specialists
Physician Produciton Analysis
(3 FTE Physicians)

	GROSS CHARGES 1997
Total Practice	$2,745,893
Practice Average/FTE	$915,298
MGMA Median/FTE	632,055
75th Percentile	805,264
90th Percentile	$996,602

Exhibit 9.3
Carmody Multi-Specialty Clinic
Specialty Production Analysis

	1997 Gross Charges/FTE	MGMA Median	Variance $	Variance %
Family Practice	$ 430,256	$ 306,544	123,712	40.36%
Internal Medicine	$ 381,456	$ 310,127	71,329	23.00%
General Surgery	$ 710,264	$ 698,681	11,583	1.66%
Orthopedic Surgery	$ 950,456	$ 974,965	(24,509)	-2.51%

Sometimes it is more appropriate to report this information by specialty FTE or location instead of by individual physician. Another way of presenting productivity comparisons without singling out individual physicians is to prepare a comparison based on specialty averages. Exhibit 9.3 is a sample worksheet showing this comparative.

You will have to evaluate all of these issues as you perform the practice assessment and at the same time develop a clear understanding of your objectives related to the physician analysis. Most practice assessments will include individual physician comparisons, as well as possibly some consolidated or practice average comparisons. This information is also available from the American Medical Group Association, which also sponsors a compensation and productivity survey.

American Group Practice Association
1422 Duke Street
Alexandria, VA 22314
703-838-0033

American Medical Association (AMA)
515 North State Street
Chicago, IL 60610
800-621-8335

The Health Care Group
Meetinghouse Business Center
140 W. Germantown Pike, Suite 200
Plymouth Meeting, PA 19462
800-441-0737

Healthcare Financial Management Association (HFMA)
2 Westbrook Corporate Center, Suite 700
Westchester, IL 60154
800-252-4362

Medical Group Management Association (MGMA)
104 Inverness Terrace East
Englewood, CO 80112-5306
303-799-1111

Society of Medical-Dental Management Consultants
Kansas City, MO
1-800-826-2264

Contact at Joey Haven's office:
Erin Granberry
Horne CPA Group
101 Madison Plaza
Hattiesburg, MS 39402
601-268-1040, ext. 26
efgranbe@hcpag.com

Another physician analysis, which will help you address the mix of fee-for-service business with capitated or prepaid business, is the analysis of encounter detail by physician. This analysis examines the number of patient encounters a physician has over a period of time. These encounters are defined as face-to-face meetings involving one-on-one physician contact with the patient. This encounter information can be related to office visits and consultations, but there is also information available in relation to surgical procedures. This information can be found in the Medical Group Management Association data, as well as the AMA's *Physician Marketplace Statistics*. Exhibit 9.4 is a worksheet comparison of individual physician encounters compared to the MGMA median levels.

Exhibit 9.5 is a comparison of the physicians' patient visits per week compared with the AMA Physician Market Place Statistics.

Once you have obtained gross charges and encounter information by individual physician, you should also calculate an average charge per encounter. This can be extremely important information since it will allow you to understand the different aspects of physician production. Obviously, if the practice is in a predominately fee-for-service environment, you are interested in seeing if the physicians are maximizing a very high average charge per encounter. However, the opposite holds true when capita-

Exhibit 9.4
Carmody Multi-Specialty Clinic
Annual Encounter Analysis

Physician	Specialty	Annual Encounters/ FTE	MGMA Median	Variance #	Variance %
Dr. Carmody	Family Practice	6,480	4,390	2,090	47.61%
Dr. Jepson	Internal Medicine	4,150	3,275	875	26.72%
Dr. Anderson	General Surgery	2,043	1,543	500	32.40%
Dr. Harman	Orthopedic Surgery	2,850	3,111	(261)	-8.39%

Exhibit 9.5
Carmody Multi-Specialty Clinic
Weekly Patient Visit Analysis

Physician	Specialty	Weekly Patient Visits	AMA Median	Variance #	Variance %
Dr. Carmody	Family Practice	135	123	12	9.76%
Dr. Jepson	Internal Medicine	86	105	(19)	-17.66%
Dr. Anderson	General Surgery	42	78	(36)	-46.55%
Dr. Harman	Orthopedic Surgery	59	111	(52)	-46.51%

This information can also be presented graphically, as shown below. Our experience has been that physician groups relate better when information like this is presented in graph format.

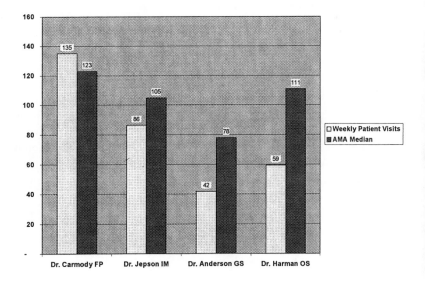

Exhibit 9.6
OB-GYN Specialists
Production Analysis

DOCTOR	ANNUAL ENCOUNTERS	GROSS CHARGES	CHARGES/ ENCOUNTER
1997			
Bolling	4,482	928,967	$ 207.27
Reid	5,050	1,032,926	$ 204.55
Mays	3,556	784,000	$ 220.49
Practice Average	4,362	915,298	$ 209.81
MGMA Median	2,988	632,055	$ 211.53
1996			
Bolling	3,855	817,491	$ 212.09
Reid	4,696	981,280	$ 208.95
Mays	3,200	717,360	$ 224.16
Practice Average	3,917	838,710	$ 214.12
MGMA Median	3,199	596,000	$ 186.31

tion represents a significant portion of practice revenues. In this situation, you need to assess the average charge per encounter to identify an overutilization of services, such as ancillary services. It is the "high cost" providers who cause the practice to lose profit in a capitated arrangement. Exhibit 9.6 shows the average charge generated by physicians over a two-year period as compared to the MGMA median levels.

PHYSICIAN COMPENSATION

Arguably the most controversial issue in any medical practice is physician compensation. Is the practice dividing its income in a fair way? If the practice has been acquired or managed by a third party, are the physicians being compensated at a reasonable and fair level? Due to the sensitivity of this issue, we suggest that you discuss with physician management how they want the assessment to evaluate compensation. Some groups will be very sensitive to analyzing physician compensation. If the practice assessment does analyze compensation by individual physician, then it is usually not necessary to make direct comparisons between or comments about physicians and their respective compensation.

The first step to analyzing physician compensation is to compare the doctor's or doctors' compensation to industry medians. Shown in Exhibit

Exhibit 9.7
Carmody Multi-Specialty Clinic
Compensation Analysis

Physician	Specialty	Annual Compensation	MGMA Median	Variance $	Variance %
Dr. Carmody	Family Practice	$155,432	$132,635	$22,797	17.19%
Dr. Jepson	Internal Medicine	140,123	139,305	818	0.59%
Dr. Anderson	General Surgery	275,001	216,679	58,322	26.92%
Dr. Harman	Orthopedic Surgery	289,456	271,469	17,987	6.63%

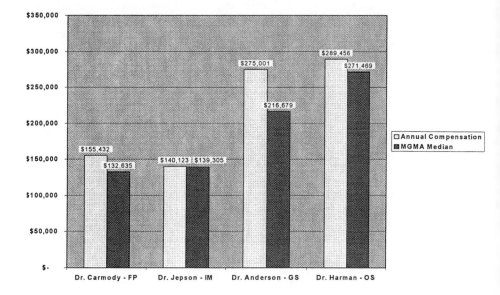

9.7 is a sample comparison of the median compensation compared to the MGMA levels for a multi-specialty practice.

As you can see, the physicians are individually compared to their respective medians. This worksheet can also be prepared based on an average compensation by specialty.

The next step in the analysis of physician compensation is to obtain a copy of the compensation formula and a copy of related computation worksheets for a recent period. This will allow you to provide a cursory review of the formula to understand how the medical practice provides incentives for its physicians and to look for any area of the formula that could be improved. Whenever you address compensation plans or income distri-

Exhibit 9.8
Physician Questionnaire
Compensation Plan

Physician's Name: _____ Date _____

1. How would you rate your medical practice's distribution plan?

   Generous   Reasonable   Marginal   Unfair   Disastrous

2. How would you rate your level of compensation?

   Extremely   Over com-   Basically   Under com-   Extremely
   over com-   pensated   fair   pensated   under compensated   pensated

3. Do you understand the present income distribution plan?   Yes   No

4. How would you rate the level of complexity of your existing income distribution plan?

   Extremely   Complex   Moderate   Simple   Very simple
   complex

5. Do you feel that your income distribution or compensation plan is adequately achieving its goals?

   _____
   _____
   _____

6. What do you like most about your existing plan?

   _____
   _____
   _____

7. What do you like least about your existing plan?

   _____
   _____
   _____

8. What would you recommend as a change to the existing income distribution or compensation plan?

   _____
   _____
   _____
   _____

bution plans with a medical practice, it is imperative that you have an understanding of the physician's perception concerning that plan. Therefore, as part of the practice assessment, it may be beneficial to gather some information on the physicians' current perception of the compensation plan.

This part of the analysis can aid physicians in a medical practice in addressing their sensitive issues and sometimes provides them with a building block for addressing changes that need to be made within the compensation formula. Exhibit 9.8 is a very simplified questionnaire which can be utilized during physician interviews or simply handed out to the physicians and returned confidentially to the evaluator to provide a better insight into how the income distribution plan is performing in its present environment. This questionnaire has been used successfully during many practice assessments, as well as in individual physician compensation analysis engagements. It may have to be modified for each separate practice assessment so it addresses unique compensatory issues and situations of the practice being evaluated.

After compiling information on the compensation plan and performing some of the compensation analyses shown previously, you may uncover additional issues which might need some further investigation. Sometimes this leads to a review of the current physician employment agreements. Although this would not necessarily be included in all practice assessments, it is sometimes necessary in order to follow up your findings. If you elect to review the physician employment agreements during the practice assessment, the review generally should be limited to standardization issues, benefit issues, and physician availability issues which can be reviewed and noted in a short period of time. This review should in no way equate to a complete analysis of the physician employment agreements. Again, it should be performed only to supplement some of the information and analyses that you have already gathered during this portion of the practice assessment.

PHYSICIAN COMPENSATION/PRODUCTION

The next step is to determine the ratio of compensation to production for the group. Obviously one of the most significant operational benchmarks is how much of the production actually results in owner or physician income. This ratio helps determine if the practice is efficient and provides a benchmark to measure compensation compared to a level of production.

As we stated earlier in the chapter, this requires a good understanding of the benchmark or survey data that you may use to compare to the medical practice. How is production defined? Does it include ancillary income? Does it only exclude the technical portion of ancillary? The medical practice's data will have to be compiled to match the benchmark data. Examples of these ratios are shown in Exhibit 9.9

As we have previously mentioned, physician reimbursement is rapidly changing and medical practices are having to struggle with changing payer mixes that are evolving from their indemnity or discounted fee-for-service business to a capitated patient base. As a result, physician production is being defined in a number of ways. Instead of looking at a physician's gross charges, which has been the predominant comparison previously, it is now more acceptable to consider comparisons like the encounters or patient visits that we discussed earlier in this chapter.

Also, the use of a relative value scale to compute RVUs (Relative Value Units) for each physician and comparing those to national norms is also a common benchmark. The logic behind this comparison is that it removes the incentives for high charge utilization and really begins to look at work units by physicians. By nature, the use of relative value scales are our best estimate of evaluating one service or procedures as compared to another. When these relative value units are utilized as a measure of production, people find a better comfort level that they are comparing apples to apples. Exhibit 9.10 shows a worksheet and graph showing individual physician relative value units compared to relative value units as shown in the American Group Medical Association Compensation and Productivity Survey.

This comparison can provide a unique way of looking at physician production and can be extremely beneficial for a medical practice which has a varying patient base. It is also very valuable when some physicians have a heavily capitated payer mix and other physicians in the same prac-

Exhibit 9.9
Compensation to Production Ratio Comparison

Physician	Specialty	Annual Compensation	Annual Production	Comp/ Prod Ratio	MGMA Norms
Dr. Carmody	Family Practice	$155,432	$430,256	0.361	0.444
Dr. Jepson	Internal Medicine	140,123	381,456	0.367	0.428
Dr. Anderson	General Surgery	275,001	710,264	0.387	0.326
Dr. Harman	Orthopedic Surgery	289,456	950,456	0.305	0.313

Exhibit 9.10
Physician Annual RVU Comparison

Physician	Specialty	Annual RVUs	AMGA Median	Variance #	Variance %
Dr. Carmody	Family Practice	7,325	5,375	1,950	36.28%
Dr. Jepson	Internal Medicine	6,143	5,043	1,100	21.81%
Dr. Anderson	General Surgery	8,732	8,819	(87)	-0.99%
Dr. Harman	Orthopedic Surgery	12,843	13,637	(794)	-5.82%

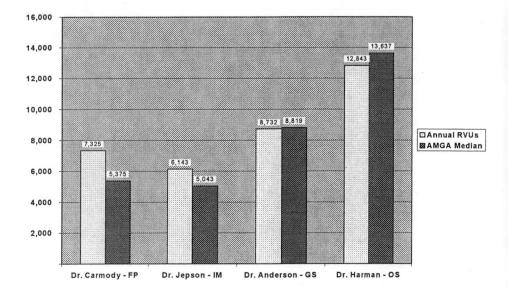

tice have a predominately fee-for-service mix. This comparison, again, allows an analysis of the work units versus the charges generated.

GOVERNANCE ISSUES

As part of the physician analysis, it might be beneficial to inquire into the organizational structure and governance of the medical practice. There is such rapid consolidation and changing practice environments that medical practices have historically not instituted a governance structure that allows for timely reaction to this type of environment. Historically, medical practices have not established an organizational chart with lines of authority and responsibility. As a result, the decision-making process has

Exhibit 9.11
Organizational/Governance Questionnaire

1. Do you have a formal organizational chart, if so, please attach. Yes_____ No_____

2. Does your practice have a board of directors or executive committee? Yes_____ No_____

3. If yes, what is their role?

_____
_____
_____

4. Does your board or executive committee have written empowerment? Yes_____ No_____

5. Please describe your organizational decision-making capabilities.

_____
_____
_____

6. How would you rate your practice's decision-making ability?

Extremely slow	Slow	Inconsistent	Responsive	Very proactive

7. How often are business goals discussed?

_____
_____
_____

8. How are business decisions made in the clinic?

_____

9. Do you feel emotions play a large role in decision-making? Yes_____ No_____; If yes, explain.

_____
_____
_____

been more or less a consensus by all the physician owners or by the solo physician himself. With this ever-changing environment, the resulting competitive pressures, new administrative roles, and rapid market consolidation, medical practices need to assess whether their organizational and governance structures are sound. As such, you should consider as part of your assessment interviewing practice physicians and management personnel as well as analyzing the medical practice's governance structure.

You would start this process by obtaining an organizational chart to see exactly how the practice has developed its organizational structure. If an organizational chart is unavailable, it is usually a good sign that this is an issue which has not been formally addressed by the medical practice. The questionnaire in Exhibit 9.11 can be a useful tool during an interview process or to have certain management or physicians to complete.

The objective of this questionnaire is to provide you, the evaluator, with an overview of what the medical practice believes to be its organizational structure and how well this structure is functioning. Does the practice have the physician leadership to make quick and hard decisions when necessary? Are they managing only for the short term or have they grasped an understanding of what it takes to be successful in the long term? Is its governance structure streamlined enough to allow quick and responsive decision-making to meet market demands?

Another possible governance issue is in regards to a group owned or managed by another entity. Is there sufficient input from the physicians within the medical practice into governance of the medical practice? How do physicians participate in the decisions concerning capital invested, staffing, protocol and guideline implementation, and managed care contracting? The most successful organizations will continue to have physician participation in the governance structure. If the organization does not have good communication and physician participation, it can lead to unresolvable differences later on. As part of the medical practice assessment, the evaluator should make some determination as to the organization's functionality between the medical practice and its management or ownership entity.

SUMMARY

As we stated in the beginning of this chapter, the physician component of any medical practice is really its most valuable asset. A properly executed practice assessment is going to include a thorough physician analysis to provide management with an understanding of the performance and compensation levels of the physicians. This analysis can be done in a number of ways as demonstrated in the worksheets included in this chapter. As additional benchmarks become available, the physician analysis component of medical practice assessments should be expanded accordingly to meet the user's needs.

CHAPTER TEN

Internal Controls Review

There are many medical practices that do not pay a whole lot of attention to internal controls. This is particularly true of smaller practices, even though we have found lackadaisical attitudes about internal controls even in larger practices. Sometimes it seems the larger the practice, the less attention that is paid to this issue. Smaller practices sometimes have trouble implementing internal controls simply because of their size—there is just not enough personnel, management expertise, or management time available to implement and monitor these measures.

Unfortunately, however, we have all heard of embezzlement situations in medical offices; many of these could have been avoided if proper internal controls had been implemented and monitored on an ongoing basis. Therefore, as a measure of checks and balances, the practice assessment should at least take a look at the existing internal control structures within the practice. This is particularly true if the practice has not had a review of its internal controls for a lengthy period of time. The following is a checklist of internal controls that your assessment should review and address. Issues found as well as related recommendations should be discussed in your assessment report to the practice's management.

1. Inquire when was the last time the practice performed a review of its internal controls.

The answer to this question should give you insight on how in-depth your review should be of the practice's internal controls. Obviously, the longer the time period, the more detailed your review should be. However, even if the review was performed recently, you should still perform this review.

2. Assess whether or not job duties are adequately divided among employees.

SEPARATION OF DUTIES

There are certain functions and job duties within a medical office that should be divided among employees. For example, one person should never be allowed to both open the mail (i.e., physically touch money) and post these same payments into the computer. Dividing these two duties prevents an employee from embezzling money from the practice and disguising the embezzlement by manipulating the patient's accounts in the computer, usually by writing off the account balances as either contractual adjustments or bad debts.

The following is a typical example: Kim Moore is responsible for opening the mail and posting payments. To conceal her planned embezzlement, Kim writes off an account as a bad debt after the patient's account statement has been mailed. She knows this patient will pay within 30 days, so she sits and waits for the check to come in the mail so she can intercept it and cash it or even deposit it into her personal account.

Obviously in this situation and others that are similar to it, the best internal control is to have one person open the mail, have another person prepare the deposit slips, and have a third person post the payments to the patients' individual accounts in the computer. If these job duties are not adequately segregated, the scope of the assessment may need to be increased to allow you to perform a detailed review of write-offs, adjustments, and trace a sample of transactions through the system.

3. Find out if selected employees are bonded.

Whether or not job duties are adequately segregated, every medical practice should have certain employees bonded. This is a form of insurance that will reimburse the practice for an embezzlement by office personnel; it is sometimes referred to as fidelity bond insurance. It is recommended that any person with access to money should be bonded; this includes front desk personnel, administrative personnel, and selected billing and collection personnel.

MANAGING WRITE-OFFS

4. Must any write-off be approved before the write-off can be posted to the computer?

Another basic internal control is to make sure than any patient receivable can never be written off as a bad debt without the prior (preferably written) consent of the practice's physician. Unapproved write-offs signal a red flag that must be investigated. Approved write-offs can be documented directly in a detailed aging of the accounts receivable each month. The doctor or practice administrator can initial each patient's account to document approval for the write-off to take place. This control should not discriminate: even though this sounds cumbersome for large practices, approval and documentation of write-offs must take place.

5. Determine if the practice performs a periodic reconciliation of patient office visits to source documents.

On a periodic basis, someone should reconcile patient names listed on the sign-in sheet and the appointment schedule to what was posted to the computer for that particular day. If employees know this type of reconciliation is taking place, hopefully it will prevent the situation where a front desk person collects (i.e., embezzles) money from a patient and does not post the related charge and payment to the computer system.

DAILY BALANCING

6. Does the practice reconcile daily deposits to the Daily Report of Payments produced by the practice's computer system?

Practices should deposit monies daily and reconcile the deposit(s) to the computer-generated report of daily payments. This is easier to perform by smaller practices than larger ones simply due to the number of transactions to reconcile. For larger practices, this reconciliation should take place at least two to three times a month.

Embezzlement can occur in a situation where bank deposits are never reconciled with what gets entered into the computer system. The more confusion that abounds, the better the chance for an embezzlement because the embezzlement is easier to hide. This is particularly true of practices with multiple offices since many times all of the offices cannot make a deposit of the funds they received at their individual office location.

7. Does any person ever check desk drawers for money that has not been deposited?

How many times have we all heard of the story where the practice administrator opens an employee's desk drawer only to find thousands of dollars of undeposited checks. It is easy to embezzle if an employee has ample time to keep their hands on the money. This is especially true for employees who handle money and post these payments to patient accounts in the computer. Another basic internal control is to check desk drawers on a weekly basis, obviously when employees are not around to see it. Practices that constantly have "money lying around the office" are excellent candidates for embezzlement.

8. Are employee vacations mandatory?

Many embezzlements can be detected when the employee is not around to cover them up. How many times have we caught an embezzlement after an employee leaves employment or has taken off for a vacation. Taking time off for vacation should be mandatory; make sure that the time taken is at least one week minimum in duration. Employees who can take vacation leave "a day here and a day there" can still cover up their embezzlement. It is usually a red flag whenever an employee refuses to take a vacation.

CHARGE TICKETS

9. Make sure all charge tickets are prenumbered and accounted for.

Accounting for charge tickets is done by checking the numerical sequence of the control numbers on each charge ticket and then tracing them back to the patient sign-in sheet or the daily appointment record. The office copy of each charge ticket should be kept in a separate file in numerical order. The file should be reviewed periodically by searching for a gap in the numerical sequence of the charge tickets. A gap may indicate that a charge ticket was used in an embezzlement scheme.

The most common form of embezzlement here is when the patient makes a payment in the office for his or her visit but the visit charge is not posted into the computer. As such, the patient's account does not reflect a charge or a payment. The employee pockets the payment and uses a charge ticket to give to the patient as a receipt (the employee hand writes the information on the "stolen" charge ticket).

10. Does the practice mail out patient account statements each and every month?

In situations where an employee takes payment and either does not post the related charge to the computer or eliminates the related posted charge entirely, embezzlement can be discovered when patients call the office inquiring why they have never received a billing statement from the office. Many patients know they might have to pay a deductible or copayment and will call the office asking why they have not received a statement. The patient probably did not receive a statement because the employee embezzled the insurance check and wrote off the entire balance to cover it up.

Embezzlement is also covered up by not sending an account statement to a particular patient because that patient could see on the statement that his or her charge and payment were not included. This applies to patients who have a prior receivables balance.

11. Does the practice monitor and review contractual adjustments on an ongoing basis?

During the financial analysis, a worksheet is prepared listing practice charges, collections, and contractual adjustments. Depending on the practice's payer mix, a high volume of contractual adjustments could indicate a possible embezzlement situation. The following is the most common example of employee embezzlement using contractual adjustments as the mechanism to conceal it:

An insurance claim for $1,000 is prepared and mailed to an insurance plan for services rendered by the practice. The patient's insurance coverage will pay 80 percent of the charge and as such, it subsequently sends a check in the amount of $800 to the practice. Shantel Henry, an employee in the practice, takes the $800 check, deposits it into her own personal bank account, and then goes to the practice's computer to write off the entire $1,000 patient account balance as a contractual adjustment.

Obviously the best way to prevent embezzlement from occurring in this situation is to make sure the person who handles money is not responsible for posting it into the computer. Another prevention technique is to see if the practice's computer can be programmed to prevent a patient's entire balance from being written off without authorization.

At a minimum, however, to prevent or detect embezzlement using contractual adjustments, the amount of these adjustments written off each month and on a year-to-date basis should be monitored. Compare the adjustments written off to the payer mix. Does it seem reasonable in light of the number of fixed-fee payers the practice does business with? Also keep in mind not all write offs are contractual write offs (Refer back to Chapter 1).

One other internal control measure is to print out and review patients' account ledgers on a periodic basis. The objective is to look for and investigate any balance that has been written off in its *entirety* without prior approval.

CHECK SIGNING

> 12. During the accounts payable administration process, find out if the vendor invoice is attached to the related disbursement for review as vendor checks are signed.

Embezzlement is not limited to accounts receivable areas; it can also occur during the accounts payable process as well. The objective of this internal control prevents sending payment to fake or nonexistent vendors. The check is really being sent to a practice employee.

> 13. Who has check signing authority in the practice?

Physicians should never refuse their responsibility for signing checks. This only invites the temptation to embezzle. In other words, make sure the office administrator or some other employee is not the only person who prepares the checks, signs them, and mails them.

> 14. Does anyone review vendor check endorsements on a periodic basis?

On a periodic basis, someone should review canceled checks to make sure the endorsements on the back of the canceled checks match the name of the persons or vendors to whom the checks were written. Third-party endorsements should be looked for specifically. Even if the practice's bank does not provide canceled checks, they should be obtained on a periodic basis and reviewed.

CHAPTER ELEVEN

Putting It All Together: Report Writing

After conducting the assessment, the next step is to present your findings to the person or persons who requested the assessment and/or to the management of the medical practice. On the following pages are three sample reports for you to review. By reviewing these reports, you should get a "flavor" of how a medical practice assessment should be performed, what you should be looking for during the assessment, and how to present your findings in a final report.

Report formats can take many forms; your goal should be to communicate as accurately as possible your findings during the assessment and your related recommendations. The presentation of recommendations is a vital component of the assessment process. You cannot just say, "These are your problems." This is like an auto mechanic saying to you what is wrong with your car but not suggesting how to fix it! For every problem found there should always be a recommendation.

Finally, attempt to quantify your recommendations in the form of a revenue impact. If your recommendation adds (or sometimes decreases) the practice's revenue, state it in your report. We believe it is very important that the individual or individuals relying on the report know firsthand how the recommendations might impact the bottom line.

PRACTICE REVIEW REPORT

The following areas of Independent Primary Care Associates of Mason were evaluated by our Firm. Many of our conclusions, recommendations, and questions are outlined within each section below. This report is based upon a review of internal practice documents, including insurance claim forms, explanation of benefits, and computer reports. It is also based upon our on-site visit to the practice and interviews with Dr. Reed and practice personnel. This report focuses on the financial health of the practice per the engagement agreement and all of the following findings are based upon this agreement.

Data and information used as a basis for our analysis, findings, and recommendations included in this report are based on information provided in whole or in part by representatives of the practice. We have not audited or attempted to confirm this information for accuracy or completeness.

Our analysis is also contingent on the following assumptions and limiting conditions:

1. We have no financial interest in Independent Primary Care Associates of Mason and the fee for this engagement is not contingent on the findings reported herein.

2. This engagement cannot be relied upon to disclose fraud or potential fraud in the medical practice.

3. This report is intended for use only by the party to whom it is provided and only for the purpose described. Mere possession of this report does not convey a right of reliance, nor may any reliance be placed on it by any party for any other purpose than that for which it was prepared.

Financial Analysis

FINDING: Exhibit 11.1 shows the 1996 Independent Primary Care Associates of Mason practice management financial statistics:

DISCUSSION: The gross collection ratio for the practice averaged just above 100 percent in the period we examined (January 1, 1996 through September 30, 1996). Obviously this gross collection rate is excellent. However, further analysis showed the high ratio of collection to production is due to the profitability generated by the monthly capitation payments received from NYLCare. These payments averaged $6,140 per month during the period we examined or 12.5 percent of production. We will discuss the capitation contract more extensively later in this report.

Exhibit 11.1
Practice Management Financial Statistics

Month	Production	Collections	Gross Collection %	Adjustments	Adj%	Net Collection %
January-96	144,048	79,799	55%	32,753	23%	72%
February-96	97,170	61,652	63%	30,452	31%	92%
March-96	117,473	72,436	62%	32,707	28%	85%
April-96	171,244	82,470	48%	29,707	17%	58%
May-96	187,365	88,700	47%	72,797	39%	77%
June-96	163,447	113,729	70%	30,927	19%	86%
July-96	183,481	117,648	64%	44,988	25%	85%
August-96	209,899	94,886	45%	59,471	28%	63%
September-96	215,272	77,888	36%	38,240	18%	44%
October-96	229,086	186,056	81%	129,262	56%	186%
Total	**1,718,485**	**975,264**		**501,304**		
'96Practice Avg.	171,848	97,526	57%	50,130	28%	85%
'95Practice Avg.	75,012	50,523	67%	22,981	31%	97%
'96 Specialty Avg. (3 FTE's)	100,998	79,914	79%	17,084	17%	95%

The net collection percentage for the practice also looks very good. The net collection percentage is the percentage of the practice's "collectible dollar" that has been collected. This percentage takes into account contractual adjustments and the write-offs. Typically a primary care practice strives to keep its net collection percentage above a 95 percent benchmark. In other words, any primary care practice should be able to collect 95 percent of its collectible monies.

RECOMMENDATION: None. However, please refer to related financial findings and recommendations throughout the various sections of this report.

FINDING: Practice production and related visits per provider are lagging.

DISCUSSION: From January, 1996 through September, 1996 the practice averaged approximately 30 new patients per week and approximately 122 established patient office visits per week. This translates to approximately 5 to 6 new patient visits per day and between 20 and 24 established patient visits per day which means the practice is only seeing 25 to 30 patients per day in the office. Since Dr. Reed was part-time at the West Brenham Family Clinic until September, the Flatonia clinic had approximately 2.6 FTE providers from January to September and thereafter has had 3 FTE providers. This includes the full-time Physician Assistant. Using the 2.6 FTE figure as a basis for analysis and assuming the practice saw 30 patients per day in a particular month, this means each doctor treated an average of only 11.54 patients per day. This obviously is way below standard for a busy primary care practice.

In our experience, a family practice physician will see between 25 to 40 patients *each* on an average day. By this measure, if the clinic were in line with other family practice clinics with three providers, it would see between 150 and 200 patients per week.

RECOMMENDATION: First, analyze provider needs for this service area. In other words, is the practice overstaffed with direct healthcare providers? It would be a strategic decision by the Southwest Regional System to employ doctors with the long-term objective of building production. There is obviously a related cost investment to implement this kind of a strategy. However, if the service area will not support this number of providers, the practice must decide whether or not continued employment is warranted. Please refer to additional commentary about this issue in the section entitled "Overhead Analysis."

If the service area can support this number of providers, we suggest the clinic develop and implement a comprehensive marketing plan and related budget. To increase production for a primary care practice, the practice must commit to an ongoing marketing program. The basic elements of a good marketing plan are to (a) Decide on the practice's target audience, (b) Decide which are the best methods to reach this audience, (c) Once methods are chosen, create a cost budget, (d) Implement chosen methods, and (e) Track the success of chosen methods. Keep in mind the success of any marketing program for a primary care practice is tied directly to its longevity. You cannot create a short-term marketing program and expect it to succeed for a primary care practice. Generally it takes a full twelve-month, annual commitment.

For family practitioners, we find the best marketing strategies are:

- Direct mail

- Advertising

- Marketing directly to employees of the area's largest employers

- Public speaking by the practice providers

- Service discounts to employees in the area for particular services (e.g., flu shots)

- After-hours appointment availability (These should be marketed heavily)

The practice should keep its eye on the growth of Medical Savings Accounts in the service area during the next year. This program becomes effective January 1, 1997. The program allows employers to adopt "high deductible" policies. If there is significant growth of these policies, employees will have greater flexibility since they will have a much higher deductible. The feeling is that many primary care doctors can increase production if the practice is willing to provide fee discounts to people enrolled in Medical Savings Accounts.

We also recommend the clinic begin marketing through managed care plans. The goal here is patient access. You want these employees to select one of the physician providers as their primary care doctor. The best way to access a patient is through visibility. Therefore, obtain a list of the major employers in each managed care plan in the service area, especially for the plans the practice currently participates in. Contact the person in charge of human resources at each employer and state that the doctors in the clinic are participating providers in that company's managed care health plan (This assumes the practice is credentialed with all of the plans to begin with; If not, consider doing so to increase production). The objective is then to find ways that will place the names of the physicians and the clinic in front of the employees. Suggestions include submitting articles for the company newsletter, presenting a lunch talk on a health related subject, or giving flu shots at a discounted rate for the company's employees.

As stated above, the practice needs to track where new patients are coming from in order to know which marketing strategies work and which ones do not. Right now the practice has the ability to document new patient information on the new patient information sheet; However, sometimes this section of the form is not completed. But even more important, where new patients are coming from is not being compiled anywhere. This information is not being entered into the computer nor tracked manually. Most practice management software systems have a built-in feature to track referral sources by entering the referral information into the system. We therefore recommend the clinic begin using this feature as a tool for identifying what patient sources the practice can take better advantage of. This report should be printed and analyzed each month.

REVENUE IMPACT: Assuming each *doctor*'s production can be raised to an average of 20 patients each per day, and assuming an average visit charge of only $50, practice production would increase by approximately

$192,000, taking into account physician time off. Assuming a gross collection percentage of 75 percent on these gross charges, the practice could expect an approximate increase in collections of $144,000.

FINDING: Exhibit 11.2 shows how the practice reported its payer mix:

DISCUSSION: The largest payer group for the practice is Medicare, comprising 33 percent of the patient load. The practice has one capitation contract, NYLCare, which represents 11 percent of its patients. An analysis of the capitation contract experience indicates that charges for capitated services were $38,616. The practice received $65,551 in capitation payments and copays.

RECOMMENDATION: Since it appears the practice is generating profit on its capitated contract, consider direct marketing activity toward the employees of the employers that contract with this plan. The objective would be to increase practice selection during the next open enrollment period and to obtain new patients as they are hired by these employers before the open enrollment period.

Also, it seems the practice should be garnering more of the commercial insurance population. Even though managed care is growing, there is still a significant commercial insurance base. Keep this in mind when developing the marketing strategy discussed above.

Overhead Analysis

For the purpose of this overhead analysis, we have combined the operations of the Independent Primary Care Associates of Mason and the West Brenham Family Clinic since Dr. Reed practiced in both offices during the time periods represented by the financial information provided to us.

Exhibit 11.2
Payer Mix

Capitation	11%
Commercial & Self Pay	26%
PPO	20%
Worker's Compensation	10%
Medicare	33%

Total overhead for the practice was 56 percent of collections previous to the merger and was 115 percent of collections for the period September 1, 1995 to August 31, 1996 excluding depreciation.

The pre-merger overhead is based upon financial information provided by Dr. Reed for the purpose of valuing his medical practice. The post-merger overhead is based upon Southwest Regional Physician Network financial statements for Independent Primary Care Associates of Mason and West Brenham Family Clinic for the period beginning September 1, 1995 and ending August 31, 1996. Pre-merger net collections were $696,960 and post-merger revenues were $644,284.

The primary increases in expenses were in the areas of salaries (excluding Dr. Reed), and building lease. The increase in building lease is due to the fact that Dr. Reed owns the building where the West Brenham Family Clinic is located. Lease payments are now being made to Dr. Reed whereas there were none before practice acquisition. The increase in salaries, as a percent of collections, is attributed to the addition of staff and an increase in Dr. Reed's salary.

Refer to related findings below in this Section.

FINDING: The office is overstaffed with clinical personnel.

DISCUSSION: The clinic currently has four full-time nurses/medical assistants. Two medical assistants are also radiology technicians but a majority of their duties are nursing oriented. *Per the service frequency report, there were only 477 x-rays taken for the first nine months of the year. This level of activity obviously does not support two technicians. Neither does the level of office visit activity per provider justify four clinical personnel in the office.*

From our on-site visit and interviews it was apparent that the clinical staff is usually very busy. However, a great deal of time is spent on the telephone making and taking phone calls. For example, Dr. Reed will routinely request the nursing staff to call patients a day or two after their office visit to check on them. Also, Dr. Reed requires that all of his prescriptions be called in to the pharmacy. While these may be nice gestures for patients, they are not an efficient use of nurse time. Messages are usually taken for incoming calls for refills and nurse calls but the front desk does not always get enough information for the nurse to be prepared when returning the call. This results in wasted time and extra phone calls.

For busy medical practices, the telephone can become a direct hindrance to the efficiency of daily office operations. One of the biggest problems a medical practice encounters, especially offices with many physicians, is managing the sheer volume of phone calls from its patients. If employees at the front desk and other staff members must spend a majority of their time fielding telephone calls, they will not be able to devote enough attention to their normal job duties and compliance with the office's internal operating systems might be impaired. For example, it is difficult for a receptionist to field telephone calls and check out patients at the front desk at the same time. In this situation, front-desk collections and the receptionist's ability to record office visit charges and payments can and usually are hindered.

Practice Point: If there are problems checking patients in and checking patients out, look to the telephones for the problem.

Practice Point: If the nurses do not have time for patient care and other office duties, look to excessive phone calls from patients about clinical matters for the problem.

Excessive telephone calls to a medical practice come from many sources. The most obvious origin cannot be minimized: patients' calls to make appointments. Other types of phone calls, however, can and should be cut short or bunched together. For example, to minimize the distraction that results from patients calling for lab test results and to improve efficiency, the office manager should designate a time during the day or week when patients can call specifically for lab results. Then the practice can assign one person to field these calls, thus freeing time for all other personnel to perform other office duties. This person usually is designated the phone nurse for the day. An alternative solution is for the office to adopt the policy of informing patients of their lab test results in writing only.

Calls from patients who want to discuss their medical problems over the phone, without making an appointment, can also waste office time. If patients continue to call the office seeking free advice regarding their medical problems, insist that they make an appointment. An office visit allows the physician an opportunity (a) to properly diagnose and treat the problem, (b) to avoid losing revenue by giving free advice over the telephone, and (c) to avoid malpractice claims should advice be given over the telephone that has negative consequences. If the physician gives advice over the telephone, make sure it is documented in the patient's medical chart.

Another way to cut down on unnecessary telephone calls is to begin charging for them. Although a practice cannot charge for this service for certain insurance plans (such as Medicare and Medicaid), it can for others. Even if an insurance plan does not pay for the call, the patient will more likely be the one responsible for payment because the telephone charge is a "noncovered benefit." When patients have to pay for these services out of their own pockets, more than likely they will quit making unnecessary calls, or at least reduce the number of calls to the office.

Practice Point: No matter what telephone policy a practice adopts, the practice should always inform its patients before implementation. Not to do so risks a backlash from patients when they are billed for services not previously explained. This is especially true if the practice charges for telephone calls.

RECOMMENDATION: Eliminate one technician. Provider clinical styles and the lack of control over patient telephone calls are inflating personnel costs. A technician can be rehired when practice production justifies it.

Develop and institute a practice telephone call policy to help manage the phone situation. The following is an example:

When a physician orders tests for a patient, the patient is routinely asked to return to the office for the test results and possible treatment orders. Only under special circumstances will a physician discuss test results over the telephone. If you insist that the physician discuss the results with you by telephone before your office appointment and the physician has not asked for the information to be handled by phone, you will be charged for the telephone conference. If you would like to discuss your lab tests with other office clinical personnel, you are instructed to call the office between the hours of _____ and _____.

It is the policy of this office for the physician to communicate with the patient directly regarding the patient's medical status. Should you have a clinical problem requiring a physician's attention, call the office to make an appointment. Please refrain from calling the office strictly for advice except for cases of medical emergency. If the patient is not capable of discussing his or her medical course of treatment with the physician, the family will need to designate one person to act on the patient's behalf.

Unless otherwise designated, the following policies will apply:

- *If the patient is married, the physician will communicate with the spouse, and the spouse will then be responsible for relaying the information to other family members.*

- *If the patient is not married but has adult children, the physician will discuss the patient's condition with one designated child.*

- *If the patient is not married and has no children, the physician will discuss the patient's status with his or her parents.*

- *If the patient is a minor, the physician will communicate with the parents or court-appointed guardian. Any other person will need to contact the parents or guardian for an update.*

If you are a personal injury patient and have an attorney, the physician will not discuss your case with the attorney by telephone or by office conference. Any communication with your attorney will need to be in writing, and you will be charged for the time.

[Insert here the office's policy on charging for telephone calls.]

REVENUE IMPACT: Elimination of the technician would save the practice approximately $24,840.

FINDING: There may not be an immediate need for a Physician's Assistant in the practice.

DISCUSSION: As stated, using the 2.6 FTE figure as a basis for analysis and assuming the practice saw 30 patients per day in a particular month, this means each doctor treated an average of only 11.54 patients per day. This obviously is way below standard for a busy primary care practice. We therefore question the need for the Physician Assistant position. The objective is to increase the production of both physicians to acceptable levels.

RECOMMENDATION: Analyze not only practice need, but system need for the Physician Assistant. Transfer her to another Southwest Regional Physician Network practice or at least have her float as a provider among all of the practices. This way the costs can be shared among practices and not isolated in the Flatonia practice.

REVENUE IMPACT: Elimination of the position will save the practice approximately $71,280.

FINDING: The clinic has a problem controlling staff overtime.

DISCUSSION: During our visit, a common complaint among staff was that they had no breaks and thus were having to expend overtime hours to take care of their duties. The phone issue was one particular problem and has been addressed by us above. We were not able to quantify overtime pay during our engagement.

RECOMMENDATION: Address this issue immediately since we were not able to address it completely during our engagement. Implementing our suggested telephone policy should eliminate some of the overtime.

Accounts Receivable Analysis

FINDING: Exhibit 11.3 shows the monthly aged accounts receivable balances for the clinic.

DISCUSSION: In general the accounts receivable for the practice look good. The amount of receivables over 90 days old is reasonable. However, the percentage of total receivables is high. The following is the benchmark: No more than 15 to 18 percent of the accounts receivable should be 90 days old and older.

RECOMMENDATION: Continue to monitor accounts receivable on an ongoing basis to ensure above benchmark is being obtained.

Exhibit 11.3
Monthlyl Aged Accounts Receivable Balance

Month	Total A/R	Current	%	31-60	%	61-90	%	91+	%
Feb-96	49,666	15,397	31%	1,437	3%	12,016	24%	7,906	16%
Mar-96	53,731	18,757	35%	13,503	25%	7,316	14%	14,155	26%
Apr-96	60,339	31,993	53%	10,045	17%	5,422	9%	12,878	21%
May-96	54,959	19,028	35%	16,721	30%	5,136	9%	14,074	26%
Jun-96	46,927	7,658	16%	12,356	26%	10,114	22%	16,799	36%
Jul-96	info	not		available					
Aug-96	47,018	23,386	50%	5,356	11%	3,310	7%	14,966	32%
Sep-96	48,931	28,526	58%	4,218	9%	2,628	5%	13,558	28%
Oct-96	38,975	27,094	70%	1,550	4%	1,019	3%	9,312	24%

FINDING: The clinic policy is to only make refunds when requested by the patient.

DISCUSSION: When insurance benefits cannot be confirmed, it is the policy of the clinic to collect the entire amount due from the patient at the time of service and file a claim with the insurance company on behalf of the patient. When payment is received from the insurance company for services that the patient has already paid for, the accounts receivable will indicate a credit balance. An analysis of the aged accounts receivable dated September 30, 1996 indicated that credit balances for the practice were $7,267. This is a significantly high amount since it represents nearly 20 percent of the total accounts receivable. In other words, if these balances had been refunded to patients, the total accounts receivable would be approximately 20 percent greater and more accurately reflect the amount to be collected.

RECOMMENDATION: Review all current account credit balances and determine appropriate disposition. Develop and implement a refund policy related to credit balances. Review the monthly aging of the accounts receivable for credit balance accounts and dispose according to practice policy.

FINDING: An analysis of the front desk collections during the month of September indicates that 87 percent of the patients are making a payment at the time of service.

DISCUSSION: This indicates that the office staff does a reasonably good job of collecting money from patients at the time of service. In most cases evaluated, if the patient did not make a payment, it was because they had a credit balance or there was no charge for the visit. Managing front desk collections is a good pro-active way to manage the accounts receivable.

Although our review indicated that front desk collections were in good shape, most of the patient balances in the 90+ category represent balances under $200. Balances less than $200 on the accounts receivable are often an indication the front desk collections person did not do a good job of collecting payments at the time of service. This seems to conflict with our finding. Since many of these balances are in the 90 days + category, it is possible these small balances represent problems in the past that have been corrected.

To clean up these accounts, the practice should be able to collect patient balances under $200 by simply contacting the patient. Some patients tend to disregard monthly statements. Therefore, they should be contacted by phone to increase the chances they will mail in a payment with the next statement.

RECOMMENDATION: Monitor front desk collection activity on an on-going basis. In addition, the practice should develop and implement the following collection policy for patient-pay accounts.

- Each day identify those scheduled patients who have a balance forward in their account; Determine if it is a patient-pay balance; If so, make sure front desk personnel ask these patients how they would like to take care of their overdue balance. At a minimum, some monies should be collected even if it is a partial payment.

- Each month print an aging of the accounts receivable; A phone call should be placed to each patient-pay balance exceeding $250 (Note: The practice should always emphasize front desk collections and the collection of unpaid insurance balances first). This telephone call must be documented, preferably in the computer.

Analysis of Billing and Collection Operations

FINDING: There are significant problems with the current computer system, resulting in unnecessary inefficiencies.

DISCUSSION: While on-site conducting this study the computer was unavailable for posting the entire day due to technical problems. We were informed by the office staff this is not an uncommon occurrence. This is causing unnecessary delays and inefficiencies. For example, it is causing employees to delay their work and catch up on it later.

RECOMMENDATION: Expedite the installation of the Southwest Regional Physician Network's standard practice management system, MOMS.

FINDING: Charges are sometimes not captured.

DISCUSSION: Our review of the daily work indicates that charges for some patients are not being captured. In one case, a patient returned the morning after an office visit for lab tests and the staff did not complete a superbill because they thought he had already been charged at the time of the visit.

RECOMMENDATION: Each patient encounter should be tracked on a superbill and each day the superbills should be checked against the sign-in log and the Procedure Day Sheet report to ensure no charges were missed. Also, prenumber the charge tickets in the future as another way to identify missing superbills and charges. Have the office staff prepare superbills for every patient who signs in and check daily for missing superbills and charges.

FINDING: Cash is not handled properly in the clinic.

DISCUSSION: The clinic currently has one cash drawer available to all employees. Also, cash is typically left on-site overnight in an unlocked drawer. This uncontrolled system leaves potential for theft. Cash should be accounted for at the beginning and end of the day and left in the custody of a responsible employee.

RECOMMENDATION: During the day keep cash in a locked drawer and allow only one person, the cashier, to have access to the cash. If scheduling requires, have a separate cash drawer and another designated employee responsible for the cash. Account for the cash at the beginning and end of the day, requiring employees to sign the cash in and out. At the end of the day, after the cash has been accounted for, place the cash in a secure place such as a safe.

FINDING: Payments are not handled properly in the office.

DISCUSSION: Currently Kala Ratliff is opening the mail, posting checks, and sometimes preparing deposit slips. Having a single person perform all three tasks allows the opportunity to embezzle or not post and deposit checks in a timely manner.

RECOMMENDATION: Opening the mail should be the responsibility of the receptionist. The receptionist can also prepare the deposit while giving the EOBs (explanation of benefits) to the cashier for posting in the system. Checks received from patients through the mail can be posted from the deposit slip.

On a periodic basis, compare the deposit slip to the Payment Day Sheet printed from the computer. This procedure can detect embezzlement.

FINDING: The practice posts its contractual adjustments to a single adjustment code.

DISCUSSION: To enable the practice to periodically analyze payers' contractual adjustments for reasonableness, we recommend posting adjustments to a separate code for each payer. The practice can see on computer practice analysis reports how high adjustments are for each payer and then assess their reasonableness. In addition to this being a good tool for monitoring managed care contracts, it also is a way of monitoring whether or not employees are adjusting off charges to conceal embezzlement. If proper controls are not in place, it is possible for an employee to adjust off the charges for a claim as contractual adjustments and deposit a payment into their personal checking account. Posting adjustments by payer will make such inappropriate adjustments noticeable. Segregating duties as mentioned above is also a preventative measure.

RECOMMENDATION: Set up an adjustment code for each contracted managed care payer and begin posting payments using these adjustment codes. Each month compare the adjustments to the payer mix to determine if contractual adjustments are reasonable. If adjustments for a specific payer increase significantly, investigate immediately. Review the EOBs from that payer to rule out inappropriate adjustments by employees.

FINDING: The practice does not currently have an operational policy and procedure manual.

DISCUSSION: The purpose of an operational policy and procedures manual is to standardize and communicate the office policies, jobs, and responsibilities. Once a sound policy and procedures manual is in place, employees will be aware of their job responsibilities and the methods to accomplish them. At that point, any future practice management problem can be traced to a specific personnel issue, and not necessarily to a systems issue.

An operational practice policy and procedure manual should at a minimum address the following areas:

- Handling telephone calls
- Appointment scheduling
- Check-in procedures
- Patient reception

- Flowchart of a patient visit
- Appointment delays
- Prescription policy
- Check-out procedures
- Payment postings
- Receivables management
- Closing out the day
- Closing out the month

RECOMMENDATION: Develop and implement a comprehensive policy and procedure manual for the clinic. Have all employees read and acknowledge receipt of the manual. Our firm is able to assist you in developing this manual.

Insurance Claims Filing

FINDING: The majority of insurance claims in the practice are filed on paper.

DISCUSSION: Typically, a practice can save time and improve the speed of cash flow by using a clearinghouse to file all claims electronically. Additionally, clearing houses provide "edit checks" as part of their services. An "edit check" will electronically verify all required fields of the claim are completed and check for invalid information in certain fields. If the clearing house finds any potential errors, the claim will be sent back to the practice to edit before it is actually filed. Thereby, recognizing the error and correcting it without waiting 30 days to receive a denial EOB in the mail, which will need to be appealed.

RECOMMENDATION: Check with the insurance companies with whom the practice files its insurance claims to see if they accept electronic claim submissions and if so, which clearinghouse they utilize. If enough payers do accept claims electronically, it may be cost and time effective to begin filing most claims electronically.

At a minimum, file all Medicare and Medicaid claims electronically.

FINDING: Based on a sample of filed insurance claim forms, it took the practice an average of 2.25 days from service date to complete and remit an insurance claim.

DISCUSSION: For primary care practices with a heavy concentration of office visits, it should take no more than two to three days on average to remit a claim form from the date of service. The practice is meeting this benchmark and no further discussion is required.

RECOMMENDATION: None.

Explanation of Benefits Review

FINDING: The average EOB turnaround for the clinic is 47.5 days after the date of service.

DISCUSSION: The EOB payment turnaround measures the length of time between the date of service and the actual insurance payment. The benchmark for any practice is to get paid by insurance companies on average 30 and 45 days from the date of service.

RECOMMENDATION: Filing as many claims as possible electronically will speed up insurance collections. Also, make sure all claims are completed correctly before they are remitted (See sample of denials in the next Finding).

Finally, the practice must implement and adhere to a strict insurance receivable follow-up process. We recommend the following:

1. Each month, identify all unpaid claims that are 28 days old from the date of service.

2. Contact each payer by telephone and make sure the telephone discussion is documented. Document the following in the computer: (a) Name of person spoken with, (b) Was claim received? (c) Was claim approved for payment? (d) If no, why was claim denied? and (e) If yes, when can payment be expected?

3. If claim denied, correct and refile.

FINDING: A review of a sample of EOBs identified the following error messages:

- Coverage not in effect at the time the service was provided.

- Duplicate claim/service.

- Physician/supplier signature missing or not in correct block on claim.

- Services provided outside your office require facility name and address or 9-digit facility provider number.

- Denied. Incomplete claim beyond 90 day deadline.

- Your claim contains incomplete and/or invalid information, and no appeal rights are afforded because the claim is unprocessable.

DISCUSSION: This is further evidence that claims are being sent out with improper or incomplete information. This coupled with the fact that the majority of claims for the clinic are filed on paper slows down the payment cycle. Other messages indicate that the staff may not be getting current insurance information from the patients.

RECOMMENDATION: Carefully examine all claims before they are sent out to minimize errors and the subsequent denials. In addition, EOBs should be kept in notebooks by payer and reviewed monthly to ensure the following:

- Claims are paid on average within 30 to 45 days.

- Denials are appealed immediately.

- Identify all specific billing problems with specific payors.

- Determine which services are approved 100 percent for payment.

- Evaluate billing effectiveness of current personnel.

Summary of Revenue Impact

The following is a summary of revenue impact detailed in this report:

Increase in doctor production	$144,000
Fee revisions	25,234
Elimination of a technician	24,840
Elimination of Physician Assistant	71,280
Control of overtime hours	Cannot Quantify
Total Revenue Impact To Practice	**$265,354**

SAMPLE MEDICAL PRACTICE ANALYSIS

Preface

In response to the challenges and opportunities of the _____ and _____ community and surrounding area, Management Company has engaged to prepare an analysis of _____ (practice name) and _____, (practice name) the purpose of which is to assess the viability of pursuing a collaborative relationship with the clinics. Specifically, _____ (your firm) has been retained to conduct a practice analysis consisting of a thorough evaluation of the practice operations including financial analysis, facility assessment, and patient origin analysis. This analysis will provide a framework to further enhance the delivery of quality healthcare services to the _____ area.

The analysis contained herein is based on information provided by Medical Associates. We have not audited such information and, accordingly, do not express an opinion or any other form of assurance on the information provided by Medical Associates.

This report has been prepared for the exclusive internal use of Management Company and Medical Associates. Copies of this report should not be distributed or otherwise reproduced except for the purpose of utilizing this information internally. Specifically, this information will not be distributed to other consultants or organizations.

We appreciate the opportunity to work with Medical Associates and Management in this practice analysis. The findings and recommendations presented herein are based upon careful analysis of all available data and represent our best professional judgment.

I. Introduction and Overview

Clinic History

The Clinic was originally founded around 1945 by Dr. Tinsley, who is deceased. The first physician to join Dr. Tinsley was Dr. Havens, who is also deceased. Dr. Hebert also practiced at the facility and is now retired. The current physicians practicing at the facility are Dr. Barcelona (joined 1965), Dr. Hinckley (joined 1977) (son of Dr. Barcelona), Dr. Granberry (joined 1990), Dr. Anderson (joined 1985), Dr. Cravitz (joined 1985), Dr. Bower (joined 1993), and Dr. Ward (joined 1994). The partners are Drs. Barcelona, Hinckley, Granberry, Ward, and Cravitz, with each holding a 20 percent interest in the partnership. Dr. Thompson is employed under a contract that expires in July of 1997 and is not expected to remain in the practice. Dr. Karling joined the practice in August of 1996 under a contract which expires in December of 1997. Dr. Bennett is expected to join the partnership in January of 1998. All physicians are board certified in Family Practice with the exception of Dr. Bennett, who is a general practitioner and is not board certified. All board-certified physicians are members of the American Academy of Family Practice.

The clinic administrator and physicians believe that the future of the clinic is best served by alignment with an integrated entity to allow for growth and take advantage of the current market for clinic acquisitions. The future vision is for a new facility to be built to provide a larger, more modern building and updated equipment. The clinic also sees future inclusion of mid-level practitioners in remote sites.

II. Financial Analysis

The key elements in examining a practice's profitability are the statements of income and expenses and balance sheets. The income statement reflects the practice's income, operating expenses, and physician compensation. The practice's income and expenses are analyzed in relation to national norms as reported by the Medical Group Management Association (MGMA) in its annual surveys. The MGMA survey results report median values, not averages, to prevent the figures being skewed by extreme high or low results. The MGMA figures provide a framework for the comparative analysis of the practice's finances. The statements of income and expenses and corresponding balance sheets for the fiscal years 1995 through 1997 are analyzed in this report.

A. Balance Sheet

Exhibit 11.4 illustrates the balance sheets as of December 31, 1997, 1996 and 1995, in a single report. In 1995, the practice reported $91,409 total assets, of which $51,044 consisted of cash, $30,513 comprised net property and equipment, and $9,852 was made up of other assets. In 1996, cash in-

Exhibit 11.4
Balance Sheets December 31, 1997, 1996 and 1995

	1997	1996	1995
Assets			
Current Assets	$ 98,411	$ 75,788	$ 51,044
Fixed Assets, Net of Depreciation	40,148	66,373	30,513
Cash Surrender Value of Life Insurance	29,533	20,256	9,627
Deposits	225	225	225
Employee Advances	582		
Total Assets	$ 168,899	$ 162,642	$ 91,409
Liabilities			
Current Liabilities	$ 99,019	$ 69,235	$ 49,321
Long Term Liabilities	33,049	46,563	
Total Liabilities	132,068	115,798	49,321
Partners' Capital	36,831	46,844	42,088
Total Liabilities and Partners' Capital	$ 168,899	$ 162,642	$ 91,409

creased to $75,788, while net property and equipment increased to $66,373. In 1997, cash increased to $98,411 at year-end, while depreciation of property and equipment decreased net fixed assets to $40,148.

Total liabilities in 1995 consisted of $49,321 in notes payable. In 1996, total liabilities increased to $115,798 as a result of medical equipment acquisitions. In 1997, total liabilities increased to $132,068.

Profits from the practice and increases in life insurance cash values resulted in an increase of $4,756 in partners' capital after draws. Draws in excess of profits during 1997 caused a decline in the capital to $36,831 at December 31, 1997.

B. Income

Exhibits 11.5 through 11.9 illustrate the practice's income and expenses in comparison to MGMA figures for the fiscal years 1995 through 1997.

Exhibit 11.5
Income and Expenses, Compared to MGMA Year Ended December 31, 1996

	Actual	Percent to Total Revenue	MGMA	Percent to MGMA Revenue
Income				
Gross Patient Revenue	$ 1,310,928	98.2%		
Interest Income	2,227	0.2%		
Deferred Annuities	34,459	2.6%		
Refunds	(12,163)	−0.9%		
Net Revenue	$ 1,335,451	100.0%	$ 1,348,975	100.0%
Expenses				
Physician:				
Compensation & Bonus	$ 595,397	44.6%		
Pension		0.0%		
Dues and Subscriptions	1,666	0.1%		
Meetings/Travel	5,540	0.4%		
Subtotal Physician	602,603	45.1%		
Nonphysician:				
Nonphysician Payroll/Benefits	356,259	26.7%	442,545	29.2%
Rent & Occupancy	75,198	5.6%	105,580	7.1%
Medical Supplies	55,159	4.1%	53,375	3.6%
Lab Supplies	57,434	4.3%	58,005	4.1%
Admin. Supplies/Services	27,403	2.1%	35,820	2.3%
Insurance	71,033	5.3%	41,480	2.6%
Interest	5,475	0.4%	6,485	0.4%
Radiology and Imaging	18,162	1.4%	17,045	1.2%
Outside Professional	6,478	0.5%	17,080	1.2%
Furniture and Equipment	22,560	1.7%	14,870	1.0%
Information Systems	24,626	1.8%	32,150	2.0%
Other	18,214	1.4%	32,490	8.3%
Subtotal Nonphysician	738,001	55.3%	856,925	57.9%
Total Expenses	$ 1,340,604	100.4%		
Net Income (Loss)	$ (5,153)	−0.4%		

Exhibit 11.6
Income and Expenses, Compared to MGMA Year Ended December 31, 1996

	Actual	Percent to Total Revenue	MGMA	Percent to MGMA Revenue
Income				
Gross Patient Revenue	$ 1,441,531	97.6%		
Interest Income	2,359	0.2%		
Deferred Annuities	39,778	2.7%		
Refunds	(6,200)	−0.4%		
Net Revenue	$ 1,447,468	100.0%	$ 1,359,870	100.0%
Expenses				
Physician:				
Compensation & Bonus	$ 698,026	47.2%		
Pension	7,562	0.5%		
Dues and Subscriptions	1,101	0.1%		
Meetings/Travel	8,881	0.6%		
Subtotal Physician	715,570	48.4%	523,405	36.7%
Nonphysician:				
Nonphysician Payroll/Benefits	315,040	21.3%	449,710	29.1%
Rent & Occupancy	79,647	5.4%	115,100	7.3%
Medical Supplies	79,440	5.4%	61,055	3.7%
Lab Supplies	69,118	4.7%	65,685	3.7%
Admin. Supplies/Services	28,355	1.9%	34,755	2.2%
Insurance	88,096	6.0%	42,525	2.6%
Interest	6,292	0.4%	6,075	0.4%
Radiology and Imaging	16,705	1.1%	18,535	1.1%
Outside Professional	8,388	0.6%	13,590	0.9%
Furniture and Equipment	33,596	2.3%	21,520	1.3%
Information Systems	25,380	1.7%	29,965	1.8%
Other	17,714	1.2%	31,040	4.1%
Subtotal Nonphysician	767,771	52.0%	889,555	58.3%
Total Expenses	$ 1,483,341	100.4%		
Net Income (Loss)	$ (5,873)	−0.4%		

Exhibit 11.7
Income and Expenses, Compared to MGMA Year Ended December 31, 1997

	Actual	Percent to Total Revenue	MGMA	Percent to MGMA Revenue
Income				
Gross Patient Revenue	$ 1,630,705	97.8%		
Interest Income	1,818	0.1%		
Deferred Annuities	41,228	2.5%		
Refunds	(6,131)	−0.4%		
Net Revenue	$ 1,667,620	100.0%	$ 1,661,370	100.0%
Expenses				
Physician:				
Compensation & Bonus	$ 798,797	47.9%		
Pension	14,801	0.9%		
Dues and Subscriptions	4,868	0.3%		
Meetings/Travel	12,030	0.7%		
Subtotal Physician	830,496	49.8%	580,020	41.7%
Nonphysician:				
Nonphysician Payroll/Benefits	354,749	21.3%	504,355	29.4%
Rent & Occupancy	72,557	4.4%	118,120	6.8%
Medical Supplies	112,785	6.8%	64,230	3.4%
Lab Supplies	79,907	4.8%	65,315	3.3%
Admin. Supplies/Services	33,449	2.0%	40,890	2.1%
Insurance	87,049	5.2%	42,910	2.0%
Interest	5,316	0.3%	9,470	0.5%
Radiology and Imaging	22,823	1.4%	22,385	1.2%
Outside Professional	8,086	0.5%	13,665	0.8%
Furniture and Equipment	31,958	1.9%	22,565	1.4%
Information Systems	32,035	1.9%	33,390	1.8%
Other	15,700	0.9%	39,005	8.9%
Subtotal Nonphysician	856,414	51.4%	976,300	56.3%
Total Expenses	$ 1,686,910	101.2%		
Net Income (Loss)	$ (19,290)	−1.2%		

Exhibit 11.8
Income and Expense Comparison: 1995–1997

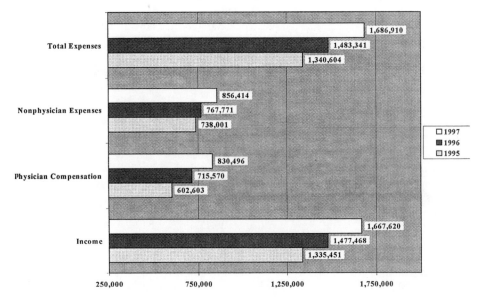

Net income before physician compensation and expenses was as follows during the analysis period:

1995	$597,450
1996	$709,697
1997	$811,506

In 1995, the practice received $1,310,928 in gross patient revenues and $36,686 in other income. After taking refunds into consideration, the practice netted $1,335,451. Compared to MGMA statistics, this is $13,524, or 1.0 percent less than the revenue generated for a typical family practice clinic.

In 1996, the practice received gross revenues in the amount of $1,441,531, representing a 10 percent increase over the amount reported in 1995. When taking refunds into consideration, the practice netted $1,477,468 or 10.6 percent more than in 1995. Comparing these statistics to MGMA indicates the practice netted $117,598 greater than norms.

In 1997, the practice received $1,630,705 in gross revenues, reflecting an increase of 13.1 percent compared to the prior year. Total net revenue was $1,667,620, reflecting an increase of 12.9 percent over the prior year.

Exhibit 11.9
Income and Expense Historical Trends Years Ended December 31, 1997, 1996 and 1995

	1997	Percent Change	1996	Percent Change	1995
Income					
Gross Patient Revenue	$ 1,630,705	13.12%	1,441,531	9.96%	1,310,928
Interest Income	1,818	−22.93%	2,359	5.93%	2,227
Deferred Annuities	41,228	3.65%	39,778	15.44%	34,459
Refunds	(6,131)	−1.11%	(6,200)	−49.03%	(12,163)
Net Revenue	1,667,620	12.87%	1,477,468	10.63%	1,335,451
Expenses					
Physician:					
Compensation & Bonus	798,797	14.44%	698,026	17.24%	595,397
Pension	14,801	95.73%	7,562		
Dues and Subscriptions	4,868	342.14%	1,101	−33.91%	1,666
Meetings/Travel	12,030	35.46%	8,881	60.31%	5,540
Subtotal Physician	830,496	16.06%	715,570	18.75%	602,603
Nonphysician:					
Nonphysician Payroll/ Benefits	354,749	12.60%	315,040	−11.57%	356,259
Rent & Occupancy	72,557	−8.90%	79,647	5.92%	75,198
Medical Supplies	112,785	41.98%	79,440	44.02%	55,159
Lab Supplies	79,907	15.61%	69,118	20.34%	57,434
Admin. Supplies/Services	33,449	17.97%	28,355	3.47%	27,403
Insurance	87,049	−1.19%	88,096	24.02%	71,033
Interest	5,316	−15.51%	6,292	14.92%	5,475
Radiology and Imaging	22,823	36.62%	16,705	−8.02%	18,162
Outside Professional	8,086	−3.60%	8,388	29.48%	6,478
Furniture and Equipment	31,958	−4.88%	33,596	48.92%	22,560
Information Systems	32,035	26.22%	25,380	3.06%	24,626
Other	15,700	−11.37%	17,714	−2.75%	18,214
Subtotal Nonphysician	856,414	11.55%	767,771	4.03%	738,001
Total Expenses	1,686,910	13.72%	1,483,341	10.65%	1,340,604
Net Income (Loss)	$ (19,290)	228.45%	(5,873)	13.97%	(5,153)

Comparing the practice's figures to MGMA norms indicates the practice received $6,250 more than the typical family practice.

C. Physician Compensation

During 1996, total physician compensation and benefits were $715,570, consisting of $698,026 in direct compensation, $8,881 in travel and seminars, $1,101 in professional dues, and $7,562 in pension expense. Total physician compensation was $192,165 more than the compensation figure reported by the MGMA of $523,405. In addition, the practice's compensation figure represents 48.4 percent of total net revenue. The MGMA compensation statistic represents 36.7 percent of net revenues.

In 1997, total physician compensation was $830,496, $798,797 of which was direct compensation, $12,030 in travel and seminars, $4,868 in dues, and $14,801 in pension plan contributions. Total compensation represented 49.8 percent of net production. The MGMA reported total compensation of $580,020 which represented 41.7 percent of total revenues.

Exhibit 11.10 documents various other categories of MGMA direct compensation and production numbers.

D. Nonphysician Expenses

Exhibit 11.11 illustrates the nonphysician expenses comprising practice overhead. These expenses are not physician related and consist of expenses as part of providing medical services.

In 1996, the practice incurred $767,711 in nonphysician expenses, which represented 52 percent of net revenue. The MGMA statistics indicate a typical family practice incurred 58.3 percent overhead. The practice incurred $121,784 less in nonphysician expenses than MGMA norms.

In 1997, nonphysician expenses were $856,414, representing 51.4 percent of total net revenues and an increase of $88,643 from the prior year. Typical overhead expenditures for a practice of this type are 56.3 percent, slightly higher than the practice's experience. The main contributors to this difference are nonphysician payroll and benefits (lower than average), rent and occupancy, and other (nonphysician expenses).

E. Contingent Liabilities

There are no contingent liabilities recorded and disclosed on the practice's books and records.

Exhibit 11.10

Physician Compensation Comparison Years Ended December 31, 1997 and 1996

1997

	MGMA*	Dr. Barcelona	Dr. Hinkcley	Dr. Granberry	Dr. Anderson	Dr. Bower	Dr. Ward
Direct Compensation							
All Groups	$ 120,000	148,000	162,000	154,000	138,000	124,000	27,400
Single Specialty	116,004						
Southern Section	127,949						
Production							
All groups	287,131						
Single Specialty	332,274						

1996

	MGMA*	Dr. Barcelona	Dr. Hinkcley	Dr. Granberry	Dr. Anderson	Dr. Bower
Direct Compensation						
All Groups	$ 112,585	150,130	164,459	131,399	126,384	118,404
Single Specialty	104,681					
Southern Section	120,547					
Production						
All groups	289,203					
Single Specialty	271,974					

* MGMA Physician Compensation and Production Survey

Note: MGMA data reflects median values

Exhibit 11.11
Practice Overhead Analysis Years Ended December 31, 1997, 1996 and 1995

Year	Total Collections	Total Overhead	Overhead as a % of Collections	MGMA Norm	Difference
1997	1,667,620	856,414	51.36%	56.34%	−4.98%
1996	1,447,468	767,771	51.97%	58.27%	−6.30%
1995	1,335,451	738,001	55.26%	57.92%	−2.66%

Analysis of Overhead Categories

	1997		1996		1995	
	Actual	Percent to Total Revenue	Actual	Percent to Total Revenue	Actual	Percent to Total Revenue
Nonphysician Payroll/Benefits	354,749	21.27%	315,040	21.32%	356,259	26.68%
Rent & Occupancy	72,557	4.35%	79,647	5.39%	75,198	5.63%
Medical Supplies	112,785	6.76%	79,440	5.38%	55,159	4.13%
Lab Supplies	79,907	4.79%	69,118	4.68%	57,434	4.30%
Admin. Supplies/ Services	33,449	2.01%	28,355	1.92%	27,403	2.05%
Insurance	87,049	5.22%	88,096	5.96%	71,033	5.32%
Interest	5,316	0.32%	6,292	0.43%	5,475	0.41%
Radiology and Imaging	22,823	1.37%	16,705	1.13%	18,162	1.36%
Outside Professional	8,086	0.48%	8,388	0.57%	6,478	0.49%
Furniture and Equipment	31,958	1.92%	33,596	2.27%	22,560	1.69%
Information Systems	32,035	1.92%	25,380	1.72%	24,626	1.84%
Other	15,700	0.94%	17,714	1.20%	18,214	1.36%
Total Overhead	856,414	51.36%	767,771	53.04%	738,001	55.26%

Legal counsel for the practice is:

(Fill in appropriate name)

Findings

1. Consistent increases in cash have resulted from debt-financing of capital purchases during the assessment period. Cash increases have amounted to $47,367 between 1995 and 1997.

2. While total property and equipment balances have increased $75,189 between 1995 and 1997, depreciation has limited the net increase to only $9,635.

3. In 1996 and 1997, net revenues of $1,477,468 and $1,667,620 have been higher than MGMA norms for family practice clinics, and revenue over the three-year practice assessment period has consistently shown increases over the previous year.

4. Physician compensation consistently exceeded norms in 1996 and 1997, by 37 percent and 43 percent, respectively. Compensation has steadily increased during the period, up by 16.1 percent in 1997 over 1996 compensation.

5. Nonphysician expenses fell below MGMA norms, by $118,924 in 1997, $121,784 in 1996 and $119,886 in 1995. Nonphysician payroll and benefits make up a sizeable portion of the difference.

6. Medical supplies expense has shown significant increases in the range of 44 and 42 percent over 1996 and 1995, respectively. The primary result of these increases is attributable to the Norplant costs in 1996 and 1997.

7. The practice has no outstanding off-balance sheet contingent liabilities.

III. Personnel Assessment

Personnel

Exhibit 11.12 lists the practice staff for both locations including position, wage rates, a comparison of compensation for the clinic staff versus recent survey data, FTE (full-time equivalent) levels, date of hire, and location assignment. There are a total of twenty-three employees for both clinic locations. Not all employees are full-time. The total FTE's for both clinics totals 17.2. The MGMA staffing norm is 21.5 FTE's. Exhibit 11.13 compares the clinic staffing levels versus MGMA norms. The clinic staff wage rates are lower than the median rates as reported in the most recent survey conducted by the Mitchell Health Care Group. Staff wage rates are reviewed and adjusted annually each July.

All full-time employees are eligible for two weeks of vacation time per year and two weeks sick leave per year. The clinic offers seven and one-half holidays per year to all employees. The clinic does not provide health in-

Exhibit 11.12
Schedule of Employees

Employee	Title	Date of hire	FTE	Hourly Salary	Range/ Hour*	Median/ Hour*
Jane Lott	Billing Clerk	8/93	1.0	6.25	5.00–8.80	7.00
Lucy Stuart	Receptionist	12/89	1.0	6.76	6.75–11.00	8.37
Suzanne Powell	Relief	8/92	.5	5.95	5.50–8.75	7.13
Julie Smith	Telephone Operator	4/71	.8	7.29	6.75–11.00	8.37
Ellen Kinsey	Insurance Clerk	8/90	.8	7.03	6.58–13.75	9.20
Leann Gable***	Receptionist	4/87	.8	8.03	6.75–11.00	8.37
Becky Ross	Front Desk	5/91	.6	8.03	5.50–8.75	7.13
Sharon Jones	Front Desk	5/81	.035	6.69	6.75–11.00	8.37
Melissa Knight	Front Desk	6/81	.035	7.80	6.75–11.00	8.37
Sabrina Miller***	Front Desk	9/93	1.0	7.00	5.50–8.50	6.43
Karen Stuart	Front Desk	9/94	1.0	5.00	5.50–8.50	6.43
Stacie Roberts	File Clerk	9/94	1.0	5.00	4.35–6.25	5.00
Michael Graham***	Medical Technologist	7/87	1.0	9.27	8.52–14.00	12.27
John Blackburn	Medical Technologist	9/93	.03	7.57	8.00–13.00	10.25
Adrian Montgomery	Medical Technologist	7/88	1.0	11.66	8.52–14.00	12.27
Caroline Downs	Phlebotomist	11/89	0.8	7.80	5.00–9.73	6.91
Sandy Brown**	Medical Assistant	7/91	1.0	6.76	4.72–13.00	7.50
Kim Anderson**	LPN	7/90	.8	8.11	4.95–17.31	8.51
Renee Fleming**	Medical Assistant	8/85	.8	7.84	4.95–17.31	8.51
Cindy Carr**	Medical Assistant	7/80	.8	7.28	4.95–17.31	8.51
Helen Johnson**	LPN	6/94	.8	7.50	4.72–13.00	7.50
Donna Myers**	LPN	10/94	.6	7.50	4.72–13.00	7.50
Lorraine Stamps	Administrator	11/89	1.00	20.67	9.50–43.61	15.11
Total	23		17.2			

* Source: Mitchell Health Care Group
** Employed at main clinic
*** Employed at satellite office

surance; however, medical care from clinic physicians is provided free of charge to all employees and their immediate family members. A retirement plan is offered which includes a 401(k) with voluntary employee contributions and employer contributions of 3 percent of employee wages, as well as a profit sharing plan, which is integrated with social security. A term life insurance policy is provided for all employees and employees are covered under the clinic's malpractice policy.

All office staff members report to the administrator who is responsible for scheduling and supervision of employees. Nursing staff report to the administrator and physicians. The clinic does not have a written personnel policy manual or written job descriptions. Performance evaluations

Exhibit 11.13
Comparison of Staffing Levels

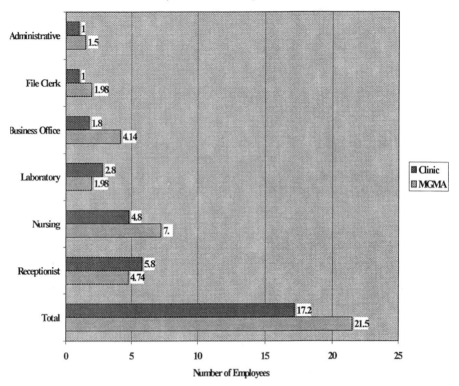

Number of Employees

and wage reviews are completed by the administrator every July. The administrator's recommendations are reviewed by the physicians.

At the clinic location, there are three employees who are responsible for patient check-in and check-out. These individuals collect payments, enter charge and payment information at check-out, and also post payments received in the mail. Each employee rotates duty for the Saturday clinic and two part-time employees also work on Saturdays to cover the front desk. One employee is specifically assigned as a telephone operator, but all front desk employees handle telephones if needed. Hospital charge information and posting workers' compensation payments is handled by one employee. One employee is responsible for submission of all insurance claims and posting all Medicare and Medicaid payment registers. A full-time employee handles all medical records filing. The lab is staffed by 1.8 FTE's. A total of three LPNs and three medical assistants work at both the main clinic and the satellite clinic depending upon the physician work schedules at both clinics.

The main clinic has 1.8 FTE's who work at the front desk and handle all patient check-in and check-out. The responsibilities are the same as those for front desk employees at the satellite clinic. One FTE medical technologist handles all lab work at the main clinic. The nurses and medical assistants from the main clinic rotate to the satellite clinic as needed. The administrator oversees operations at both clinics and is on-site at the main clinic each morning before going to the satellite clinic.

Findings

1. The practice currently has a total of 23 employees at both locations.

2. The staffing level of 17.2 FTE's is significantly lower than national norms of 21.5 for family practice specialties.

3. There is no employee personnel manual or written job descriptions.

IV. Facility/Ancillary Services

Location

The main clinic is located at 123 Broadside Street and is approximately one mile from the intersection of Fannin and Holcombe. The location is approximately two miles from Interstate 40. The clinic has occupied this location for over 40 years.

The satellite clinic is located 10 miles north of the main clinic, located at 542 Avenue North. The location is approximately two miles from Interstate 20. The clinic has occupied this location since 1992. The satellite clinic was established in 1985; however, it outgrew the original facility and was relocated in 1992.

Facility Description

Main Clinic

Clinic was originally constructed in the mid 1940s and has not been updated significantly from the original building. Over the years, two side wings and one front wing were added to the original structure. A new building has been constructed to the north of the original structure and additions. This facility is not utilized by the clinic, but is rented to a home health agency and an orthodontist. The new building is joined to the old facility and could be accessed through the old facility with some minor construction. The clinic has no plans to utilize the new addition for its own purposes and plans to continue to rent this property.

Entry into the clinic is through a front door directly off a paved parking area which accomodates approximately 40 vehicles. Patients enter directly into the waiting area. The waiting area is furnished with metal and vinyl seating which is not in good condition. The waiting room has a magazine rack and a soft drink machine. The area seats approximately 40 people. A front reception desk with a partial glass partition separates the waiting area from the business office. Medical records are located behind the business office area in a corridor and small medical records room.

Exam rooms, physician offices, and rooms for ancillary services are located off a hallway which runs the width of the building. There are seven exam rooms which are used exclusively as exam rooms. There are four exam rooms which are used as a combination exam room and physician office. At the north end of the building there are two adjoining rooms which are used as the laboratory. A room across the hall is used for phlebotomy. There is also a minor surgery/trauma room and a room housing x-ray equipment. A separate room is dedicated to EKGs. There are two patient restrooms designated for women and one designated for men. There is also a private restroom for staff which is kept locked. A storage room is located at the north end of the building which contains refrigerators and shelving. Sample medications are stored in this area. The area is not locked. There is one physician office which is not combined with an exam room. The overall condition of the facility is cramped and in need of updated decor and minor repairs.

The facility has approximately 5,500 square feet. It is owned by Crack-aWall Corporation. The shareholders of this corporation are Dr. Hinckley, Dr. Barcelona, Dr. Cravitz, Dr. Granberry, and Dr. Anderson. Each shareholder owns 20 percent of the corporate stock. Medical Associates reported rent expense of $50,072 in 1997, $56,138 in 1996 and $50,022 in 1995.

Satellite Clinic

The facility was constructed in 1992. The facility is relatively new and in good condition. On-street parking is available for approximately fifteen vehicles directly in front of the clinic. The clinic utilizes a gravel parking lot for a mini-warehouse facility across the street for overflow parking.

Entry to the clinic is through a door off a sidewalk in front of the on-street parking area. Entry is directly into the waiting area which seats approximately 15 patients. The waiting area is furnished with chrome and fabric side chairs positioned around the perimeter of the waiting room. A wall with a glass window separates the business office/reception desk from the waiting area. Medical records are stored at the rear of the business office area. The business office area is accessible through a single door.

Nine exam rooms and two physician offices are located off of a square hallway which circles a central area housing the x-ray room, the lab, a minor surgery room that is also used as an exam room, and a storage closet. One exam room is used as a combination exam room and physician office. One exam room is used for overflow only and one is used for storage. An employee lounge and private employee restroom is located behind the business office area. One men's and one women's restroom are available for patients and are accessible from the waiting area and the hallway to exam rooms.

The property is leased from Dr. Barcelona and has approximately 3,000 square feet. There is no formal lease agreement for this facility.

The main clinic has approximately 31,500 medical records which include active and inactive charts. Approximately 400 charts have been set aside as "deceased" patient charts. Records have never been purged and many charts are included which have been inactive for many years. The satellite clinic has approximately 15,000 charts, including active and inactive charts. Deceased charts at both locations were not available for estimate. Charts have never been purged to inactive status at either location and many charts have been inactive for many years. Medical records are filed in a numeric color-coded file. The charts do not include dividers and there are loose records in a majority of the charts. Progress notes are handwritten. Records are faxed between the two clinics when patients are being seen in the other location. The records at the main clinic are stored in shelves along a corridor beside the business office and in a small room at the end of the corridor. Shelf space is available for some additional growth. Records at the satellite clinic are located in shelves directly behind the reception desk. The shelves allow for some additional growth.

Hospital Services and Referrals

The physicians are on staff at Evergreen Hospital. Patients admitted to this facility average 22 per month for all physicians. Patients requiring diagnostic procedures beyond the scope of clinic services (such as mammography and treadmills) are referred to Evergreen Hospital. Patients requiring the care or evaluation of a specialist are referred to other physicians.

Findings

1. The practice has one main clinic and one satellite clinic.

2. The main facility is approximately 5,500 square feet and is leased at a rate that varies each year. The facility is over 40 years old.

3. The satellite facility has approximately 3,000 square feet and is under no formal lease agreement.

4. Ample parking is available at both facilities.

5. The main facility has limited exam rooms and physician office space. A new addition adjacent to the old facility could be accessed for clinic use but is now leased to a home health agency and orthodontist.

6. The satellite facility is in need of minor repairs and an overall update in decor.

7. The satellite facility has adequate exam rooms and office space available for three physicians if all exam rooms were utilized.

8. The physicians are on staff at one hospital.

V. Operational Assessment

The operational assessment includes analyzing the accounts receivable in comparison to national norms, assessing the billing and collection policies and procedures, and cash management procedures.

A. Accounts Receivable Management

At November 30, 1997, the clinic reported $1,525,817 in outstanding accounts receivable. This represents approximately 8.75 months of charges in outstanding receivables. This compares unfavorably with the MGMA norm for family practice of 2.44 months of charges in accounts receivable. Approximately 78 percent of the outstanding receivables are patient responsible balances. The remaining 22 percent is reported as assigned insurance receivables.

The aged breakdown of receivables reports 82 percent of total receivables over 90 days old. Slightly over 3 percent of receivables are over 60 days old. Ten percent of total receivables are current.

The aged breakdown of patient-responsible balances indicates 90 percent of patient receivables over 90 days old. The aged breakdown of insurance assigned receivables indicates 51 percent of insurance receivables over 90 days old.

Information for detailed analysis of the payer mix for the clinic was not available. Estimates provided by the clinic administrator for 1997 report 47 percent of gross receipts as "private" and 53 percent of gross receipts as "Medicare/Medicaid assignment."

Findings

1. The clinic has 8.76 months of average charges in outstanding accounts receivable.

2. Eighty-two percent of total receivables are over 90 days old.

B. Billing and Collection Process

Combined billings net of adjustments for both clinic locations for January through November of 1997 totaled $1,918,694. Collections for this same time period totaled $1,632,896. This equates to a net collection ratio of 85 percent versus a norm of 98.5 percent as reported by MGMA's *Cost Report: 1996 Report Based on 1995 Data* net. Collection percentage for the fiscal year ended December 31, 1996, was 83 percent. Annualized net billings for 1997 equal $2,093,121, which will exceed 1996 net billings by 9 percent. Annualized net collections for 1994 equal $1,781,340, which will exceed 1996 collections by 13 percent. Individual physician net production averages between $350,000 and $400,000 per year, which is about average when compared to specialty norms.

The clinic has established a credit policy for collection at the time of service for all patients for the first five or six visits. After this time, patients are allowed to charge their services. New patients are requested to pay a $50 deposit at check-in prior to seeing the physician. The new patients are advised of this policy at the time the appointment is made.

The clinic sees all patients without restriction. The clinic accepts all Medicaid and Medicare patients. The physicians are not participating physicians for the Medicare program. The physicians do participate in the Blue Cross Key Physician program and accept assignment on all Blue Cross claims.

Patients are billed monthly with approximately 2,100 statements mailed each month. An aged accounts receivable report is reviewed each month by the administrator who is responsible for follow-up on delinquent accounts. A combination of letters and telephone calls is used for delinquent account follow-up. Extended payment arrangements are determined on a case-by-case basis by the administrator. Delinquent accounts appear on the screen at the time an appointment is made, and the patients are advised that they must pay the delinquent balance in full prior to seeing the physician. The clinic does not use an outside collection agency for delinquent accounts. No accounts are written off as bad debts. All delinquent accounts remain in the clinic's accounts receivable.

Findings

1. Net billings for 1997 should exceed 1996 by 9 percent.

2. Net collections for 1997 should exceed 1996 by 13 percent.

3. The clinic requests payment at time of service for patients for first five or six visits, and new patients are requested to pay prior to seeing the physician.

4. The clinic physicians are not Medicare participating physicians but are Blue Cross Key Physicians.

5. Patients are advised of credit policy at the time the appointment is made and delinquent account balances appear on screen when appointments are made.

6. The clinic uses a combination of letters and telephone calls for delinquent account follow-up without any established system or policy.

7. The clinic does not write off any accounts as bad debt.

C. Computer System

The clinic is utilizing software and hardware provided by TinsTech. TinsTech was acquired in 1994 by Medical Software Solutions, which has their own medical software billing system. The clinic has chosen not to make the additional investment to move up to the Medical Software Solutions package. Medical Software Solutions is still providing support for the TinsTech software, but no upgrades will be made. The only revisions which have been made to the program are those changes required for insurance filing to comply with Medicare regulations or a change in the HCFA insurance form. The clinic still has two years left on the support contract with ICS, but it is uncertain whether ICS will be willing to renew the support contract for this product. ICS has no other clinics still using this software.

All insurance billing, patient billing, and appointment scheduling is done on the system. Electronic claim filing capabilities are available for Medicare and Medicaid claims only. The reporting capabilities of the software are very limited. Charges, collections, and adjustments are accumulated only by provider. Information by payer type or location of service is not available. General ledger and payroll is also completed on the system. The satellite clinic is directly connected to the main system at the main location and handles their own data entry.

Findings

1. The clinic is utilizing TinsTech software which is no longer marketed but is still supported by Medical Software Solutions with two years remaining on the support contract.

2. All insurance, patient billing, and appointment scheduling is done on the software.

3. The software has limited reporting capabilities.

D. Cash Management

The clinic accepts cash, checks, and credit cards as payment. Patients are asked to pay at the completion of their visit. The physician marks the superbill for services rendered and diagnosis. The superbill is a one-part form with procedures on the front of the form. Diagnosis codes are listed on the front and back of the form. The superbill is numbered but is not generated by computer.

Payments made at check-out are received and posted by the same individual. There are four employees at the front desk who could perform this responsibility. Checks received in the mail are opened by the administrator and routed to the employees for posting. Medicare and Medicaid checks are posted by the insurance clerk. Workers' compensation checks are posted by the same individual who posts hospital charges. Patient payments and other payments are posted by any one of the four front desk employees. The bank deposit is prepared by one of two front desk employees who alternate this responsibility. The deposit is taken to the bank by the same individual who makes up the deposit. The deposit is balanced daily against a computer printout of payments entered in the system.

A cash drawer for change in the amount of $200 is maintained at the front desk. Anyone at the front desk has access to the drawer. It is balanced daily at the end of the day. A petty cash fund in the amount of $50 is also maintained at the front desk. This fund is balanced and replenished monthly.

Checks for accounts payable and payroll are written and signed by the administrator. The clinic has established a policy that requires two signatures on a check if the amount exceeds $1,000. The bank statement is reconciled monthly by the CPA for the clinic.

Refunds are prepared only when the patient requests a refund of a credit balance. The refund is made by manual check prepared by the administrator.

Findings

1. The practice accepts cash, checks, and credit cards as payment.

2. Four front desk employees are responsible for handling cash received at check-out, posting these payments in the computer, and making up the bank deposit.

3. The clinic administrator balances the deposits against the daily computer reports.

4. Refunds are made as requested by the patient.

5. A change drawer of $200 is maintained. A petty cash fund of $50 is maintained.

6. Checks for accounts payable and payroll are written and signed by the clinic administrator.

VI. Fee Schedule

Exhibit 11.14 illustrates the practice's fee schedule for the most commonly provided services in comparison to fees for the central geographic region as indicated in a national data base of fees for all physician specialties. The

Exhibit 11.14
Fee Comparison For Top Codes

CPT Code	Description	Fee	National Data Base
59410	Delivery	$1,200.00	$1,271.0
71010	Chest X-Ray	31.00	42.0
80003	Multichannel Chemistry	17.00	26.0
80019	Multichannel Chemistry	35.00	47.0
81000	Urinalysis	10.00	18.0
82947	Glucose	12.00	18.0
85024	CBC	24.00	24.0
88150	Pap Smear	15.00	17.0
99213	Office Visit	28.60	46.0
99214	Office Visit	30.00	62.0
99222	Hospital Admit	85.00	120.0
99231	Hospital Visit	35.00	58.0

clinic's fees are significantly lower than the typical fees for most of the services surveyed. In particular, the clinic fees for the evaluation and management services are much lower than typical. These procedures represent a substantial portion of the clinic revenues. When the procedures are analyzed utilizing the McGraw-Hill Relative Value Scale, the conversion factors for the evaluation and management services are much lower than norms for family practice. The laboratory fees for the clinic compare more favorably with the typical fees, even though they are lower in most cases. The conversion factors for the laboratory fees are more consistent with national norms.

The clinic fee schedule was last updated early in 1996. The clinic reviews and adjusts fees annually. There is no standard methodology in place for the annual fee analysis. The administrator indicates that each procedure is analyzed individually and compared to allowables for Blue Cross and the Medicare limiting charges.

Findings

1. The clinic's fees for evaluation and management services are lower than typical fees.

2. The clinic reviews and adjusts fees annually.

Exhibit 11.15
Patient Distribution by Area

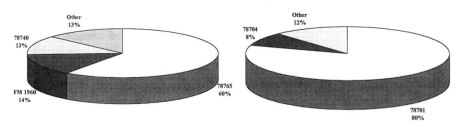

Main Clinic   Satellite Clinic

VII. Patient Analysis

A. Patient Origin and Age

Patient demographic data was obtained by sampling 312 charts at the main clinic and 98 charts at the satellite clinic. The sample included only patients who had been seen in the clinic within the last two years.

Exhibit 11.15 illustrates the patient distribution by area. Sixty percent of the patients in the main clinic originate from the 78765 zip code. Twelve and one-half percent of the patients in the main clinic originate from 78740. Over fourteen percent of the patients are from the FM 1960 area south of the main location. The balance of the patients originate from rural areas within a 30-mile radius of the main location.

Eighty percent of the patients in the satellite clinic are from 78701. Eight percent originate from 78704 and the balance is from surrounding areas.

The same record samples were analyzed for patient age which is depicted in Exhibit 11.16. In the main clinic, the patient base is rather evenly split among the age groups. The satellite clinic sees a much higher percentage of children under age 13 than the main clinic. The satellite clinic also sees a lower percentage of patients ages 21 to 62. Both clinics have around one-fourth of their patient base in the over 63 category.

Findings

1. Sixty-seven percent of the patients treated at the main location originate from the 78765 zip code.

Exhibit 11.16
Patient Distribution by Age

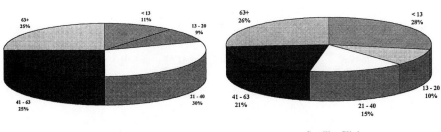

Main Clinic   Satellite Clinic

2. Twelve and one-half percent treated at the main location originate from 78740.

3. Fourteen percent of the main location patients originate from the FM 1960 area.

4. Eighty percent of the patients treated at the satellite location originate from 78701.

5. Eight percent of the satellite patients originate from 78704.

6. Patients over 63 represent over 25 percent of the patient base at both clinics.

B. Patient Volume

Each physician works four days per week and all physicians participate in a rotation schedule for Saturdays at the main clinic. Dr. Barcelona and Dr. Hinckley work primarily at the main location. All other physicians split their four days between the two locations. The main office schedule usually calls for four physicians on Monday and Friday, three physicians on Tuesday and Thursday, and two physicians on Wednesday. The satellite office schedule usually calls for three physicians on Monday and two or three physicians the balance of the week.

Exhibit 11.17 illustrates the weekly patient volumes by physician and compares this to AMA norms for family practice for the southeast region. All physicians fall below the weekly volume norms. Dr. Barcelona has the highest volume with an average of 106 patients per week. Dr. Granberry has the lowest volume with an average of 84 patients per week. All other physician volumes fall within a range between 86 and 98 patients per week.

Even though the patient volumes are lower than the norm, the average charge per visit exceeds norms. Consequently, the gross production of the physicians in terms of dollars is comparable to norms.

The volume at the main clinic is approximately 300 patients per week while satellite office volume is about 190 patients per week. This results from fewer FTE physicians working at the satellite locations. The physicians who work at both clinic locations equally see a slightly lower volume of patients at the satellite location than at the main location.

Findings

1. Each physician works four days per week and rotates with the other physicians on Saturday.

2. Weekly patient volumes for all physicians are below AMA norms for family practice.

3. Volume at the main clinic is approximately 300 patients per week, and volume at the satellite location is approximately 190 patients per week.

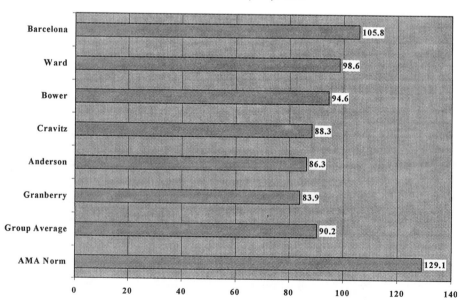

Exhibit 11.17
Patient Volumes by Physician

VIII. Recommendations

1. Financial Assessment

Findings

1. Consistent increases in cash have resulted from debt-financing of capital purchases during the assessment period. Cash increases have amounted to $47,367 between 1995 and 1997.

2. While total property and equipment balances have increased $75,189 between 1995 and 1997, depreciation has limited the net increase to only $9,635.

3. In 1996 and 1997, net revenues of $1,477,468 and $1,667,620 have been higher than MGMA norms for family practice clinics, and revenue over the three-year practice assessment period has consistently shown increases over the previous year.

4. Physician compensation consistently exceeded norms in 1996 and 1997, by 37 percent and 43 percent, respectively. Compensation has steadily increased during the period, up by 16.1 percent in 1997 over 1992 compensation.

5. Nonphysician expenses fell below MGMA norms, by $118,924 in 1997, $121,784 in 1996 and $119,886 in 1995. Nonphysician payroll and benefits make up a sizeable portion of the difference.

6. Medical supplies expense has shown significant increases in the range of 44 and 42 percent over 1996 and 1995, respectively. The primary result of these increases are attributable to the Norplant costs in 1996 and 1995.

Recommendations

1. Develop an annual budget and use the budget to monitor actual income and expenses.

In order to maintain better control over the finances of the practice, it is recommended to establish annual budgets to project income and expenses, and monitor the projected figures by comparing the actual monthly figures to the budgeted figures. A budget assists in planning specific goals and objectives, analyzing the practice's strengths and weaknesses, and enables the manager to keep control over the finances of the practice.

2. Develop a plan for working capital maintenance.

The practice has accumulated sufficient liquidity to apply a portion of cash toward outstanding debt or utilize working capital to fund expected equipment or facility improvements. Planned use of available capital to achieve the optimal return requires projection of working capital needs in conjunction with fiscal budgeting.

3. Evaluate the identified nonphysician expense categories that are above the norms and determine where improvements can be made.

In conjunction with developing an annual budget, the administrator should review the categories which are above the norm, primarily medical and lab supplies, insurance, and furniture and equipment, to determine which expenses are out of line and recommend action to the physicians.

2. Personnel Assessment

Findings

1. The practice currently has a total of 23 employees at both locations.

2. The staffing level of 17.2 FTEs is significantly lower than national norms of 21.5 for family practice specialties.

3. There is no employee personnel manual or written job descriptions.

Recommendations

1. Hire two FTEs.

Staffing levels are 4.3 FTEs lower than MGMA norms; however, volume of patients is also much lower than norms. The addition of 2 FTEs in the area of billing and collections should allow implementation of more systematic follow-up on accounts receivable and implementation of better internal controls.

2. Develop and maintain a personnel manual and written job descriptions.

At the present time, the clinic does not have a written personnel policy manual or written job descriptions. It is extremely important to have written personnel policies and job descriptions to clearly communicate policies and responsibilities to the employees. Both of these documents provide a good source for communication to employees and decrease legal risks.

3. Facilities/Ancillary Services Assessment

Findings

1. The practice has one main clinic and one satellite.

2. The main facility is approximately 5,500 square feet and is leased at a rate that varies each year. The facility is over 40 years old.

3. The satellite facility has approximately 3,000 square feet and is under no formal lease agreement.

4. Ample parking is available at both facilities.

5. The main facility has limited exam rooms and physician office space. A new addition adjacent to the old facility could be accessed for clinic use but is now leased to a home health agency and orthodontist.

6. The satellite facility is in need of minor repairs and an overall update in decor.

7. The satellite facility has adequate exam rooms and office space available for three physicians if all exam rooms were utilized.

8. The physicians are on staff at Evergreen Hospital.

Recommendations

1. Develop formal written lease agreements and rental rates for both the main and satellite clinic facilities.

Formal written lease agreements and established rental rates will provide assurance for continued occupancy and establish cash flow requirements for rental expense. This will also reduce the risk of problems associated with an Internal Revenue Service audit.

2. Analyze the cost-benefit of utilizing the adjacent addition on the facility for clinic operations versus construction of a new facility.

The addition is currently rented to others and provides rental revenue for the main facility. By accessing the addition for clinic use, the clinic will solve some of the space limitations of the present facility. The cost-benefit of this option can then be compared to construction of a new facility.

3. Analyze how all available space at both main and satellite facilities are currently utilized to optimize use of existing facilities.

At the main facility, an analysis of the revenues generated by the various service centers (EKG, x-ray, laboratory, and ambulatory surgery) could be compared to the space allocated to each service to determine if the revenues justify the allocation of space. At the satellite, the facility will accommodate three physicians with sufficient exam rooms if all exam rooms are utilized as such.

4. Consider reinvestment of available working capital in updating the facility.

A general face-lift including making needed repairs, painting, and modernizing furnishings would greatly enhance the clinic environment. Patients and staff would benefit from a more modern decor and more cheerful environment. Working capital is available that has been accumulated over the past few years which could be used for this purpose. Microfilming and purging will eliminate the need to allocate extensive floor space for medical records.

5. Purge medical records regularly. Establish active and inactive chart status.

Medical records at both clinic locations have never been purged and all charts are filed as active. Designate specific space for active and inactive records. Review all records and assign each an active or inactive status. Records for patients who have not been treated in some time can be microfilmed. Add date labels to charts to facilitate annual purging process. Microfilming and purging will eliminate the need to allocate extensive floor space for medical records.

6. Begin updating all patient information in medical records and eliminate all loose items in records.

As patients appear in the clinics for treatment, the patient information can be updated to assist in billing and collection efforts. Loose items in all charts should be secured under fasteners.

4. Operational Assessment

A. Accounts Receivable Management

Findings

1. The clinic has 8.76 months of average charges in outstanding accounts receivable.

2. Eighty-two percent of total receivables are over 90 days old.

Recommendations

Reduce age and amount of outstanding accounts receivable through implementation of a systematic process for follow-up.

B. Billing and Collection Process

Findings

1. Net billings for 1996 should exceed 1995 by 9 percent.

2. Net collections for 1996 should exceed 1995 by 13 percent.

3. The clinic requests payment at time of service for patients for first five or six visits, and new patients are requested to pay prior to seeing the physician.

4. The clinic physicians are not Medicare participating physicians but are Blue Cross Key Physicians.

5. Patients are advised of credit policy at the time the appointment is made and delinquent account balances appear on screen when appointments are made.

6. The clinic uses a combination of letters and telephone calls for delinquent account follow up without any established system or policy.

7. The clinic does not write off any accounts as bad debt.

Recommendations

1. Establish policy for collection at time of service for all patient responsible balances.

Collection of all patient responsible amounts at the time of service reduces costs associated with billing and follow-up on deliquent accounts. This is essential in primary care.

2. Consider Medicare participation.

An analysis should be conducted to determine if Medicare participation could be of benefit to the clinic. Factors to consider include the percentage of Medicare claims that are now being filed as assigned claims, the amount of expense associated with collecting payments from patients on nonassigned claims, the reduced allowable amount for nonpar physicians on assigned claims, and the limitation on the amount that can be balance billed to the patient.

3. Establish systematic collection and follow-up policies for patient balances and assigned insurance claims.

A systematic process, including timetables, can be established for both patient account and insurance claim follow-up. The established process should include the use of telephone contact and letters. Delinquent patient accounts which cannot be collected in-house should be referred to an outside collector and written off as bad debt.

C. Computer System

Findings

1. The clinic is utilizing TinsTech software which is no longer marketed but is still supported by Medical Software Solutions, with two years remaining on the support contract.

2. All insurance, patient billing, and appointment scheduling is done on the software.

3. The software has limited reporting capabilities.

Recommendations

1. Upgrade the software to the latest version of the MENDS software.

The limited capabilities of the existing software coupled with the question of continuing support for the old software dictate the need for an upgrade. The expanded capabilities of the MENDS software, as well as the assurance of continued support and upgrades, should more than justify the investment. The new software will greatly enhance accounts receivable management.

D. Cash Management

Findings

1. The practice accepts cash, checks, and credit cards as payment.

2. Four front desk employees are responsible for handling cash received at check-out, posting these payments in the computer and making up the bank deposit.

3. The clinic administrator balances the deposits against the daily computer reports.

4. Refunds are made as requested by the patient.

5. A change drawer of $200 is maintained. A petty cash fund of $50 is maintained.

6. Checks for accounts payable and payroll are written and signed by the clinic administrator.

Recommendations

1. Divide responsibilities for accepting, posting, and depositing payments to provide improved internal controls.

The size of the staff provides sufficient personnel for these responsibilities to be handled by separate individuals. Implementation of control procedures for balancing and cross-checking will provide less opportunity for diversion of funds.

2. Have a physician sign all checks.

This procedure will improve internal controls and help keep the physicians informed on cash disbursements. This responsibility could be rotated weekly or monthly among the partners in the practice.

5. Fee Schedule

Findings

1. The clinic's fees for evaluation and management services are lower than typical fees.

2. The clinic reviews and adjusts fees annually.

Recommendations

1. Have a complete fee schedule analysis prepared.

A complete analysis of all fees utilizing a relative value scale, as well as an analysis of the practice's current reimbursement patterns, will provide more consistent and competitive pricing.

2. Analyze fees annually utilizing a relative value scale.

The annual fee schedule analysis should incorporate current reimbursement patterns, as well as relative value scale analysis.

6. Patient Analysis

Recommendations

1. Development plans for future growth based on origin of current patients.

Any plans for future satellite facilities should include an analysis of the existing patient origins.

2. Develop marketing plans to target a higher percentage of employed patients who are between ages 20 and 62.

Targeting this market segment can improve the clinic payer mix by including a higher percentage of commercial payers. Marketing plans can include developing closer relationships with local industry to provide all needed services, including physicals and workers' compensation case needs.

B. Patient Volume

Findings

1. Each physician works four days per week and rotates with the other physicians on Saturday.

2. Weekly patient volumes for all physicians are below AMA norms for family practice.

3. Volume at the main clinic is approximately 300 patients per week, and volume at the satellite clinic is approximately 190 patients per week.

Recommendations

1. Develop marketing plans to increase patient volume.

Developing good working relationships with area industry and identifying other target markets can increase patient volume. Expanding the service area beyond the current geographic scope could also improve patient volume.

2. Improve patient relations to develop a strong patient base.

Good communication and high quality service are keys to patient retention. Provide all employees with training on developing good patient relations.

FINDING: The practice's production, collections, and adjustments for the fiscal year ended September 30, 1996 are shown in Exhibit 11.18.

DISCUSSION: The specialty averages are based upon Medical Group Management Association's (MGMA) *Cost Survey: 1995 Report Based Upon 1994 Data,* using family practice physicians. The practice's 1995 and 1996 average monthly production is approximately 9 percent below MGMA's average for family practice physicians. The collections are well below the industry average. Collections will be addressed later in this report under the heading, "Analysis of Billing and Collections."

The collections process has been dramatically impacted. During the first seven months of the fiscal year the practice has a gross collection percentage of 74.92 percent. Since June 15, 1996, the date the clinic began using its new computer system, the gross collection percentage has been 36.40 percent.

During our interview with Mrs. Hinckley we learned the accounts receivable balances were not transferred to the new computer system at the time of implementation. To avoid sending out more than one statement to each patient, the clinic decided to only send out statements on the accounts still maintained in the old system. Later, as the collections from these ac-

Exhibit 11.18
Production, Collections, Adjustments FYE September 30, 1996

Period	Production	Collections	Adjustments	Gross Coll. %	Net Coll. %
Oct.'95-Jun14'96	$470,044	$352,162	$35,164	74.92%	80.98%
Jun15'96*-Sept.'96	$263,515	$95,801	$20,378	36.40%	39.40%
FYTD 1995	**$733,559**	**$447,963**	**$55,542**	**61.07%**	**66.07%**
Specialty Average (2M.D.s)	**$807,988**	**$666,832**	**$131,887**	**82.53%**	**98.63%**

* Transition to new AMOS computer system.

counts tapered off, the clinic discontinued sending patient statements completely.

The clinic has a high self-pay A/R (see finding later in this section) and therefore collects a great deal of its revenue from patient statements. Delaying issuing statements for charges on the new computer system is the primary reason for the decrease in the gross collections percentage.

RECOMMENDATION: Monitor production and collections on a monthly basis and investigate any negative trends. One method of monitoring a clinic is a practice management report (PMR). A PMR will highlight production collections and adjustments each month, making trends more evident. We can assist in the implementation of a PMR for Continental Medical Center. Attached is a sample PMR. Also, refer to the recommendations later in this section regarding patient statements.

FINDING: As of June 15, a total of $54,329.74 has been transferred from the old system to the new AMOS system.

DISCUSSION: Transferring of any balances to the new system from the old only occurs when a patient or that patient's insurer submits payment. The prolonging of transferring balances has caused the A/R to increase substantially and the collections to fall by over 50 percent during the last quarter alone. The main reason for the decrease in collections is due to the nontransferred balances going uncollected with no effort being made to remedy the situation. This indicates the staff was not prepared for the additional responsibilities of performing billing and collections for the transition.

According to the last A/R report from the old system, there is approximately $326,928 that needs to be entered into the AMOS computer system. Prior to the transition the clinic should purge its old accounts receivable system by going through a detailed aged accounts receivable report and determining which accounts are too old to collect and which patients may still pay. Accounts that are too old to collect should be written off. The accounts that belong to patients that are still visiting the office should remain in the A/R and be transferred to AMOS. Any accounts that are over 120 days old should be turned over to a collection agency. Please see the "Analysis of Billing and Collections" for more information concerning a collection agency.

RECOMMENDATION: Purge the old A/R and transfer the rest of the "active" patients off of the old system immediately to the new system.

FINDING: Patient statements have not been mailed since July (as of 10/22/96).

DISCUSSION: The clinic has decided not to issue statements until the full transferring of all old patient accounts to the new system has been completed. This decision was based on patients possibly complaining about receiving two bills instead of one.

During our visit we spoke with Mrs. Hinckley concerning statements and the policy of when they are sent to patients. Mrs. Hinckley has refrained from sending any statements due to the overwhelming cost in relation to the recovery of any of the debts.

RECOMMENDATION: Issue statements immediately for all outstanding account balances. Once all the statements have gone out, make calls to these patients and document each call on a log which gives a status of the account and when a payment can be expected. Continue this process monthly. It is crucial that the full transition to the new system be implemented and completed immediately. The longer this process takes, the greater the chances are that the accounts receivable will become uncollectible.

FINDING: The adjustments for the practice are unusually low.

DISCUSSION: Adjustments for the practice were only 7.57 percent of total charges for the period beginning October 1, 1995 and ending September

30, 1996. The adjustments made on the old system, which range from 10/1/95 to 6/14/96, were $35,164 or roughly 7.50 percent of total charges. The new AMOS system data reflects adjustments of $20,378 for the period 6/14/96 to 9/30/96, or 6.41 percent of total charges.

When a practice's payer mix has a high concentration of Medicare and the clinic charges its regular fees for these Medicare patients, a significant amount of adjusting should have to be made when a payment is received. For example: when a Medicare patient comes in and a 99213 is charged, which is $51.41 according to the fee schedule, Medicare will pay $32.88, leaving $18.53 to be adjusted off of the patient's account. If roughly half of Dr. Hinckley's patients are Medicare patients and a 99213 is assigned to an estimated 95 percent of them, then assuming on average there are 25 patients per day, there should be approximately $4,900 in adjustments per month for Dr. Hinckley.

An adjustment percentage below 15 percent is a possible identifier of the adjustments not being made. The practice currently has a large A/R (when combining the old and new), and although there is some indication that fees may be low, the primary reason for the low adjustments appears to be a Medicare issue. Any Medicare not covered or paid is being filed with a secondary insurer and not being followed up and written off if payment is never received. The nonadjusted zero EOBs are refiled but not followed up or appealed and are ending up in the A/R left to age and eventually inflate the true collectible amount in the A/R.

Another payer that will impact your adjustment percentage is the HMO/PPO patients. Managed care patients make up 42 percent of the practice's payer mix. Similar to the Medicare scenario above, the same principles may apply to managed care patients. It is highly unusual for an HMO or PPO to pay a clinic's standard fee.

RECOMMENDATION: Review the A/R and adjust all unpaid Medicare balances. Set up an adjustment code for each major payer and begin posting payments using these adjustment codes. Each month, compare the adjustments to the payer mix to determine if contractual adjustments are reasonable. If adjustments for a specific type of payer increase significantly, investigate immediately by reviewing EOBs from that payer to rule out error or any inappropriate adjustments being made.

FINDING: Exhibit 11.19 shows the practice's payer mix.

DISCUSSION: The practice obviously has a high concentration of HMO/PPO patients. Many of these patients are part of the CIGNA HMO

Exhibit 11.19
Payer Mix

HMO/PPO	42.00%
Self Pay	5.00%
Commercial	2.00%
Workers' Compensation	1.00%
Medicare	14.00%
Medicaid	36.00%

and BC/BS PPO. The other large portion of the payer mix is Medicare and Medicaid combining for a total of 50 percent of the total mix.

RECOMMENDATION: Market the practice to patients with commercial insurance and PPO insurance. With half of the payer mix consisting of Medicare and Medicaid, it is a good time to begin preparing the practice for managed care for these payers. It is imminent that managed care will be implemented into these government programs and a good cost accounting system will allow the practice to stay profitable when this change occurs.

Accounts Receivable Analysis

FINDING: The current accounts receivable ratio for the practice is 6.63. This represents the amount of average monthly production contained in the accounts receivable balance.

DISCUSSION: Family practice clinics should have an A/R ratio between 1 and 2. In other words, there should be no more than 1 to 2 times the average monthly production contained in the accounts receivable. The clinic's accounts receivable ratio of 6.63 represents over half of a year's production.

The accounts receivable ratio is one key indicator of the financial health of a medical practice. If the ratio increases month to month, which is currently happening, it could signal potential problems with the office collection efforts, capturing charges, or the patient payer mix. The issue now is a problem of collecting billed charges.

The A/R ratio is also skewed to yield a higher figure due to an overwhelming amount of uncollectible accounts sitting in the 180+ day category of the aging report. Please refer to the finding regarding the aging analysis.

RECOMMENDATION: Monitor the A/R ratio on a monthly basis. The PMR report mentioned previously can assist in tracking the A/R ratio from month to month.

FINDING: The Accounts Receivable has increased dramatically.

DISCUSSION: Since August of this year, the A/R from the old system has only decreased $17,369, while the new system's A/R is currently at $227,464 with only billing being done and no follow-up collection efforts being made. The total A/R, including both the old system and the new, was $554,390 as of October 22, 1996.

This increasing A/R is a direct result of improperly implementing the new computer system. As of June 15, 1996, as mentioned before, the clinic has been entering charges and filing claims using the AMOS computer system. As of October 22, 1996, when our site visit occurred, patient balances from the old system have not been transferred to the new AMOS system. This means that collections on production from June 15 to the present are limited to what has been paid by third-party payers. Balances that patients are responsible for have been on the books for as much as 120 days with no collection effort. It is the experience of our firm that the collectibility of accounts diminishes greatly if collections are not made within the first 30 to 60 days. All patients should receive statements on a monthly basis.

RECOMMENDATION: The prior recommendation regarding purging the old system and transferring balances and issuing statements along with calling patients to collect on these accounts should reduce the A/R considerably since the old A/R consists entirely of accounts over 120 days old. It will take approximately three to six months to clean up the accounts receivable. It may be more effective if the practice turns over all accounts over 120 days old to a collection agency immediately.

Another option we recommend is issuing a "10 day letter." A "10 day letter" is a demand for payment or the account will be turned over to a collection agency. The physicians and staff should perform a review of the detailed aged A/R and decide which patients to send this letter to. A sample of this letter is attached. This letter will help justify the quick assignment of the 120 days and older accounts to a collection agency.

Exhibit 11.20
Accounts Receivable Aging Report

Month	Total A/R	Current	30+	60+	90+
New System 10/22/96*	227,464.06	N/A	N/A	N/A	N/A
Old System 10/22/96	326,926.12	−13,314.69 −4.07%	728.37 0.22%	0.00 0%	339,512.44 103.85%
Specialty Average (2 M.D.s)	**137,579**	**44.0%**	**17.0%**	**8.0%**	**31.0%**

*Aging for the new system was not available due to the incapability of the system to age without processing a statement.

FINDING: The practice's aged accounts receivable is shown in Exhibit 11.20.

DISCUSSION: The accounts receivable aging is vital to monitoring a practice's patient accounts. For example: if the 90+ category is 26 percent of the A/R one month and the next month's aging report it represents 45 percent of the accounts receivable, then this will indicate that 16 percent of the 601 category from last month was allowed to age rather than be collected by the practice.

The accounts receivable aging report for the old system indicates that all of the A/R is residing in the 90+ category. This category needs immediate attention. The practice should be making collection calls on each account in this category and performing proper follow-up. The collection duties will need to be assigned to someone. In the "Overhead Analysis" an individual has been selected to perform as a collector. The following section entitled "Analysis of Billing and Collection Operations" will describe proper collection procedures and follow-up. The negative balance that is in the current category are accounts that have been transferred during that period to the new system.

The new AMOS system has not aged any of the accounts because a statement has not been generated from this system. Unless a statement cycle is run on the A/R of AMOS, the system has no way of aging the accounts. This leads to an A/R with its entire balances sitting in the "current" category.

The practice's A/R consists of the following payer types, broken down by patient and insurance balances in Exhibit 11.21.

Exhibit 11.21
Accounts Receivable Payer Mix

HMO/PPO	1.54%
Self-Pay & Private Portion	51.64%
MC/MD	46.08%
Workers' Compensation	0.74%

The figures above support the previous findings pertaining to Medicare and self-pay payers being the main reason for a large A/R. Collection calls or letters not being made or used will only allow these percentages to stay stagnant. The self-pay and private portion consists of accounts that may have been a different payer's responsibility at one time but now have been transferred to the patients as their own liability. This explains how it is possible to have such a small percentage of private payers in the mix but a large portion of that same payer making up the A/R.

RECOMMENDATION: Monitor the accounts receivable aging report on a monthly basis and identify areas that need additional collection efforts. Currently, this area is the 90+ category. It is important to focus much of the efforts on this category, but it is equally important to get statements out on unbilled patients and begin collecting on the new accounts before they end up in the 90+ category as well. The purging of the old A/R and making collection calls, along with issuing "10 day letters," will heavily impact the entire A/R.

FINDING: Over 40 percent of the old system's balance is comprised of patient balances under $200 which are over 90 days old.

DISCUSSION: The practice should be able to collect patient balances under $200 by simply contacting the patient. Some patients will tend to disregard monthly statements. Issuing a "10 day letter" or contacting the patient by telephone will increase the chances of collecting from these patients.

The front desk is attempting to collect the patient's outstanding balance as the patient checks out. However, the practice cannot rely on the front desk as their only effort to collect from the patient outside of mailing monthly statements.

RECOMMENDATION: The practice should make collection calls to patients each month with each call being documented. Another way of flagging a patient that has a balance due is to note it on the superbill. When the superbill is developed, a box should be placed in a corner that notes the balance on that patient's account. This will assure that the patient is reminded by the staff of their balance due prior to the services being rendered.

Analysis of Billing and Collection Operations

FINDING: The front desk does not routinely ask every patient if their address or insurance has changed since the last visit.

DISCUSSION: To ensure proper insurance filing and to maximize collections, it is very important the practice have current patient information in the computer. If the patient's insurance has changed since the last visit, payment will be delayed while the claim is filed to the old insurance company and then has to be refiled when the claim is denied. If the patient's address has changed since the last visit, the practice will not be able to notify the patient when there is an outstanding balance due from them. As a result, payment is again delayed.

RECOMMENDATION: The practice should confirm each patient's address and insurance information each visit. A sign should be posted in the waiting room stating patients should inform the front desk if their insurance has changed since their last visit.

FINDING: It does not appear the office policy is to follow up on unpaid insurance claim forms when they are older than 25 days. An established unpaid insurance claim collection policy could not be detected in the office.

DISCUSSION: All unpaid insurance claim forms must be followed up within 25 days of submission to the payer. This procedure is performed at this time for two specific reasons: (1) To identify potential claims have not reached the insurance carrier, and (2) To identify problems the insurance company may have with the way the insurance claim forms were completed.

RECOMMENDATION: When an insurance claim form is filed, the office copy should be placed in an alphabetized, expandable folder, which is now not being done. Each week, the file should be reviewed for any claim that is older than 25 days. Once identified, the insurance company should be telephoned and the following *documented*: (a) Name of the person spoken to, (b) The reason the claim has not yet been paid, and (c) When payment can be expected. At this time the staff should refile or submit any additional documentation needed to get the claim paid. Since it would be difficult to document all of this information in the computer, I suggest using the attached follow-up form for each phone call. After preparation, attach it to the claim form and refile in the alphabetized folder. Each week, these forms should be reviewed to assess the follow up efforts of the staff.

FINDING: The clinic does not utilize a superbill.

DISCUSSION: The physician uses the patient chart to document all information regarding the visit and this data (i.e., the chart), is then forwarded to the cashier who in turn codes out the visit. This system of coding without a superbill will lead to possible missed charges and a high potential for miscoding.

RECOMMENDATION: The practice should create and begin utilizing a superbill immediately. This will improve the coding habits of the physician and may eventually reflect an increase in charges since the office visits will be more accurately tracked, which will ultimately increase collections. We can help develop a customized superbill that will make the coding process more efficient for the practice and the physician.

FINDING: The office visits are all coded identically with a 99213 unless otherwise instructed by the doctor.

DISCUSSION: Coding is a clinical decision and should be made based upon the criteria set forth by the American Medical Association's *Physician's Current Procedural Terminology* manual. Medicare, and some private payers, will compare a physician's coding for office visits with national norms. If it appears the physician has a tendency to code services above the national norms, they may conduct an audit to determine if the documentation in the chart justifies the code. The current coding practice used by the physicians reflects that the same things are being done for each patient.

If for some reason the physician did not meet the criteria to justify that code, the practice would be liable to repay the overpayment to the insurance company. As penalties, Medicare can request up to three times the amount in repayment. In addition, it is authorized to impose criminal and civil penalties against a person or entity making false or improper claims to government programs, with fines up to $2,000 per occurrence.

Exhibit 11.22
Utilization of Office Visit Codes

Description	CPT Code Used	% Utilized
Office Visit - New Patient	99202	97.97%
Office Visit - Established Visit	99213	98.65%

Exhibit 11.22 illustrates the overutilization of codes for established and new patients. The reason for these high utilization numbers may be due to the cashier being responsible for coding instead of the provider. Each office visit, new and established, has five different levels of service. It is the clinic's responsibility to support with documentation, the level of service provided.

RECOMMENDATION: In addition to developing a superbill, as discussed above, the physicians should review all coding criteria pertaining to office visits and be certain their coding decisions or the decisions of their staff are appropriate and well supported by their documentation in the chart.

FINDING: The physicians do not utilize a hospital charge ticket.

DISCUSSION: When a patient is admitted the clinic receives a "notice of admission," and the clinic then charges an admission code or 99223 to the patient. Every day following admission a 99232 is charged unless the physician instructs the cashier that he did not see that patient. The discharge code (99238) appears to be charged correctly.

This method may not capture all potential revenues. Initial hospital care has three different levels of service. It is the physician's responsibility to select the proper level based upon the actual services rendered. Subsequent hospital visits also have three different levels of codes that should be selected based upon the actual services rendered.

RECOMMENDATION: Begin utilizing a Hospital Charge Card to record hospital services and report them to the billing staff. The card allows the physician to indicate different levels of admission, daily visits, and discharges. It is also important to support all coding with proper documentation in the chart.

FINDING: The clinic is assuming that the physician visited the hospital every day the patient was admitted to the hospital. Therefore, the clinic is billing CPT code 99232, subsequent care, for every day after the initial day the patient is in the hospital.

DISCUSSION: The American Medical Association has defined explicit criteria for coding of hospital visits. These criteria are as follows:

99221

- Detailed or comprehensive history

- Detailed or comprehensive examination

- Medical decision making that is straightforward or of low complexity

99222

- Comprehensive history

- Comprehensive examination

- Medical decision making of moderate complexity

99223

- Comprehensive history

- Comprehensive examination

- Medical decision making of high complexity

The following are the criteria that must be met for each of the levels of subsequent hospital care. Each visit must meet two of the three criteria:

99231

- Problem focused interval history

- Problem focused examination

- Medical decision making that is straightforward or of low complexity

99232

- Expanded problem focused interval history

- Expanded problem focused examination

- Medical decision making of moderate complexity

99233

- Detailed interval history

- Detailed examination

- Medical decision making of high complexity.

Hospital discharges are coded based upon the time spent managing the patient on the discharge day. If the total time is 30 minutes or less, the discharge is 99238. If the total time is more than 30 minutes, the discharge is a 99239.

RECOMMENDATION: This is another reason to follow the recommendation above and begin using Hospital Charge Cards for billing hospital services.

FINDING: The practice files claims electronically for Medicare, Medicaid, and Blue Cross Blue Shield. All other carriers are filed using paper claims.

DISCUSSION: The practice can save time and improve accuracy by using a clearinghouse to file all claims electronically. Clearinghouses provide "edit checks" as part of their services. An "edit check" will electronically verify all required fields of the claim are completed and check for invalid information in certain fields. If the clearinghouse finds any potential errors, the claim will be sent back to the practice to edit before it is actually filed. Thereby, recognizing the error and correcting it without waiting 30 days to receive a denial EOB in the mail, which will need to be appealed.

With the addition of the clearinghouse, time will be available to spend more time on the collection of the accounts receivable instead of perforating and mailing paper claims.

RECOMMENDATION: Obtain bids from various clearinghouses and select a service to use for filing all claims that are not Medicare, Medicaid, or

Blue Cross Blue Shield. During the assessment, Mrs. Hinckley did comment that with the new AMOS system they will be filing more claims electronically.

FINDING: The practice does not use a collection agency.

DISCUSSION: To complete the collection cycle, the practice should have a means to actually send accounts to a collection agency. Without this final step, the collection efforts may be pointless. Eventually, the patients will disregard the collection letters just as they have disregarded patient statements.

RECOMMENDATION: We recommend turning over accounts to a collection agency once they have exceeded the 90th day without any payment agreement or terms being reached. Obtain bids from collection agencies and select an agency for the practice to use. CSC in Houston is used by several practices as their collection agency. This option may be a more effective way to collect from the private pay accounts that are already over six months old.

FINDING: The practice does not currently have an operational policy and procedure manual.

DISCUSSION: The purpose of an operational policy and procedures manual is to standardize and communicate the office policies, jobs, and responsibilities. Once a sound policy and procedures manual is in place, employees will be aware of their job responsibilities and the methods to accomplish them. At that point, any future practice management problem can be traced to a specific personnel issue, and not necessarily to a systems issue.

An operational practice policy and procedure manual should at a minimum address the following areas:

- Handling telephone calls

- Check-in procedures

- Patient reception

- Flowchart of a patient visit

- Prescription policy

- Check-out procedures

- Payment postings

- Receivable management

- Closing out the day

- Closing out the month

RECOMMENDATION: Develop and implement a comprehensive policy and procedure manual for the clinic. Have all employees read and acknowledge receipt of the manual. Our firm is able to assist you in developing this manual.

INSURANCE CLAIMS FILING

FINDING: For the period June 16 to September 30, 1996, new and established office visits were billed in comparison to the National Distribution Average for family practice physicians as shown in Exhibit 11.23.

DISCUSSION: National Distribution Averages are used as a benchmark for providers to identify trends in over and under utilization of evaluation and management codes. It is important to remember that coding is based upon defined criteria and physicians, clinicians, and billing personnel should be familiar with these criteria.

The above analysis shows the practice primarily uses CPT codes 99202 and 99213 for its office visits. The practice appears to be locking itself in to using code 99202 for its established patient visits. This could trigger an audit at some point in time if the chart documentation does not support this code. Also, payers may be downcoding this service if there is a conflict with the related diagnosis code that was billed. Overuse of code 99213 may trigger an audit, fines, and penalties if the documentation in the medical chart does not support the higher level of service.

The effects that this type of coding may impact upon the practice financially are significant. This type of coding reflects the same level of service is performed on each patient. This chart indicates possible overbilling to established patients and underbilling of new patients. It may also be perceived that the majority of established patients are more ill than new patients consistently.

RECOMMENDATION: As recommended earlier, a superbill should be utilized. A meeting between the physicians and the staff members who are

Exhibit 11.23
Office Visits, New and Established National Distribution Comparison

CPT Code	Frequency	% of New Office Visits	% of All Office Visits	National Distribution Averages	% of All E&M Codes
99201	2	0.51	0.06	8.86	0
99202	387	97.97	12.30	31.09	10.00
99203	5	1.27	0.17	34.19	6.82
99204	1	0.25	0.03	16.86	2.19
99205	0	0	0	9.00	0.21

CPT Code	Frequency	% of New Established Office Visits	% of All Office Visits	National Distribution Averages	% of All E&M Codes
99211	5	0.18	.17	4.06	3.44
99212	14	0.51	0.45	22.24	2.5
99213	2,713	98.62	86.24	57.45	68.07
99214	15	0.55	0.48	13.29	4.95
99215	3	0.11	0.10	2.96	0

responsible for coding should take place to review criteria for common codes being utilized and what codes are appropriate for different diagnoses.

FINDING: For year-to-date 1996, the practice coded almost all initial hospital care as CPT code 99223.

DISCUSSION: This utilization pattern is consistent with the practice's procedures of using the front desk "coding system" described in the "Analysis of Billing and Collection Operations" section of this report. As described above, initial hospital care has three different levels of services from which to select your CPT code. The practice needs to make sure they are billing for the same level of service they are actually providing.

The current use of the highest level of admittance and following up with a moderate subsequent level is not consistent.

RECOMMENDATION: As mentioned previously, the practice should begin using Hospital Charge Cards to capture all charges at the point of service.

FINDING: For the same period of June 16 to September 30, 1996, subsequent hospital care was coded as in Exhibit 11.24 compared to the National Distribution Average for family practice physicians:

DISCUSSION: This utilization pattern is consistent with the practice's procedures of using the front desk "coding system" described in the "Analysis of Billing and Collection Operations" section of this report. National Distribution Averages are used as a benchmark for providers to identify trends in over and under utilization of evaluation and management codes. It is important to remember that coding is based upon defined criteria and physicians, clinicians, and billing personnel should be familiar with these criteria.

RECOMMENDATION: Review the definitions for subsequent hospital care in the same manner described in the previous recommendation for reviewing new and established patient office visits.

FINDING: The office may not be billing out office visits related to starred surgical procedures.

DISCUSSION: Under the CPT coding system, a physician can bill an office visit along with a starred surgical procedure if the visit is a separate, identifiable service. We were not able to identify, according to the clinic's CPT frequency reports, a significant amount of starred procedures and how often they were billed or determine if the related office visits were billed out when they could have been.

Exhibit 11.24
Hospital Visits National Distribution Comparison

CPT Code	Frequency	% of Established Hospital Visits	National Distribution Averages	% of All E&M Codes
99231	103	15.06	41.44	1.15
99232	581	84.94	46.92	0.16
99233	0	0	11.64	0.16

CPT code 99025 did not show up on the frequency report either. This code can be billed out with a starred surgical procedure if the patient is a new patient and the actual visit is not a separately identifiable service.

RECOMMENDATION: The office staff and providers should be educated on the coding definitions for when it is appropriate to bill an office visit with a starred procedure and when to use CPT Code 99025. By educating all persons involved with coding and billing, you can ensure these services will not be missed in the future. CPT Code 99025 should be included when developing the superbill. If necessary, somehow highlight starred procedures on the superbill.

Fee Analysis

FINDING: Fees for this sample of evaluation and management codes are below the norm according to our experience in the Mason/Port Arthur area.

DISCUSSION: As described above, since the practice's fees are below the norm, a fee increase is indicated. However, an increase in office visit fees to the standard will not be effective unless fully utilized by the clinic and followed for each patient. Current fees are being adjusted frequently to accommodate established patients. Therefore, we would recommend increasing new patient visits, hospital visits, and consultations to the current standard and only increasing established patient office visit fees between roughly $5 to $10. This method would allow the practice to increase fees without upsetting the current patients. However, the practice should continue to increase established patient office visit fees in small amounts over the next two years until these fees are closer to the industry average.

RECOMMENDATION: The evaluation and management fees in Exhibit 11.25 should be increased.

REVENUE IMPACT: If the above fees were increased, practice charges would be increased by $23,480 with approximately $4,700 realized in collections with a 20 percent impact to the practice.

FINDING: Fees related to surgical procedures require adjustment.

DISCUSSION: We analyzed the practice fee schedule, in particular the fees of the clinic's most common codes. Based upon review of EOBs and

Exhibit 11.25
Evaluation and Management Codes Fee Recommendation

CPT	Current Fee	Recommended Fee
99211	20.14	25.00
99212	36.04	40.00
99213	51.41	60.00
99214	79.50	85.00
99215	125.61	130.00

our experience in other family practices in similar locales, it appears the practice could adjust upward certain fees. However, keep in mind any fee adjustment should be tempered against public perception. This is particularly important for primary care practices. The office does not want to price itself outside competing family practices in the area.

RECOMMENDATION: Exhibit 11.26 shows recommended fee adjustments for the practice's most commonly utilized surgical procedures; We also recommend a complete review of the entire fee schedule to identify potential fee increases for other services.

REVENUE IMPACT: Based upon the suggested fee revisions, practice revenues would increase $8,136 for the services listed above. Assuming 20 percent of the practice is impacted by these changes, the practice would expect to receive an additional $1,627 in collections.

Overhead Analysis

FINDING: Overhead for the nine months ending June 30, 1996 is 63.97 percent of total collections.

DISCUSSION: The Society of Medical-Dental Management Consultants (SMD) publishes a survey of national averages for practices from all specialties. The national average for family practice is 58.3 percent overhead. Therefore, your practice's overhead is slightly higher than the national averages. Overhead is presented as a percentage of practice collections. Since practice collections are lagging, the overhead appears high.

RECOMMENDATION: Implement all collection-related recommendations contained throughout this report.

Exhibit 11.26
Surgical Procedures Fee Recommendation

CPT Code	Current Fee	Recommended Fee	Difference	Frequency Annualized	Impact
10060	35.00	70.00	35.00	16	560.00
10120	50.00	115.00	65.00	8	520.00
11400	77.00	150.00	73.00	4	292.00
11402	121.00	150.00	29.00	12	348.00
11406	136.00	240.00	104.00	16	1,664.00
11750	180.00	285.00	105.00	24	2,520.00
12002	60.00	125.00	65.00	16	1,040.00
16010	22.00	100.00	78.00	4	312.00
17110	20.00	70.00	50.00	12	600.00
16020	30.00	75.00	45.00	4	180.00
69210	20.00	25.00	5.00	20	100.00

FINDING: An analysis of the full-time equivalent (FTE) employees indicates the practice has eight FTE employees (or four per physician).

DISCUSSION: Per the SMD surveys for family practices, the average FTE employees is 3.75 per physician (or 7.5 FTE for the entire practice). Although your practice's FTE's are in line with the norm, it should be possible to utilize the extra half of an employee to perform extra collection efforts.

Based upon all of the findings in the "Analysis of Billing and Collection Operations" section of this report, the practice needs to assign collection duties to one of the staff. The collectors would be responsible for making the phone calls to follow-up on outstanding insurance claims, mailing patient statements, calling on past due patient balances, and all other collection activities. Then, the practice will have adequate billing and collection staff to implement the recommendations necessary to improve the practice's billing and collections.

It is our recommendation that Mrs. Hinckley perform these collection duties. Mrs. Hinckley has experience in collecting, having done it for this practice previously.

RECOMMENDATION: The practice should assign collection duties to Mrs. Hinckley. In the future it is our understanding that Mrs. Hinckley will be leaving the clinic. Prior to her departure, the clinic should seek a qualified collector to take her place.

Explanation of Benefits Review

FINDING: The average EOB turnaround for the clinic is 30.8 days after the date of service.

DISCUSSION: The EOB payment turnaround measures the length of time between the date of service and the actual insurance payment. The benchmark for any practice is to get paid by insurance companies on average 30 to 45 days from the date of service. The practice falls within this range.

RECOMMENDATION: None

FINDING: A review of a sample of EOBs identified the following error messages:

- Our records indicate this client is enrolled with Medicaid; Please bill Medicaid first.
- Client is covered by other insurance which must be billed prior to this program.
- This client is eligible for deductible and/or coinsurance payments for Medicare covered services only.
- These charges were incurred after the patient's cancellation date with the Texas Plan.
- This charge is not covered by the subscriber's benefit plan.
- Your claim lacks information which is needed for adjudication.
- Incomplete/invalid patient's diagnosis (es) and condition (s).
- Your claim contains incomplete and/or invalid information, and no appeal rights are afforded because the claim is unprocessable.

DISCUSSION: This is further evidence that insurance verification is not being performed. Most messages indicate that the staff may not be getting current insurance information from the patients. This is also evidence that claims are being sent out with improper or incomplete information.

RECOMMENDATION: Carefully examine all claims before they are sent out to minimize errors and the subsequent denials. Since EOBs are already kept in notebooks by payer, it should be easy to review them monthly to ensure the following:

- Claims are paid on average within 30 to 45 days.
- Denials are appealed immediately.
- Identify all specific billing problems with specific payers.
- Determine which services are approved 100 percent for payment.
- Evaluate billing effectiveness of current personnel.

OSHA and CLIA Compliance

FINDING: We did not evaluate whether or not the practice is currently in compliance with OSHA regulations.

DISCUSSION: Make sure your office is in compliance with the worker safety regulations that are part of OSHA. Many offices concentrate solely on the bloodborne compliance portion of OSHA.

RECOMMENDATION: To make sure your office is in compliance with OSHA guidelines, contact your local office to have a voluntary audit conducted. There are no penalties associated with this audit; it is informational only.

Appendix A

ANALYSIS OF SMALL RECEIVABLE BALANCES
Practice Name: _____
Worksheet Preparation Date: _____

Accounts receivable balance as of _____	$
Total of balances that are $200 or less (small balances)	$
% of small balances to total accounts receivable	%

Appendix B

PATIENT DEMOGRAPHICS SHEET
PLEASE PRINT ✐   Date: _____

Name: _____ Date of birth: ____/____/____
         (Last)   (First)   (Middle)   (Month) (Day) (Year)

Address: _____Age_____
         (Street Number & Name)   (City)   (State)   (Zip)

Phone (_____) _____-_____Marital status: ☐ Married ☐ Single ☐ Divorced

Patient's employer: _____Work phone (_____) _____-_____

Spouse's name: _____

Spouse's employer: _____Work phone (_____) _____-_____

Person responsible for bill (if other than above) _____Relationship to patient _____

Address: _____Phone (_____) _____-_____
         (Street Number & Name)   (City)   (State)   (Zip)

Nearest relative (Not living with patient) _____Relationship to patient _____

Address: _____Phone (_____) _____-_____
         (Street Number & Name)   (City)   (State)   (Zip)

Were you referred by another physician? If so, whom? _____ Phone (_____) _____

Address: _____
         (Street Number & Name)   (City)   (State)   (Zip)

Primary Insurance Company (#1)

Insurance name: _____

Member name: _____

Employer: _____

Address for mailing claims: _____
                           (Street Number & Name)   (City)   (State)   (Zip)

Policy #, Certificate #, or ID #: _____ Group #: _____ Phone: (_____) _____-_____

Reason for visit: _____Last menstrual period ____/____/____

AUTHORIZATION TO RELEASE INFORMATION AND TO PAY BENEFITS
I hereby authorize any physician who has treated or attended me or my dependent to furnish any medical information requested. In consideration of services rendered, I hereby transfer and assign to David Berry, M.D., who has treated me or my dependent, any benefits of insurance that I may have. A photocopy of this authorization shall be considered as effective and valid as the original.

Patient's Social Security #: ____/____/_____   Spouse's Social Security # ____/____/_____

Drivers License #: _____(State) _____   Medicare #: _____

Signature: _____   Medicaid #: _____

Please check insurance type   ☐ STANDARD   ☐ HMO   ☐ PPO   ☐ MEDICAID   ☐ OTHER

Appendix C

TODAY'S DATE _____
INITIAL'S _____

<u>INSURANCE PRECERTIFICATION INFORMATION</u>

<u>PATIENT INFO</u>

NAME _____   ADDRESS _____
PHONE _____   _____
DOB _____   _____
SS # _____   _____

NEAREST RELATIVE NOT LIVING WITH PATIENT (NAME) _____
RELATION _____
ADDRESS _____
PHONE _____

EMPLOYER _____   INSURANCE _____
ADDRESS _____   ADDRESS _____
_____   _____

PHONE _____ CONTACT _____   PHONE _____ CONTACT ____
REF. PHYSICIAN _____   GROUP # _____
SYMPTOMS _____   POLICY _____
_____   PRE-CERT # _____
_____   CONTACT (s) _____
TYPE SURGERY _____   COVERAGE _____
_____   _____
_____   OTHER NOTES: _____

PROPOSED DATE OF SURG. _____   _____
PHYSICIAN _____   _____

_____
_____
_____
_____
_____
_____
_____
_____
_____
_____
_____

Appendix D

ANALYSIS OF PHYSICIAN REFERRAL PATTERNS
Practice Name: _____
Worksheet Preparation Date: _____

Referring Doctor/Source	Referrals Current Year	Referrals Last Year	Referrals for Year ___	Reason for Decline in Referrals

Appendix E

MARION HILLS MEDICAL CLINIC RICHARD L. ROSS, MD 967 Medical Drive, Marion Hills, MS 32095 (228) 394-2905 Tax ID# 73-0195863	Patient Name		DATE
			ENCOUNTER FORM NO.
	Acct #	Pt's DOB	Appointment Time
	Address		**Previous Balance**
Referring Doctor	City, State, Zip		**Today's Charge**
Primary Insurance	Phone #		**Today's Payment**
Secondary Insurance	Payment:___Cash ___Credit Card		**New Balance**
RETURN APPOINTMENT:	Check No.		

	OFFICE VISIT				LABORATORY				INJECTIONS		
X	**NEW PATIENT**	**CODE**	**AMT**	**X**	**DESCRIPTION**	**CODE**	**AMT**	**X**	**DESCRIPTION**	**CODE**	**AMT**
	Focused / Straightforward	99201			CBC, Partial diff	85024			Allergy Injection	95115	
	Expanded / Straightforward	99202			Cholesterol	82465			Bicillin 1.2ml	J0540	
	Detailed / Low Complexity	99203			CULTURE, Throat	87060			Celestone	J0702	
	Comprehensive / Moderate Comp	99204			CULTURE, Urine	87088			Decadron 4mg/ml	J1100	
	Comprehensive / High Complexity	99205			Glucose, strip	82948			Decadron LA	J1095	
	Initial OV for * Procedure	99025			H. Pylori Kit	87082			DepoMedrol 40mg	J1030	
X	**ESTABLISHED**	**CODE**	**AMT**		Hemoccult	82270					
	Minimal / May not require physicia	99211			Mono Spot Test	86310			Phenergan 50mg	J2550	
	Focused / Straightforward	99212			PPD, TB	86585			Rocephin 250mg	J0696	
	Expanded / Low Complexity	99213			Pregnancy, serum	84702					
	Detailed / Moderate Complexity	99214			Specimen transfer	99000			Tetanus Toxoid	90703	
	Comprehensive / High Complexity	99215			Strep ID	83518			Toradol 15mg	J1885	
X	**PREVENTIVE OFFICE VISIT**	**CODE**	**AMT**		UA Pregnancy	81025			Vitamin B-12	J3420	
	New Patient/12-17 years	99384			Urinalysis, w/o microsc	81003			OTHER:		
	New Patient/18-39 years	99385			Venipuncture	36415					
	New Patient/40-64 years	99386			OTHER:						
	Est Patient/12-17 years	99394								**X-RAYS**		
	Est Patient/18-39 years	99395						**X**	**DESCRIPTION**	**CODE**	**AMT**
	Est Patient/40-64 years	99396							Ankle	73600	
									Chest 1-view	71010	
					SUPPLIES				Chest 2-views	71020	
	OFFICE PROCEDURES			**X**	**DESCRIPTIONS**	**CODE**	**AMT**				
X	**DESCRIPTION**	**CODE**	**AMT**		Ace S M L	A4460			Elbow 2-views	73070	
	Biopsy Skin (Cytology)	11100			Crutches	EO112			Femur 2-views	73550	
	Cryotherapy, Warts	17340*			Dressing S M L				Fingers 2-views	73140	
	Ear Irrigation	69210			Eye Tray/Patch				Foot 2-views	73620	
	EKG, Complete	93000			Knee Imobilizer	L2999			Forearm 2-views	73090	
	Excision Lesion/Site (Size)	113_*			Rib Belt	A4572			Hand 2-views	73120	
	I & D Abscess, simple	10060			Sling	A4565			Humerus 2-views	73060	
	Removal Foreign Body, eye	65220*			Splint	A4570			Knee 2-views	73560	
	Simple Repair, Superficial	12002*			Steri Strip	A4454			Ribs 2-views	71100	
	OTHER:				Surgical Tray	A4550			Spine, CX, 2 views	72040	
					Tennis Elbow Sleeve	L6100			Spine, LS, 2 views	72100	
					OTHER:				OTHER:		

	DIAGNOSES			DIAGNOSES			DIAGNOSES	
X	**DESCRIPTION**	**CODE**		**DESCRIPTION**	**CODE**		**DESCRIPTION**	**CODE**
	Abdominal Pain, Unsp.	789.0_		Edema, unspecified cause	782.3		Upper Respiratory Infection	465.9
	Adenitis, cervical	289.3		Esophageal Reflux	530.81		Urinary Tract Infection	599.0
	Allergic Reaction	995.2		Fatigue	780.7		Urethritis	597.80
	Allergy	995.3		Foreign Body, Eye	930._		Vaginitis	616.10
	Amenorrhea	256.8		Gastritis	535.5		Venereal Disease	099.9
	Anemia, Iron Deficiency	280.9		Headache	784.0		Vertigo	780.4
	Angina, unstable	411.1		Hernia, Hiatal	553.3		Wart, common	078.10
	Anxiety	300.00		Herpes, Simplex	054.9		OTHER:	
	Arthritis,_____			Hypercholesterolemia	272.0			
	Asthma, unspecified_	493.9_		Hypertension	401.1			
	Bleeding, rectal	569.3		Lower back pain	724.2			
	Bronchitis, acute	466.0		Influenza with resp manifest	487.1			
	Bursitis, unspecified	727.3						
	Cellulitis, leg	682.6		Menopause Syndrome	627.2			
	Chest pain, unspecified	786.59		Migraine	346.9_			
	Cholelithiasis	574.1_		Nausea and Vomiting	787.01			
	Congestive heart failure	428.0		Otitis Media	382.9			
	Conjunctivitis	372.03		Pap Smear	V72.3			
	Constipation	564.0		Pelvic Inflammatory Dis--P.I.D.	614._			
	Contact Dermatitis, unspecified cause	692.9		Pharyngitis	462			
	Cyst, Sebaceous	706.2		Phlebitis, unspecified site	451.9			
	Cystitis, unspecified	595.9		Physical Exam, General	V70.0			
	Dehydration	276.5		Pneumonia	486			
	Depression, major	296.30		Prostatitis	601.9		Outpatient Tests:	
	Diabetes Mellitus, Insulin Dep	250.01		Sinusitis, maxillary	473.0			
	Diabetes Mellitus, Non-Insulin Dep	250.00					Referrals:	
	Diarrhea	787.91		Strep Throat	034.0			
	Dysfunctional/func uterine hemorrhage	626.8		Stye	373.11		Remarks:	
	Dyspepsia	536.8		Tendonitis	726.90			
	Eczema	692.9		Tonsilitis	474.0			

Appendix F

FRONT DESK COLLECTION ANALYSIS WORKSHEET
Practice Name: _____
Worksheet Preparation Date: _____

Date	Patient Name	Type of Insurance	Office Charge	Amount Collected

Total visits per worksheet _____
Total visits where collection occurred _____
Percent of visits collected _____%

Appendix G

INSURANCE FILING WORKSHEET

Type of Service: __Inpatient __Office __ Surgical __ Other _____

Practice Name: _____

Worksheet Preparation Date: _____

Patient Last Name	Type of Insurance	Date Claim Prepared	Date of Last Service	Number of Days

Total number of days _____
Total number of claims _____
Average time to file a claim form _____

Appendix H

✓	CODE	DIAGNOSIS (cont.)
	6584	Infection of Amniotic Cavity
	65623	Isoimmunization, Oth. Bld. Grp. Incompat.
	65613	Isoimmunization, Rhesus
	65113	Multiple Gestation, Triplets
	65103	Multiple Gestation, Twins
		Multiple Gestation, Unspecified
	6._._	Obstetrical Pulmonary Embolism
	6580_	Oligohydramnios
	V288	Other Specified Antenatal Screening
	67133	Phlebothrombosis, Deep, Antepartum
	64103	Placenta Previa, without Hemorrhage
	64113	Placenta Previa, with Hemorrhage
	64243	Pre-eclampsia, Mild
	64253	Pre-eclampsia, Severe (HELLP)
	64273	Pre-eclampsia, Superimposed
	64421	Premature Delivery
	64403	Premature Labor, Threatened
	6581	Premature Rupture of Membranes
	6542_	Previous Cesarean Section
	V234	Previous Poor Obstetric History
	64503	Prolonged Pregnancy
	6582	Prolonged Rupture of Membranes
	67002	Puerperal Infection, Major
	4633	Recurrent Pregnancy Loss
	64623	Renal Disease without Hypertension
	V	Elevated MSAFP
		Supervision of Normal Pregnancy
	65553	Suspected Damage to Fetus from Drugs
	65533	Suspected Damage to Fetus from Viral Dis.
	7100	Systemic Lupus Erythematosus
	64813	Thyroid Dysfunction
	65233	Transverse or Oblique Presentation

Patient Name: _____ Patient No.: _____

Physician: _____ Date: _____

HOSPITAL VISIT & CONSULTATION									
	✓	CONSULT	✓	FOLLOW UP	✓	ADMISSION	✓	ROUNDS	✓	OBSERV.
Level I		99251		99261		99221		99231		
Level II		99252		99262		99222		99232		
Level III		99253		99263		99223		99233		99218
Level IV		99254								99219
Level V		99255								99220
					✓	DISCHARGE				
						99238				
ADMISSION DATE				ROUNDS DATE				DISCHARGE DATE		

Appendix I

UVALDE
BONE & JOINT
CLINIC, P.A.

Gloria G. Box, M.D.
1025 Garner Field Road
P.O. Drawer 1340
Uvalde, TX 78802
Phone: 210/278-2292
Fax: 210-278-1409

S 419
SURGERY FEE SLIP

☐ Gloria G Box, M.D.
☐ _____

Patient's Name _____

Date of Service _____ Diagnosis No. _____

Surgery Assistant _____

☐ Place of Service: _____
_____
_____

☐ Right ☐ Left

CODE	TREATMENT	FEE	CODE	TREATMENT	FEE	CODE	TREATMENT	FEE	CODE	TREATMENT	FEE	CODE	TREATMENT	FEE
	GENERAL			**SPINE** (cont'd)			**FOREARM-WRIST** (cont'd)			**PELVIS-HIP JOINT** (cont'd)			**TIB/FIB-ANKLE** (cont'd)	
20000	Incision Abscess		63035	Add Lami Level		25240	Darrach Procedu		27176	SCFE in situ pin		27696	Rpr Both Coll Ligam	
20005	Deep/Com		63042	Laminotomy/Re-Do		25260	Rpr Flexor Each		27177	SCFE ORIF		27698	Sec Rpr Rup Ligament	
20200	Biopsy Muscle		63047	Laminectomy/Decom		25270	Rpr Extensor Ea		27187	Prophyla Tr Fem		27705	Osteotomy Tibia	
20205	Deep		63048	Add Lami Level		25300	Rpr NoUn Rad/Ul		27284	Arthrodesis Hip		27707	Osteotomy Fibula	
20206	Biopsy Mus. Needle			**SHOULDER**		25105	w/graft		27236	Gilberty/FX		27709	Osteotomy Tib/Fib	
20240	Biopsy Bone		23040	Arthrotomy G-H Jt		25310	Rpr NoUn Navicu			**FEMUR KNEE JOINT**		27870	Arthrodesis Ankle	
20245	Deep		23044	Arth A-C, S-C Jt		25400	Arthrodesis, Wr		27310	Arthrotomy Knee		27880	BK Amputation	
	INTRODUCE REMOVAL		23120	Claviculectomy, Pt		25320	Intercarpal Fus		27332	Meniscectomy One		27888	Amputation Syme	
20650	Insert/Skel Tx		23130	Acromioplasty		25900	Amp Forearm		27333	Meniscectomy Both		27889	Ankle Disartic	
20680	Rem of Implant		23160	Sauceriz Clavicle		61719	Ulnar Nerve Wri		27334	Arth Synovectomy		29894	M-A Loose Body	
20690	External Fixation		23182	Sauceriz Scapula		64721	Carpal Tunnel		27340	Exc Prepat Bursa		29895	M-A Synovec-Partial	
			23184	Sauceriz Prox Hum			**HAND-FINGERS**		27345	Exc Baker's Cyst		29897	M-A Debride-Limited	
	I&D ABSCESS HEMATOMA		23410	Rpr Rot Cuff/Acute		26055	Rel Trig Finger		27350	Patellectomy		29898	M-A Debrde-Extensi	
10060	SO Abscess		23412	Chronic		26121	Fasciectomy Pal		27380	Rpt Infrapatel Ten		27892	Fasciotomy-Ant &/or Lat	
10140	SO Hematoma		23415	Rel Cor-Acro Lig		26123	Fasciectomy Fin		27385	Rpt Quad/Ham Rup		27893	Fasciotomy-Post Comp.	
23030	Shoulder, deep		23420	Rep Cuff Avulsion		26125	add finger		27403	Meniscal Repair		27894	Fasciotomy Ant &/or Post	
23930	Upper Arm/Elbow		23430	Tendodesis Bicep		26115	Synovectomy M-P		27405	Repari MCL, LCL			**FOOT**	
25028	Forearm/Wrist		23450	Magnuson/Put Plat		26150	1° Flexor Repair		27418	Maguel Epip Arr		28003	I&D Subfascial	
26011	Finger		23455	Bankart		26356	1° Flex RepNoMan		27425	Lateral Relcase		28005	I&D/Osteomyelitis	
26990	Pelvis/Hips		23462	Bristow		26110	Ext Ten Rep Hand		27427	X-Art Rpr ACL		28008	Fasciotomy	
27301	Thigh/Knee		23470	Near Implant		26418	Ext Ten Rep Fing		27428	inter-art open		28035	Tarsal Tunnel	
27803	Leg/Ankle		23472	Total Shoulder		26132	Mallet Fin Perc		27447	TKA		28060	Fasciectomy Plantar	
28001	Foot		23332	Rom Total Shoulder		26133	Mallet Fin Open		27486	Rev TKA 1 comp		28080	Morton Neuroma	
			23700	Manipulation		26450	Tenotomy FlPalm		27487	Rev TKA all		28090	Exc Ganglion/Cysil	
	FOREIGN BODY-REMOVAL		29819	M-A Loose Body		26455	Tenotomy FlFing		27457	High Tibial Oste		28110	Bunionette	
10120	SO		29820	M-A Synovec-Partial		26460	Tenotomy Extens		27475	Dis Fem Epip Arr		28111	Exc 1st Metatarsal	
20520	Mus/Ten Shoath		29822	M-A Debride-Limited			Hand/Finger		27477	Prox Tib Epip Arr		28112	Exc 2-4th Metatarsal	
20525	deep/com		29823	M-A Debride-Extens		26500	Pulley Repair		27570	Manipulation		28113	Exc 5th Metatarsal	
23330	Shoulder, SQ		29826	M-A Decom/Acromio		26525	Capsulotomy I-P		27590	AK Amputation		28285	Hammertoe	
23331	deep		29821	M-A Synovec - Comp.		26727	Arthroplasty C-M		27598	Disartic Knee		28288	Ostectomy	
24200	Up Arm/Elb, SQ		29825	M-A Debride-w-w/n Man		26530	Arthroplasty M-P		29874	M-A Loose Body		28290	Silver Procedure	
24201	deep					26531	w/implant		29875	M-A Synovec-Limit		28292	Keller Prcedure	
26070	C-M Jt			**HUMERUS-ELBOW**		26535	Arthroplasty 11-P		29876	M-A Synovec-Major		28293	w/implant	
27086	Pel/Hip, SQ		24000	Arthrotomy/Drainage		26536	w/implant		29877	M-A Debrid/Shaving		28294	w/tendon transfer	
27087	deep		24101	Arthrotomy Loose Bod		26540	Col Lig Rpt M-P		29879	M-A Abras Arthropl		28296	1st Metatarsal Osteotomy	
27372	Th/Knee, Deep		24105	Exc Olecranon Bursa		26565	Osteotomy Metaca		29880	M-A Menisc Both		28299	Double Osteotomy	
28190	Foot, Sq		24130	Exc Radial Head		26567	Osteotomy Phal		29881	M-A Menisc One		28715	Triple Arthrodesis	
28192	deep		24342	Reinsert Bicep Ton		26820	Fusion Thumb		29882	M-A Men Repair One		28725	Subtalar Arthrodesis	
			24351	Tennis Elbow Relea		26841	Fusion C-M Thumb		29883	M-A Men Rapir Both		28750	Fusion Gr Toe M-P	
	SKIN DEBRIDEMENT		24356	w/ostectomy		26843	Fusion Q-M Other		29888	M-A ACL Repair		28755	Fusion Gr Toe 1-P	
11040	Partial Thickness		24400	Osteotomy, Humerus		26850	Fusion M-P		29889	M-A PCL Repair		28810	Amp Metatarsal	
11041	Full Thickness		29534	M-A Loose Body		26860	Fusion L-P		29850	Knee FX-w-w/o Man		28820	Amp M-P	
11042	Skin & SQ		29835	M-A Synovec-Partial		26861	Amp Fin/Thumb		29851	KneeFX-w-w/o I or E Fix		28825	Amp 1-P	
11043	Skin, SQ, Muscle		29837	M-A Debride-Limited					29855	Tib FX-w-w/o I or E Fix				
11044	Skin, SQ, Musc, Bone		29838	M-A Debride-Extens			**PELVIS-HIP JOINT**		29856	CondyleFX-w-w/o I or E				
			64718	Ulnar Nerve Transfer		27031	Tenotomy Adduc							
	SPINE					27030	Arthrotomy/Sep.			**TIB/FIB-ANKLE**				
22625	Fusion-Lumbar			**FOREARM-WRIST**		27030	Coecygectomy		27600	Decom Fasciotomy Ant				
22520	Harvest Bone Gr.		25000	Release DeQuervens		27130	THA		27601	Posterior Compart				
22840	Harrington Rod		25101	Arthrotomy Wrist		27132	THA Conversion		27602	Both Compartments				
22842	Segmental Fixation		25111	Exc Ganglion		27134	Revision THA		27610	Arthr Ankle/Sepsis				
22852	Rem Post Seg Inst.		25115	Synovec Rheuma		27137	Acetabulum Only		27620	Arthr Ank/Loose Body				
62292	Chemonucleolysis		25118	Synovectomy, Wri		27138	Femoral Only		27650	Repair Achilles				
63010	Gill Type Opera								27652	w/graft		**PAYMENT** _____		
63030	Laminotomy/l-1								27695	1 Rpr Rup Ligament		**TYPE** _____		

NOTES/COMMENTS

Appendix J

INSURANCE CLAIM FORM FOLLOW-UP INFORMATION

Patients Name:_____Date of call:_____

Account number:_____

Insurance company:_____Phone #:_____

Spoke with:_____Fax #:_____
      (get first and last name)

1)   Status on claim for date of service;_____

2)   Was claim received:_____
     a. if NO-always check to see if claim was mailed to correct address.
     b. if address is incorrect---MAKE SURE YOU CORRECT THE COMPUTER!!

3)   Claim being processed:_____

4)   When will payment be mailed:_____Amount:_____

5)   Was claim denied: yes_____ no_____
     a. reason for denial or delay:_____

     _____

ADDITIONAL COMMENTS:

_____

_____

_____

_____

Follow up date:_____by_____

Index

About the Disk

INTRODUCTION

The forms on the enclosed disk are saved in Microsoft Word for Windows Version 7.0. In order to use the forms, you will need to have word processing software capable of reading Microsoft Word for Windows version 7.0 files.

SYSTEM REQUIREMENTS

- IBM PC or compatible computer
- 3.5" floppy disk drive

- Windows 95 or later

- Microsoft Word for Windows version 7.0 or later or other word processing software capable of reading Microsoft Word for Windows 7.0 files.

NOTE: Many popular word processing programs are capable of reading Microsoft Word for Windows 7.0 files. However, users should be aware that a slight amount of formatting might be lost when using a program other than Microsoft Word. If your word processor cannot read Microsoft Word for Windows 7.0 files, unformatted text files have been provided in the TXT directory on the floppy disk.

HOW TO INSTALL THE FILES ONTO YOUR COMPUTER

To install the files follow the instructions below.

1. Insert the enclosed disk into the floppy disk drive of your computer.

2. From the Start Menu, choose **Run**.

3. Type **A:\SETUP** and press **OK**.

4. The opening screen of the installation program will appear. Press **OK** to continue.

5. The default destination directory is C:\TINSLEY. If you wish to change the default destination, you may do so now.

6. Press **OK** to continue. The installation program will copy all files to your hard drive in the C:\TINSLEY or user-designated directory.

USING THE FILES

Loading Files

To use the word processing files, launch your word processing program. Select **File, Open** from the pull-down menu. Select the appropriate drive and directory. If you installed the files to the default directory, the files will be located in the C:\TINSLEY directory. A list of files should appear. If you do not see a list of files in the directory, you need to select **WORD DOCUMENT (*.DOC)** under **Files of Type**. Double click on the file you want to open. Edit the file according to your needs.

Printing Files

If you want to print the files, select **File, Print** from the pull-down menu.

Saving Files

When you have finished editing a file, you should save it under a new file name by selecting **File, Save As** from the pull-down menu.

USER ASSISTANCE

If you need assistance with installation or if you have a damaged disk, please contact Wiley Technical Support at:

Phone: (212) 850-6753
Fax: (212) 850-6800 (Attention: Wiley Technical Support)
Email: techhelp@wiley.com

To place additional orders or to request information about other Wiley products, please call (800) 225-5945.

For information about the disk see the About the Disk section on page 255.

CUSTOMER NOTE: IF THIS BOOK IS ACCOMPANIED BY SOFTWARE, PLEASE READ THE FOLLOWING BEFORE OPENING THE PACKAGE.

This software contains files to help you utilize the models described in the accompanying book. By opening the package, you are agreeing to be bound by the following agreement:

This software product is protected by copyright and all rights are reserved by the author, John Wiley & Sons, Inc., or their licensors. You are licensed to use this software on a single computer. Copying the software to another medium or format for use on a single computer does not violate the U.S. Copyright Law. Copying the software for any other purpose is a violation of the U.S. Copyright Law.

This software product is sold as is without warranty of any kind, either express or implied, including but not limited to the implied warranty of merchantability and fitness for a particular purpose. Neither Wiley nor its dealers or distributors assumes any liability for any alleged or actual damages arising from the use of or the inability to use this software. (Some states do not allow the exclusion of implied warranties, so the exclusion may not apply to you.)